THE 4 STAGES OF PSYCHOLOGICAL SAFETY

SECOND EDITION

THE 4 STAGES OF PSYCHOLOGICAL SAFETY

How to Build a High-Performance Culture

TIMOTHY R. CLARK

Berrett-Koehler
PUBLISHERS

Berrett-Koehler Publishers, Inc.
1333 Broadway, Suite P100
Oakland, CA 94612-1921
(510) 817-2277
bkconnection.com

Ordering Information
Quantity sales. Special discounts are available on quantity purchases by corporations, associations, individuals, and others. For details, please go to bkconnection.com to see our bulk discounts or contact bookorders@bkpub.com for more information.
Textbook exam/desk copies. Please consult the General FAQ at bkconnection.com.
Bookstore orders for trade or textbook use. For print books, please contact Penguin Random House Publisher Services at customerservice@penguinrandomhouse.com. For ebooks, contact your favorite distributor.

Distributed to the US trade and internationally by Penguin Random House Publisher Services.

The authorized representative in the EU for product safety and compliance is
EU Compliance Partner, Pärnu mnt. 139b-14, 11317 Tallinn, Estonia,
www.eucompliancepartner.com, +372 5368 65 02.

Printed in the United States of America

Berrett-Koehler books are printed on long-lasting acid-free paper. When it is available, we choose paper that has been manufactured by environmentally responsible processes. These may include using trees grown in sustainable forests, incorporating recycled paper, minimizing chlorine in bleaching, or recycling the energy produced at the paper mill.

Library of Congress Cataloging-in-Publication Data
Names: Clark, Timothy R., 1964- author
Title: The 4 stages of psychological safety : how to build a high-performance culture / Timothy R. Clark.
Other titles: Four stages of psychological safety
Description: Second edition. | Oakland, CA : Berrett-Koehler Publishers, Inc, [2026] | Previous edition: 2020. | Includes bibliographical references and index.
Identifiers: LCCN 2025053980 (print) | LCCN 2025053981 (ebook) | ISBN 9798890572035 paperback | ISBN 9798890572042 pdf | ISBN 9798890572059 epub
Subjects: LCSH: Leadership | Organizational behavior—Psychological aspects | Corporate culture—Psychological aspects | Employee morale
Classification: LCC HD57.7 .C5376 2026 (print) | LCC HD57.7 (ebook)
LC record available at https://lccn.loc.gov/2025053980
LC ebook record available at https://lccn.loc.gov/2025053981

Second Edition
35 34 33 32 31 30 29 28 27 26   10 9 8 7 6 5 4 3 2 1

Book production: Happenstance Type-O-Rama
Cover design: Ashley Ingram
Cover illustration: Generated with Nano Banana

To Tracey

Contents

Preface to the Second Edition

You are a cultural architect. You radiate influence to your colleagues every day and there's no off switch. You can't go to work tomorrow and say, "I don't want to be a cultural architect. I think I'll take the day off." While it may not be written in your job description, the role of cultural architect is *embedded* in everything you do. Even if you want to, you can't delegate or abdicate it.

Consider how culture forms from three building blocks (figure 1):

- *Habits* (patterns of individual behavior)
- *Norms* (patterns of shared behavior)
- *Culture* (a collection of norms)

What does it mean to be a cultural architect? It means that you *shape norms*. If the norms are positive and productive, you move the culture away from pathology to health, away from fear to courage, away from stagnation to

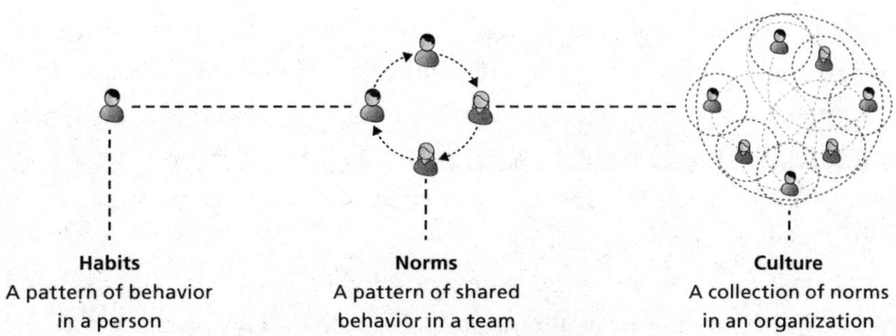

Figure 1. Culture formation

resilience. If the norms are negative, the opposite is true. How do people learn and perpetuate culture? Simple: *through observation and imitation.*[1] Finally, whom do they observe and imitate? You.

Now let's add a corollary principle: If you occupy a formal leadership position, you are, by virtue of your position, the "chief" cultural architect of that social collective. That means you have the most influence in shaping the prevailing norms. In many ways, the culture will become your lengthened shadow.[2]

What is culture, anyway? You know, that amorphous, elusive thing that is so hard to nail down. Let's reduce the complexity. Here's the working definition of culture I recommend: Culture is *the way we interact*. Period.

Really? Yes, four words. Now you might say culture is far more complex. What about attitudes, beliefs, assumptions, values, traditions, customs, mores, and artifacts? Aren't those part of culture? They are, but here's the point: All of those things find expression—or become irrelevant—at the human interface. If you simply focus on human interaction, you will capture 99 percent of what you're looking for: culture on full display.

Think about it this way. Fish have water. Humans have culture. Yet we are born cultureless.[3] That fact notwithstanding, from the day you are born until the day you die, you swim in culture. And you can't step out of it and dry off with a towel. What you *can* do is swim in other cultures. We do this all the time. In the course of a single day, you might swim in several: home, work, gym, store, school, church, restaurant, doctor's office, social media platform. It goes on and on. If you're interacting with another human being, you're swimming in culture.

Question: If culture isn't genetically inherited, where does it come from? Answer: We make it. It's socially constructed. Human beings are "incomplete or unfinished animals who complete themselves through culture."[4] *You shape culture and culture shapes you*. It has reciprocal influence, acting as both cause and effect. But that's not all. If we say that culture is the way we interact, we have to acknowledge that human interaction comes with risk—social, emotional, political, and economic.

Human interaction is a vulnerable activity. Paradoxically, the risks and rewards of life come from the same place: vulnerability. You are a social animal, a relational creature. As a result, psychological safety, as we will see, is an enduring need. As a *culture of rewarded vulnerability*, psychological safety is crucial to your happiness in work and life because it allows you to satisfy your *Workplace Hierarchy of Needs*.[5] More on that later.

The Backstory

Several years ago, my wife and I moved back to the United States from England as I neared the completion of a PhD at Oxford University. The ramen budget was gone. I would get a job, work for a year, finish my dissertation, teach at a university, and live happily ever after. That was the plan.

Here's what actually happened. I stepped out of the ivory tower into the gritty, sweaty megaton realm of a steel plant. Constructed by United States Steel Corporation during World War II, Geneva Steel was the last fully integrated steel mill west of the Mississippi River, a hulking mass of machinery spread across 1,700 acres, the industrial equivalent of the Vatican—a self-contained enclave within a larger metropolis, with its own trains, fire station, hospital, and towering blast furnace cathedral. The plant supplied steel plate, sheet, and pipe to manufacturers, including Caterpillar, to make earthmovers, graders, and bulldozers. With my working-class sympathies, I thought I knew what I was getting into. I didn't have a clue.[6]

This was another world. I found myself working with shift-work-hardened, layoff-endured welders, millwrights, pipefitters, and crane operators. These shadows under the hard hats became my friends, but there was nothing romantic about this heaving, grinding, snorting place. The shop floor was a high-stakes, no-margin-for-error arena where precision mattered and assumptions could kill. With thousands of safe-job procedures to govern every task for every job in every operation, nothing was left to chance. They preached safety so incessantly that workers often ignored the preaching.

Then came the fateful day. A maintenance worker was crushed under a sixteen-ton load of iron ore pellets. He died instantly. I remember wondering what agony would sweep through the man's family. Later that day, I was given the assignment to accompany the CEO to deliver the dreadful news. We learned later that this tragedy was the result of several employees breaking safety rules. In the days ahead, safety would become my obsession, but not in the way you might think. I would come to learn that psychological safety is the most important cultural lever a leader can pull. My planned one-year stay turned into three. With my degree finally in hand, I was ready to trade my hard hat and steel-toed boots for tweed, chalk, and the classroom. Then something unexpected happened. The CEO asked me to become the plant manager. Now I faced an unusual decision: settle into the tranquil life of an academic or lead a team of twenty-five hundred employees working in the bowels of an industrial beast. My wife and I decided to accept the offer. Why? Because it represented a rare opportunity to study human behavior in a unique setting as a participant observer. The experience would thrust me into a real-world tutorial that would challenge the elegant theory I had learned at Oxford.

On my first day as plant manager, I called to order the morning operating meeting and came face-to-face with the indigenous culture. A stoic silence fell over the room as I peered into the faces of twenty superintendents, many of whom were old enough to be my father. Now they reported to me.

They had been deeply socialized to self-censor, constrained by deference to positional power and a slavish adherence to the chain of command. Power mattered. And these men (and they were all men) understood where power lay. It lay with me. Despite my youth and inexperience, they would render obedience to that source of power. Indeed, I was now the command center, the control tower, the alpha male. I had what the sociologist C. Wright Mills called "the most of what there is to have."[7] Experience had taught these managers that it was expensive to say what they really thought, so they smiled and nodded politely.

Inhabiting this fertile setting for field study was a social scientist's dream. What I was observing cried out for interpretation. But I had to be more than an observer; I had to be a reformer. To improve the company's performance, we needed a transformation. The tired old plant was struggling to compete with the mini-mills that had disrupted the industry and were dominating the market. To increase throughput and yield, we needed to vacate the rules of naked force and disabuse people of their worship of coercive authority and their inclination to induce fear through intimidation. The entire organization needed to be cleansed of its status-bound model of authoritarian rule. Defang the place or die in the next downturn.

Commercial organizations survive by maintaining competitive advantage, which ultimately means incubating innovation. If you watch closely, you will notice that innovation is almost always a collaborative process and almost never a light-bulb moment of lone genius. To paraphrase the historian Robert Conquest, "What is easy to understand may have not been easy to think of."[8]

Innovation is never easy to think of. It requires creative abrasion and constructive dissent—processes that rely on high *intellectual* friction and low *social* friction (figure 2).[9]

Most leaders don't comprehend that managing these two categories of friction to create an ecosystem of candid collaboration is at the heart of leadership as an applied discipline. It is perhaps the supreme test of a leader and a direct reflection of personal character. Without skill, integrity, and respect for people, it doesn't happen. Nor can perks such as foosball tables, free lunch, an open office environment, and the aesthetic of a hip organization bring it to life.

As a new plant manager, I witnessed the lethality of fear and the psychic damage of social rejection.[10] I soon realized that my stewardship was to protect people not only physically but also psychologically. The absence of physical safety can bring injury or death, but the absence of psychological safety can inflict devastating emotional wounds, neutralize performance, paralyze potential, and crater an individual's sense of self-worth.[11]

Only recently has science taught us that the human brain "does not discriminate between physical and psychological dangers."[12] There's a neural basis for social rejection and it's different from social connection. Social pain hurts the way physical pain hurts. While psychological safety activates the pleasure and reward centers of your brain, fear and rejection activate the pain centers of your brain. As we interact, we engage different neural regions in each other's

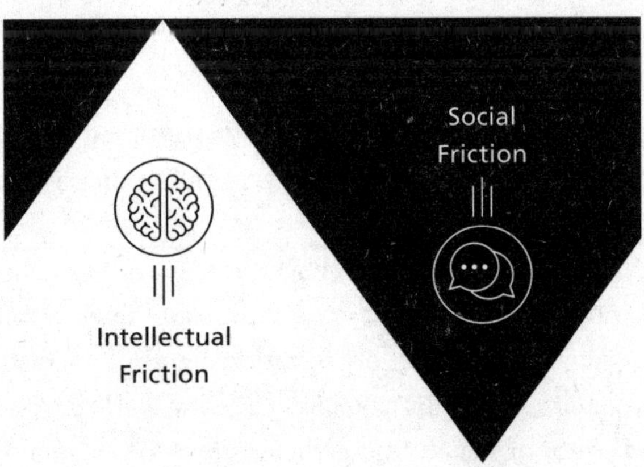

Figure 2. Increasing intellectual friction, decreasing social friction

brains.[13] One of the things you learn when leading a team is that culture has a profound influence on the way people behave and that you as the leader are, straight up, responsible for that culture.

The economist Albert Hirschman suggested that when an organization begins to fail in its performance, the members of that organization have two options: express their dissatisfaction ("voice") or leave ("exit"). In a consumer relationship, that makes sense. For instance, if you had a bad meal, don't go back. But if you're an employee, it's more complicated. Many people fear the repercussions of giving voice and have no other job options that would allow them to leave. The reality is that most employees take a third option: silence. Not out of loyalty, but out of necessity. They don't attempt to initiate change. Nor will they try to escape the organization. Both options are unrealistic, so the incentive structure motivates them, as we like to say, to quit softly.[14]

The quality guru W. Edwards Deming said, "Where there is fear, there will be wrong figures."[15] He's saying that fear drives truth underground, especially inconvenient truths, such as when someone commits an error. Here's the punchline: *Fear breaks the feedback loop.* It tempts the individual to hide mistakes. And yet what are mistakes? They represent the clinical material we use to make things better, solve wicked problems, discover breakthroughs, and innovate. But you can't fix a secret.

Psychological safety is not a luxury aesthetic. It's the crucial, indispensable condition that must fill our interpersonal space. It's social oxygen that allows us to be seen, heard, understood, and respected. Now, a final question: Whose primary job is it to ensure that psychological safety prevails? The leader is always and forever the chief cultural architect of the team. The leader sets the tone and models the way. *If a team is dominated by fear, that is the first sign of poor leadership.*

If you can banish fear, install true performance-based accountability, and create a nurturing environment that rewards people in their vulnerability, they will perform beyond your expectations.

The five years I spent as plant manager at Geneva Steel changed the arc of my career and set me on a course to understand how to unleash human potential in organizations. As an organizational anthropologist and sociologist, I'm in the pattern recognition business. Having worked with thousands of teams in every sector of society and gathered close to two million data points in global survey research, I can tell you that the patterns are unmistakable and the challenges universal. What I have to say is both empirical and normative. I make no apologies for combining cold, dispassionate research with warm, passionate pleas, because the use case—the job to be done—is to offer practical guidance for those who lead and work in organizations.

Here's the thing: Sometimes we're noble and good to each other. Sometimes we're criminally irresponsible. Our track record as a species is, for the most part, a chilling history—a pageant of war and a chronicle of conquest. Maya Angelou rendered the lamentable past as few literary voices can: "Throughout our nervous history, we have constructed pyramidic towers of evil, ofttimes in the name of good. Our greed, fear and lasciviousness have enabled us to murder our poets, who are ourselves, to castigate our priests, who are ourselves. The lists of our subversions of the good stretch from before recorded history to this moment."[16]

As social creatures, we act like free electrons, demonstrating both connection and contention. We need each other to flourish, yet despite knowing this, we suffer from compassion fatigue, are handicapped by our blind spots, and chronically regress to the mean. We snap back and exile each other. Indeed, the study of humans in social settings is largely the study of exclusion and fear. A mere third of US workers believe their opinions count.[17] Why do we hire people if we don't want their opinions?

Despite our unique life stories, we share common experiences. We have all felt the pain of reproach. At the same time, we've all done some excluding and segregating, some manipulating and controlling, some depriving and belittling, some friending and unfriending. We've all drawn racial, social, or other demographic or psychographic lines, and rendered unjust judgments on others and treated them poorly. We know something about marginality because we've all been marginalized. We can be benevolent, compassionate, and kind. We can also be, as the Harlem Renaissance poet Langston Hughes put it, "stinkin', low-down, mean."[18]

We have constructive and destructive tendencies. Sometimes we classify each other the way I classified moths in the fourth grade. We invite and disinvite, include and exclude, listen and ignore, heal and abuse, sanctify and scar. We love and hate our diversity. In all my years of working with leaders and organizations, I've never met an infallible human. Each is a work in progress, an apprentice to greatness. We're all broken, damaged, wounded, and guilty, and yet we possess amazing gifts.

It's an idealized notion to think we can undock from society and live deliberately in isolation. The monastic, cloistered alternative never works, and virtual reality is a bubble of indulgence. The truth is, we're embedded in, implicated with, bound to, and shaped by one another. Hannah Arendt wisely observed, "The world lies between people, and this in-between . . . is today the object of the greatest concern and the most obvious upheaval in almost all the countries of the globe."[19]

Crack Yourself Open

I invite you to crack yourself open. Summon the courage and brave the hazards to conduct a fearless personal inventory. And if you happen to lead a family, team, or organization, conduct an institutional examination of conscience while you're at it.

I have four questions to ask you:

- Do you truly believe that all people are created equal, and do you accept others and welcome them into your society simply because they possess flesh and blood, even if their values differ from your own?
- Without bias or discrimination, do you encourage others to learn and grow, and do you support them in that process even when they lack confidence or make mistakes?
- Do you grant others maximum autonomy to contribute in their own way as they demonstrate their ability to deliver results?
- Do you consistently invite others to challenge the status quo in order to make things better, and are you personally prepared to be wrong?

These four questions align with the *Workplace Hierarchy of Needs* and the *4 Stages of Psychological Safety* I'm about to share with you. In large measure, the way you answer these questions will define the way you value human beings. It will define the way you draw people out or shut them down, create confidence or induce fear. The philosopher Thomas Hobbes said that there is "a general inclination of all mankind, a perpetual and restless desire of power after power, that ceaseth only in death."[20] That lust for power, wealth, and aggrandizement runs counter to human flourishing, because we're connected, not self-contained. "We are," as the former archbishop of Canterbury Rowan Williams said, "healed by relation, not isolation."[21]

Is drawing lines of exclusion a primal tendency rooted in our biology? This is a matter of debate. One group of scholars is convinced that tribalism and distinction forming are prewired.[22] Another is convinced that the behavior is biocultural, an interplay of evolutionary biology and socialization. I'll come back to this later.

It's insecurity, ordinary selfishness, and the adoration of power and distinction that lead us to partition ourselves. As humans, we look for loyalties to attach to. Out of our attachments emerge our differences. Out of our differences emerge our divisions. Out of our divisions emerge our classes, ranks, and stations. And it is out of those spaces between us that the comparisons begin, the empathy flees, the fear and envy emerge, the conflicts arise, the antagonisms gestate, the destructive instincts and impulses for abuse and cruelty arise. In the spirit of our bigotry, we invent dogmas to justify the ways we torment each other. Ironically, in our digital age, we connect and feel alone, compare and feel inadequate.[23]

Indeed, if you have a sudden urge to feel "less than," do a little doomscrolling on your favorite social media platform. Do that every day, and you will suffer from digital isolation and status anxiety—the distress that comes from comparing your status to others and relying on social validation. All this so-called connection leads to nothing but demeaning self-appraisal. *When you compare and compete, you lose the ability to connect.*

Though we can be false friends to each other, we can also be ministers, healers, and good neighbors. We are capable of breathtaking compassion, generosity, and selfless service. I'm not advocating heroism and grand expressions of self-sacrifice. No, my charge is, in the most basic sense, to treat human beings as they deserve to be treated—without arbitrary distinctions. Accept them, encourage them, respect them, and allow them. If you want to be happy, come to terms with your fellow creatures. Lose the mock superiority. Stop nursing wrongs and start reaching out. Too many of us live far beneath our privileges, locked in what W. B. Yeats called the "foul rag and bone shop of the heart."[24]

If you can create a little more psychological safety for your fellow travelers, it will change your life and theirs. As AI pushes out the frontier of modernity and devours routine and complex tasks, value shifts to creativity, empathy, and judgment. A psychologically safe culture empowers people to bring those uniquely human strengths forward with confidence rather than fear of being replaced.

Introduction

Without psychological safety, it's impossible for human beings to flourish. Why? Because it's the enabling precondition for productive interaction. I define it as *a culture of rewarded vulnerability*. In the study of organizational culture, no other independent variable rivals its scope, impact, or predictive strength: It literally sets in motion a cascade of ten compounding and mutually reinforcing outcomes, as shown in figure 3. (In research, an *x* variable is a cause and a *y* variable is an outcome.)

What the Science Says: One Lever = Ten Outcomes

In the last twenty years, researchers around the world have contributed to the study of psychological safety. What they have found is astonishing. Psychological safety correlates significantly with ten organizational outcomes. Without getting too technical, let me share how this works. In social science research, we use statistical tests to understand relationships. Of course, we always remind ourselves that correlation isn't causation. But we also know that if a measure of correlation (a correlation or regression coefficient) is high enough,

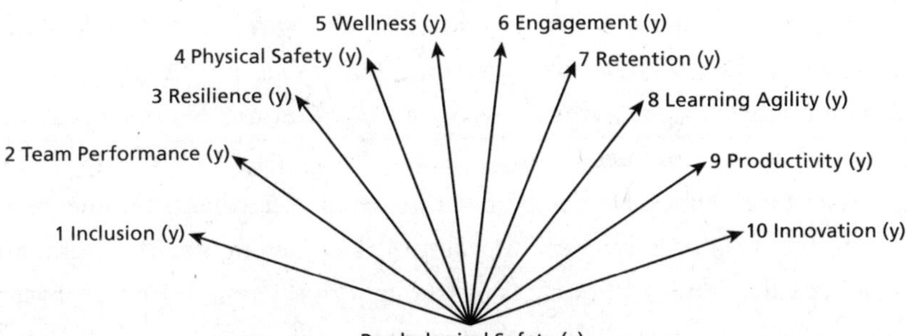

Figure 3. Ten outcomes of psychological safety

and we're not missing any lurking, mediating, or confounding variables or complex intertwined causation, we are witnessing cause and effect.

A positive correlation or regression coefficient is usually considered meaningful once it reaches a value of .30. We call this "the critical threshold." It basically means we've discovered something valuable in the human world.[25] The amazing part is that, based on peer-reviewed academic research, psychological safety surpasses the critical threshold with each of the ten outcomes:

1. Inclusion[26]
2. Team performance[27]
3. Resilience[28]
4. Physical safety[29]
5. Wellness[30]
6. Engagement[31]
7. Retention[32]
8. Learning agility[33]
9. Productivity[34]
10. Innovation[35]

Do I have your attention now? I don't know anyone who can look at these outcomes and say, "Oh, that's nice. What's next on the agenda?" The discovery of psychological safety may be the biggest breakthrough in the study of organizational culture in the last century. But why? How can psychological safety do all that? How is it possible that you can pull one lever and create transformation?

The answer is simple and yet profound: *Psychological safety enables people to satisfy their basic human needs at work.* Remember, people go to work to satisfy not only their economic needs but also their non-economic needs.

And what are those needs? You probably learned about Maslow's Hierarchy of Needs in school. He named five categories of need and a sequence for fulfilling them: 1) physiological, 2) safety, 3) love/belonging, 4) esteem, and 5) self-actualization.[36] At first, Maslow thought of safety in terms of physical safety, but he later revised that need category to include psychological safety as well, stating, "The healthy society must provide a feeling of safety, not only in the physical sense but also in the *psychological sense*—freedom from fear, from anxiety, from chaos, and from the unpredictable actions of others."[37]

With that in mind, I asked a similar question: *Is there a Workplace Hierarchy of Needs?* Is there a dominant sequence in the way individuals seek to satisfy their basic human needs in the workplace? This became my primary research question.

Based on ethnographic qualitative research with organizations around the world, I identified a dominant sequence and formed a hypothesis: Assuming employees had their basic economic and physical safety needs met, they would attempt to satisfy their non-economic needs in the workplace in this order:

1. Inclusion and belonging
2. Learning and growth
3. Choice and contribution
4. Challenge and improvement

The next step was to empirically verify the hypothesis using quantitative data and both descriptive and inferential statistics. In our PSindex® survey, my colleagues and I gathered responses from 3,366 employees in more than 20 organizations around the world and asked this question:[38]

> If you were assigned to work with a new team at work, in what order would you engage in the following activities?
>
> 1. Meet and get to know the members of the team.
> 2. Learn my role.
> 3. Contribute and add value.
> 4. Challenge the way things are done.

We randomized the response categories in order to prevent display order bias. In table 1, you can see the frequency distribution for each selection. The hypothesis is clearly confirmed. Nearly two-thirds of respondents (65 percent) selected the inclusion and belonging response as their first choice. Nearly two-thirds again (63 percent) selected the learning and growth response as their second choice. A full 81 percent of respondents chose the choice and contribution selection as their third choice, and nearly nine in ten (86 percent) chose the challenge and improvement selection as their fourth choice.

Table 1. Cross-tabulation of need category by selection order (N = 3,366)

Actual stage	1st selection *n*	1st selection %	2nd selection *n*	2nd selection %	3rd selection *n*	3rd selection %	4th selection *n*	4th selection %	Dominant stage position
Inclusion	2190	**65%**	977	29%	136	4%	63	2%	1st (65%)
Learner	1031	31%	2116	**63%**	138	4%	81	2%	2nd (63%)
Contributor	107	3%	231	7%	2713	**81%**	315	9%	3rd (81%)
Challenger	38	1%	42	1%	379	11%	2907	**86%**	4th (86%)

Note: Percentages represent the proportion of participants selecting each stage in a given sequence position. The diagonal dominance of higher percentages supports the expected progression: *inclusion* → *learner* → *contributor* → *challenger*.

(Table shows the percentage distribution for the first, second, third, and fourth participant selections.)

To further validate this Workplace Hierarchy of Needs, I conducted a comprehensive validation study using a series of ranking/order statistical model testing. In all cases, the results clearly confirm the sequence.[39] (See the appendix for a full explanation of results.) In other words, there is a dominant sequence and Workplace Hierarchy of Needs (figure 4).

Here's where psychological safety comes in: It is the enabling condition for all four need categories. In other words, *psychological safety creates conditions*

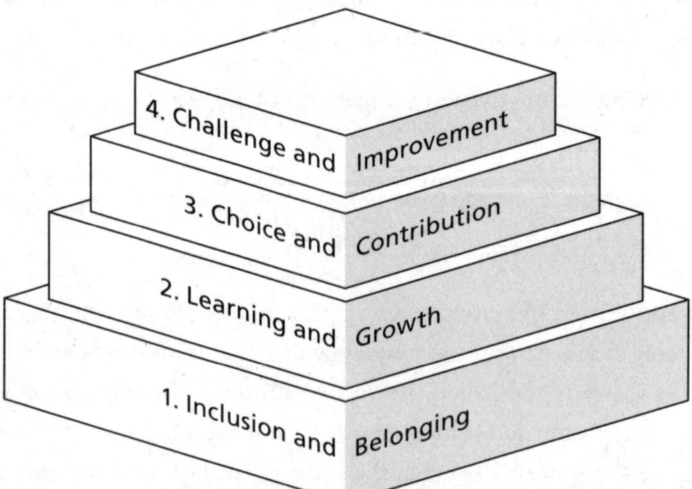

Figure 4. The Workplace Hierarchy of Needs

necessary to meet the unique requirements of each of the four need categories (figure 5). For example, the expression of psychological safety that nurtures inclusion and belonging is qualitatively different from the expression that nurtures the other three categories.

The Workplace Hierarchy of Needs maps directly to the 4 Stages of Psychological Safety. Each stage functions as the enabling condition for its corresponding need category. **Inclusion safety** makes *inclusion and belonging* possible by assuring people they are valued and accepted. **Learner safety** enables *learning and growth* by removing the interpersonal risk associated with asking questions, making mistakes, or committing other acts of learning vulnerability. **Contributor safety** supports *choice and contribution* by granting individuals autonomy and support in applying their skills, exercising judgment, and adding value without fear of negative consequences. Finally, **challenger safety** underpins *challenge and improvement* by protecting and promoting those who question the status quo, surface problems, or propose better ways forward. In this way, the 4 Stages of Psychological Safety are the foundational mechanism that allows each need category to be met.

Without each stage of psychological safety, it becomes difficult or impossible for the individual to satisfy their needs. Although the concept of psychological safety has formally evolved since Carl Rogers coined the term in 1954, it was conceived as a general condition instead of stage-specific. Let's go over a quick history of its evolution.[40]

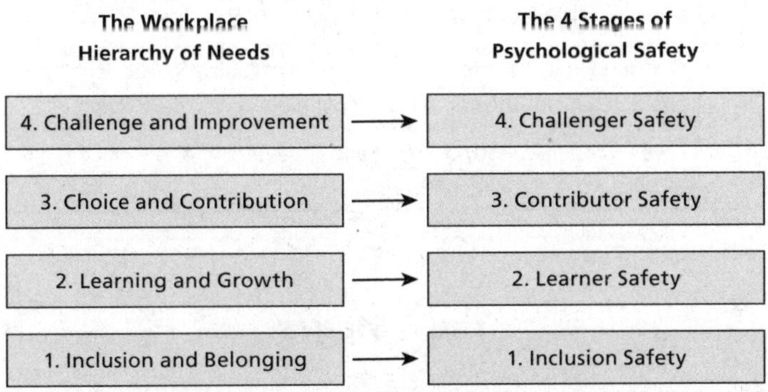

Figure 5. How the need categories correspond to the stages of psychological safety

A Quick History of Psychological Safety

The concept of psychological safety is as old as the first human interaction. But it's only been in recent years that we have consolidated the concept under a unifying term.

1844	Søren Kierkegaard identifies creativity as both a generative and destructive force that produces anxiety in the person who engages in the process.[41]
1942	Joseph Schumpeter identifies a pattern of creative destruction where continuous innovation mutates and destroys the status quo in the process.[42]
1943	Abraham Maslow identifies "belongingness needs," stating that "if both the physiological and the safety needs are fairly well gratified, then there will emerge the love and affection and belongingness needs."[43]
1947	Herbert Simon suggests that fully functioning organizations need "attitudes of friendliness and cooperation."[44]
1954	Carl Rogers discusses unconditional positive regard, contributing to the theory that inclusion starts with acknowledgment and appreciation of the humanity in each one of us. He then coins the term *psychological safety* in the context of a therapeutic relationship.[45]
1960	Douglas McGregor refers to nonphysical "security needs."[46]
1964	Edgar H. Schein and Warren G. Bennis publish the second mention of the term *psychological safety*, defining it as "the climate that reduces interpersonal risk."[47]
1990	William Kahn further develops the concept, suggesting that in order for employees to feel engaged at work, they need to feel safe to express themselves authentically.[48]
1999	Amy Edmondson proves that psychological safety is critical to team learning and performance.[49]
2014	Google's Project Aristotle identifies psychological safety as the defining characteristic of the company's most high-performing teams.[50]
2020	I publish *The 4 Stages of Psychological Safety* and introduce the 4 Stages model.

The 4 Stages

Think of a time when you were embarrassed, marginalized, or otherwise rejected in a social setting—a teacher ignored your question, a boss criticized your idea, a coworker mocked your English pronunciation, a casting director ridiculed your audition, a coach yelled at you for making an unforced error, your team ditched you and went to lunch. I'm referring to times when you were deprived of psychological safety. Do you remember those wounding experiences? They're sticky because they sting.

Do those occasions influence your behavior? As the sociologist Arlie Russell Hochschild reminds us, "Feeling is a form of pre-action."[51] When we're snubbed, ignored, silenced, brushed off, ostracized, or humiliated; when we're bullied, harassed, or shamed; when we're scorned, passed over, or neglected, those experiences are not neutral events. They're demoralizing events that lead to alienation and activate the pain centers of the brain. They crush self-confidence and leave us in resentful, stupefied silence. In fact, sometimes the fear of these experiences can be more debilitating than the actual event. Clearly, how we feel influences what we think, believe, and do.

Not being given a voice and being mistreated can have a profound impact on our ability to perform, create value, and thrive. As humans, we instinctively sense the vibe, tone, and atmosphere around us and respond accordingly. But it's not a binary proposition—psychological safety is not something you either have or don't. From the nuclear family to the Navy SEALs, from the food truck to the president's cabinet, every social unit registers some level of psychological safety. It's context-sensitive and that context can change at any time.[52]

Google's Project Aristotle proved that IQ points and money don't necessarily produce results. After studying 180 of its teams, Google found that smarts and resources can't compensate for what a team may lack in psychological safety. In fact, the company landed on psychological safety as the single most important factor in explaining high performance.

When psychological safety is high, people take more ownership, release more discretionary effort, and demonstrate greater mental toughness, resulting in higher-velocity learning and problem-solving.[53] When it's low, people usually don't just muscle through the fear. Instead, they shut down, self-censor, and redirect their energy toward risk management, pain avoidance, and self-preservation. *As a result, psychological safety will increasingly become a term of employment, and organizations that don't supply it will bleed out their top talent.*

When we operationalize psychological safety and turn it into an observable and measurable construct, it's clear that it lives at the intersection of respect and permission. By *respect*, I mean the general level of regard and esteem we give each other. To respect someone is to value and appreciate them. By *permission*, I mean the permission we give to others to be themselves and participate as members of a social unit, allowing them to interact with and influence us and to participate in what we are doing.

As organizations grant increasing levels of respect and permission, individuals generally behave in a way that reflects the level of psychological safety offered to them. Each stage encourages individuals to satisfy the corresponding category in the Workplace Hierarchy of Needs. Thus, the 4 Stages framework mirrors the dominant sequence in which human beings seek to satisfy their basic needs in the workplace (figure 6).

Let me briefly explain each of the four stages and then I will explore them in greater detail in the subsequent chapters.

Stage 1: Inclusion Safety

The social psychologist Erich Fromm said, "Unless he belonged somewhere, unless his life had some meaning and direction, he would feel like a particle of dust and be overcome by his individual insignificance. He would not be able to relate himself to any system which would give meaning and direction to his

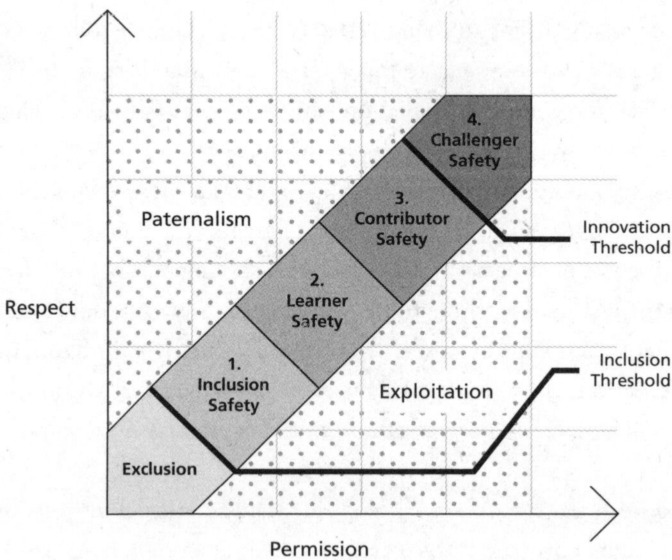

Figure 6. The 4 Stages of Psychological Safety

life, he would be filled with doubt, and this doubt eventually would paralyze his ability to act—that is, to live."[54]

The first stage of psychological safety is knowing that you're not a particle of dust. The people around you accept and acknowledge you and grant you shared identity. You are now destigmatized as an outsider and brought into the fold. But it's important to understand that inclusion safety isn't merely tolerance; it's not an attempt to cover up differences or politely pretend they're not there. No, we give inclusion safety when we genuinely invite others into our society based on the sole qualification that they possess flesh and blood. This transcendent connection supersedes all other differences. *Thus, the need to be accepted precedes the need to be heard.* As a species, we have both natural instincts and acquired socialization to detect social boundaries as well as gestures of invitation or rejection across those boundaries—to perceive the levels of respect and permission offered to us.

For example, when a new high school student asks her peers, "Can I eat lunch with you guys?" the response to that question extends inclusion safety if the students say yes. If they say no, the student is not allowed to cross the threshold of inclusion. In a subtler version of this encounter, the student is simply ignored by her peers as she passes by. In some cases, we ignore each other as a silent way to pour scorn. Regardless of the method, it hurts when you're cast off and acceptance is denied. As one poignant example of the acute need for inclusion, an American College Health Association survey of undergraduate college students found that 63 percent of the students surveyed reported feeling "very lonely." That's nearly two-thirds of the student population.[55] In spite of our material abundance, we increasingly suffer from social and emotional poverty.[56] *Being ignored is often as painful as being rejected.*

William James, the father of American psychology, said, "No more fiendish punishment could be devised, were such a thing physically possible, than that one should be turned loose in society and remain absolutely unnoticed by all the members thereof. If not one turned around when we entered, answered when we spoke, or minded what we did, but if every person we met 'cut us dead,' and acted as if we were nonexistent things, a kind of rage and impotent despair would before long well up in us, from which the cruelest bodily torture would be a relief."[57]

Why do active shooters kill innocent victims? Why do citizens spew vitriol and hate? Why has the suicide rate in the United States increased by 33 percent in just the last eighteen years?[58] What explains these outcomes? One factor is unmet needs. These tragic outcomes are directly linked to alienation, disaffection, and ostracism. Clearly, granting and receiving inclusion safety is a matter of not only happiness but, indeed, life and death. *When human beings fail to gain acceptance or approval from each other, they often seek attention as a replacement, even if that attention is destructive.*

Inclusion safety is created and sustained through renewed admittance to the group and repeated indications of acceptance. In the business world, we are formally admitted to a team when we're hired, but informal membership is granted or withheld by the people with whom we work. You may be the new hire on the product development team, which gives you official membership status, but you still need the team's sociocultural acceptance to gain inclusion safety. Giving inclusion safety is a moral imperative, but it doesn't mean team members need to surrender their personal interests and preferences.

Stage 2: Learner Safety

Learner safety indicates that you feel safe to engage in the discovery process, ask questions, experiment, and even make mistakes—not if, but when, you make them. Without learner safety, you will likely remain passive due to the risk of acting beyond a tacit line of permission. In children, adolescents, and adults, the pattern is the same: We all bring inhibitions and fear to the learning process. When the environment belittles, demeans, or harshly corrects people in the learning process, learner safety is destroyed. *But an environment that grants safe passage to learning opens the buds of potential, cultivating confidence, resilience, and independence.*

While individuals can remain relatively passive in the stage of inclusion safety, learner safety motivates them to exert themselves and develop self-efficacy. The transition means crossing into the anxiety of the unknown. When learner safety is present, the leader and team may even supply some of the confidence that the individual lacks. For instance, days after the French philosopher Albert Camus won the Nobel Prize in literature in 1957, he wrote a letter of gratitude to his elementary school teacher. He said, "Dear Monsieur Germain, without you, without the affectionate hand you extended to the small poor child that I was, without your teaching and example, none of this would have happened."[59]

Learner safety implies activity and participation within defined limits. For example, I observed an apprentice plumber assisting a more experienced master plumber at a job site. The apprentice was given learner safety to observe, ask questions, prepare tools and materials, and contribute in a limited way to the repair work. As the master plumber responded positively to the apprentice's questions, the apprentice released more discretionary effort to learn, do, and become.

In a contrasting case, I watched a hotel manager's frustration escalate with a front desk clerk who was trying to resolve a pressing customer problem. The more questions the clerk asked, the more frustrated the manager became. That frustration replaced respect and permission, creating an emotional barrier that shut down the clerk's willingness to ask more questions and initiate action. As expected, the clerk began to behave as a compliant victim, losing both initiative and enthusiasm.

Stage 3: Contributor Safety

As individual performances climb higher in a nurturing environment that offers respect and permission, we enter the stage of contributor safety, which invites the individual to participate as an active and full-fledged member of the team. Contributor safety is an invitation and an expectation to perform work in an assigned role with appropriate boundaries, on the assumption that you can perform competently in your role. If you don't offend the social norms of the team, you're normally granted contributor safety when you gain competency in the required skills and assigned tasks. You feel safe and are given the opportunity to make decisions and contributions. *As the individual demonstrates more competence, the organization grants more autonomy to contribute.*

The transition to contributor safety may also be tied to credentials, title, position, and the formal conferral of authority. For example, when a coach selects a player on an athletic team to join the starting lineup, there's often an immediate transition to contributor safety. When a hospital hires a well-qualified surgeon, she's formally granted contributor safety. Thus, where formal authority or credentials are prerequisite to a role, they act as a partial proxy for psychological safety based on the official or legal right to contribute.

Despite an ability to do the job, an individual may nonetheless be denied contributor safety for illegitimate reasons, including the arrogance or insecurity of the leader, personal or institutional bias, prejudice or discrimination, prevailing team norms that reinforce insensitivity, a lack of empathy, or aloofness. Contributor safety emerges when the individual performs well, but the leader and team must do their part to provide encouragement and appropriate autonomy.

Stage 4: Challenger Safety

The final stage of psychological safety allows you to challenge the status quo without retribution, reprisal, or the risk of damaging your personal standing or reputation. It gives you the confidence to speak truth to power when you think something needs to change and it's time to say so. Armed with challenger safety, people overcome the pressure to conform and can enlist themselves in the creative process.

Analyzing its massive database of more than fifty thousand skills, LinkedIn conducted a study to identify the most important soft skills. Can you guess what skill was most in demand? Creativity.[60] But creativity is never enough. Only when people feel free and able do they apply their creativity. Each of us protects our creativity under emotional lock and key. We turn the key from the inside out—when it's safe to do so. Without challenger safety, there's little chance of that. How likely are you to innovate if you expect to be punished for challenging the status quo?

A middle manager from a global corporation summed it up to me this way: "I'm very careful to stick my neck out and challenge the status quo. If I do and don't get my head chopped off, I'll do it again. If I get my head chopped off, you can rest assured I'll keep my ideas to myself."

This statement illustrates the self-censoring instinct all humans possess and the inherent competitive advantage that challenger safety provides. The open climate of challenger safety allows the organization to circulate local knowledge from the bottom of the organization to the top to increase its adaptive capacity. But that's not all: It also empowers people to be curious and creative.

If you conduct a postmortem analysis of failure for almost any commercial organization that dies, you can trace the cause of death to a lack of challenger safety. For example, why did WeWork, Toys "R" Us, Jawbone, MoviePass, Bed Bath & Beyond, Thomas Cook Group, Sears/Kmart, Quibi, Silicon Valley Bank, and Virgin America fail?

They lost their competitive advantage by failing to innovate, but why? These organizations were filled with large numbers of highly intelligent people, and yet they all fell prey to competitive threats that were hiding in plain sight. The countervailing strategies their competitors put in place were not mysterious. They were, in fact, obvious. What these organizations failed to do was challenge the status quo and disrupt themselves. They were, as Thoreau observed, "buried in the grave of custom."[61] They wouldn't allow themselves to change.

The process of scrutinizing the status quo normally injects a degree of conflict, confrontation, creative abrasion, and even a measure of chaos. When there's censure or punishment, when intellectual conflict turns into interpersonal conflict, when fear becomes a motivator, the process collapses and people go silent. *When there is no tolerance for candor, there is no constructive dissent.*

Challenger safety is essentially a license to innovate. It's the leader's job to manage the tension and draw out the collective genius of people, and then sustain that recursive process through trial and error. Brilliance emerges from the interdependence of the team. But organizations are often reluctant to grant challenger safety, because it threatens the power structure, allocation of resources, incentives, reward system, and speed of operation. Innovation is the lifeblood of growth and yet a formidable cultural challenge. Some organizations never get it. Others get it and then lose it. Organizations often cling to their habits until inertia and complacency threaten survival.

For many leaders, being personally vulnerable is beyond their moral, emotional, and intellectual capacity. That's why they're unable to cross the threshold of innovation and create this high level of psychological safety in their organizations. Consider the *Challenger* space shuttle disaster caused by the failure of O-ring seals used in the field joints of the solid rocket boosters. The seals were not designed to function properly under the cold conditions that existed on the day of launch. Experts warned NASA not to launch the shuttle at temperatures below 53 degrees, but, feeling the pressure of previous launch delays, senior leadership silenced the detractors, dismissed the warnings, and proceeded. A lack of challenger safety, created by a combination of arrogance and cowardice, led to tragedy.

As I work with leaders in organizations that operate in highly dynamic environments, those that create challenger safety have a competitive advantage: They accelerate the process of innovation. Those prone to cherish formal status and amass power can't do it. They don't, as chess grandmaster Garry

Kasparov said, "have the guts to explode the game."[62] Unable to embrace vulnerability, sacrifice personal interests, and escape their ego needs, they're not up to the job.

Finally, to scale innovation throughout the organization, leaders must learn to normalize challenging the status quo. And yet no technology-enabled suggestion box or collaborative jam session lasts if leadership doesn't follow up and follow through. Not responding to a suggestion can be worse than rejecting it outright—which is at least an acknowledgment.

In the twenty-first century, the need for challenger safety is becoming more important as accelerating markets squeeze the average span of competitive advantage. In 1966, the average tenure of an S&P 500 company was thirty-three years. It shrank to twenty-four years by 2016 and is projected to plummet to twelve years by 2027.[63]

The assumption going forward is that this pattern will continue without a new equilibrium or state of normalcy. Except for a few organizations that seem to have an impenetrable moat of competitive advantage, organizations will need to create and sustain challenger safety as the incubating force that enables perpetual innovation. Without it, they won't have the agility to compete.

What if an organization has not purged its legacy of prejudice toward women, minorities, religious identities, or other characteristics? Most organizations grant equality and inclusion as a matter of policy; few live and breathe it as a matter of culture and behavior. How, then, can an organization convert diversity in composition into active, confident, and fearless diversity in action? Without psychological safety, true intellectual diversity will lie fallow. Those who live and work in the shadows will repress their instinct to explore. They won't engage in constructive dissent, because they've never seen it done. Nor have they been granted the respect and permission to participate.

The Ladder of Vulnerability

If you're interacting with other humans, you're being vulnerable. Ironically, the same exposure that brings the possibilities of rejection, ridicule, and embarrassment also brings the possibilities of connection and fulfillment, and the joys and satisfactions of the human experience. *Ultimately, where there is no exposure, there is no experience; and where there is no experience, there is no reward.* As a rule, humans step into vulnerability to feel connected and step out of it to feel protected. For example, one woman told me that just showing up with her team was a high-risk behavior, so she masked her true self and said as little as possible. Another woman I spoke with said she had never experienced a more complete sense of belonging than with her current work team.

Because vulnerability is necessary to satisfy each of the four categories in the Workplace Hierarchy of Needs, there must be psychological safety to reward acts of vulnerability throughout the sequence. Here's where it gets even more interesting: Interpersonal risk is objective, but vulnerability is subjective. For example, there may be a 60 percent chance that your boss will disapprove if you speak up in a meeting. But the level of emotional exposure (vulnerability you feel based on your self-image, status, and sense of belonging) is subjective. Your vulnerability, or perception of risk, is influenced by factors such as personality, cognitive schemas, lived experience, acquired socialization, work environment, norms, job role, colleagues, and your direct supervisor. Based on life circumstances and biological factors, different types of vulnerable behaviors create different perceptions of risk. *While vulnerability is a universal condition, the level of vulnerability we feel is personal.*

Vulnerability at Work

My team and I set out to measure vulnerability at work by developing a comprehensive list of acts of vulnerability. We identified over 150 specific behaviors, such as asking a question, pointing out a mistake, setting a boundary, apologizing, communicating bad news, saying no, admitting an error, or speaking with an accent. We then narrowed the list to 20 of the most common forms to account for the majority of vulnerable encounters in the workplace.

Applying an 11-point scale to measure the relative level of risk associated with each of the 20 behaviors, we surveyed 2,025 individuals from 834 organizations worldwide by asking this question: "Using a scale from 0 to 10 where 0 means no personal risk and 10 means extremely high personal risk, please rate the level of personal risk you feel at work when you engage in each of the following activities." The results reveal a fascinating pattern in the way people experience vulnerability at work (figure 7).

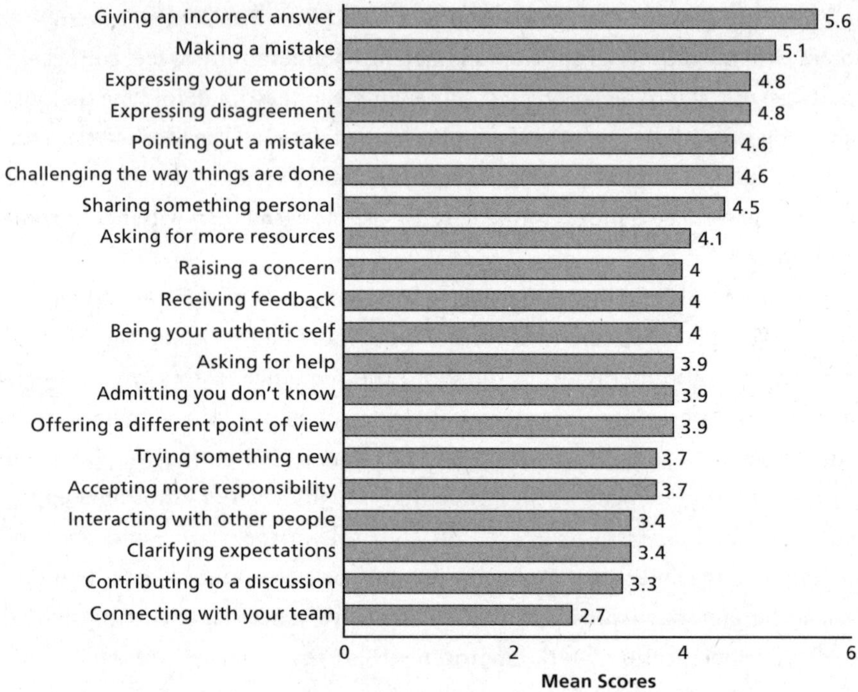

Figure 7. The Ladder of Vulnerability

Not All Acts of Vulnerability Are Created Equal

Variation at the respondent level is significant as reflected in an overall average score of 4.1 and a standard deviation of 2.6. This high level of data dispersion shows that people both perceive and experience vulnerability differently. Yet the mean scores reveal an overall hierarchy of interpersonal risk in professional life, with average scores ranging from 5.6 at the high end to 2.7 at the low end. Here are the mean scores, listed highest to lowest, for the 20 acts of vulnerability:

GIVING AN INCORRECT ANSWER Of the 20 behaviors, respondents rated "Giving an incorrect answer" as the single most vulnerable behavior in the workplace with a mean score of 5.6. In fact, to the average employee, that behavior carries more than double the risk of "Connecting with your team," which, as the lowest-risk behavior, registered a mean score of 2.7.

MAKING A MISTAKE The second-highest-risk behavior is "Making a mistake," with a mean score of 5.3. Perhaps not surprisingly, both "Giving an incorrect answer" and "Making a mistake" are behaviors that reflect directly and negatively on the performance of the individual. In the workplace, where reputation and opportunities for growth and advancement are directly tied to performance, these results help us understand more clearly why employees assign them the highest risk.

EXPRESSING YOUR EMOTIONS "Expressing your emotions" ranks as the third-highest-risk behavior. Research demonstrates that showing, rather than suppressing, emotions at work leads to greater mental health and well-being, provided the expression of emotion is regulated and nondestructive. The corporate persona of perfection and fearlessness that many employees were socialized to maintain works against building emotional resilience, collaborating effectively, motivating others, and showing empathy. Despite these liabilities, hiding emotions remains a firmly entrenched norm in the workplace.

EXPRESSING DISAGREEMENT The fourth-highest-risk behavior, with a mean score of 4.8, is "Expressing disagreement." This finding is problematic when we consider that innovation, by its very nature, requires challenging the status quo. What is the raw material for deviation? Intellectual friction, of course. Without a norm that rewards divergent thinking, teams tend towards groupthink, nurturing echo chambers instead of incubators.

The Central Mechanism of Positive Culture Formation

The way team members perceive different vulnerable behaviors depends largely on whether those behaviors have been consistently rewarded or punished in the past. Ultimately, rewarded vulnerability becomes the central mechanism for creating psychological safety and the key to a healthy and high-performing culture (figure 8).

Understanding the Ladder of Vulnerability can sensitize you to the vulnerability of others. You become more skilled at monitoring group dynamics and identifying vulnerable acts in real time. When you do, those behaviors create higher levels of psychological safety in each stage. For example, I know a leader who listens carefully for even the subtlest signs of disagreement. He makes it a point to reward those early signals of dissent to further encourage the behavior.

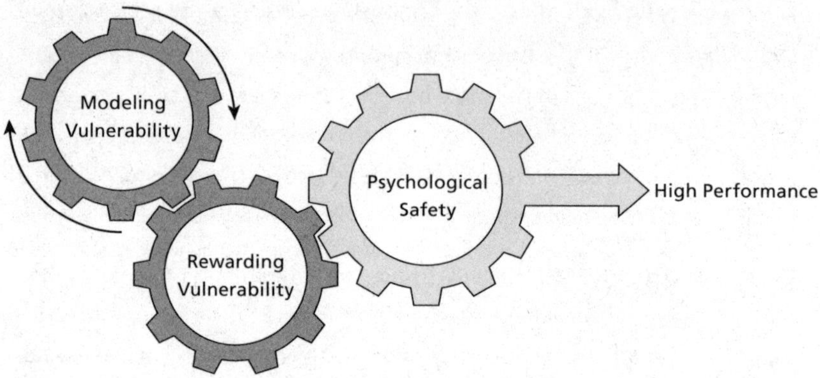

Figure 8. Model and reward vulnerability

Almost every cultural pathology in organizations is traceable to patterns of punished vulnerability and a lack of psychological safety. On the other hand, if a team strives to reward rather than punish vulnerability, that mechanism nurtures psychological safety, which activates the Workplace Hierarchy of Needs. *Modeling and rewarding vulnerability represent the central mechanism of positive culture formation.*

Paternalism and Exploitation

Finally, let me point out two leadership failure patterns that adversely affect psychological safety. Think about what happens when a leader fails to consistently reward acts of vulnerability—when they grant either respect or permission to team members, but not both.

When a leader offers respect but little permission, the leader is demonstrating *paternalism*. Paternalistic leaders act like benevolent dictators or helicopter parents who micromanage their children, patting them on the head and telling them not to touch anything. Early in my career, the CEO of a small company for whom I worked asked the members of our team for feedback on the structure of the organization. I misread the signals and mistakenly believed I had been granted challenger safety, so I spent several hours preparing some recommendations. I never heard back from the CEO and later learned from my colleagues that such requests were a charade. I also learned from my own feelings that paternalism breeds cynicism and disengagement. When a leader is paternalistic, the leader becomes the obstacle, holding people back, reducing organizational leverage, and revealing a fundamental misunderstanding of leadership.

Conversely, when a leader offers permission but little respect, the leader is demonstrating *exploitation*—a condition in which the leader attempts to extract value while not valuing those who create it. Think of exploitation on a spectrum. At one end, we find mild and subtle forms, such as stealing a little credit from a direct report, or praising someone's work only to overload them with more work. The less obvious examples always come with plausible deniability.

At the other end of the spectrum are blatant and severely destructive forms of exploitation, such as public shaming, harassing, and bullying behavior. You would think it would incite a populist revolt, and yet people often endure this treatment out of fear of losing their jobs. This is one reason why patterns of exploitation become normalized. As a plant manager, I witnessed a command-and-control, fear-and-intimidation style of leadership that had little regard for humanity and often viewed workers as commoditized flesh. Demeaning, belittling, and humiliating remarks and gestures had become normalized in many parts of the mill.

So what is the goal? The goal is to move your team or organization successfully through the 4 Stages of Psychological Safety to stage 4, challenger safety, and then stay there. Foster the conditions to preserve those patterns of interaction.

Conclusion

A leader's most important job—above that of creating a vision and setting strategy—is to act in the role of cultural architect and nourish a context in which people are given respect and permission to feel (1) included and accepted, (2) safe to learn and grow, (3) safe to choose and contribute, and (4) safe to challenge and improve the status quo. Remember, the level of psychological safety will always trace its origins to the leader. *You either lead the way or get in the way.* You can't be a neutral party.

We'll now turn to stage 1, inclusion safety, the foundation for everything that follows.

Introduction Summary

- **Core idea:** Psychological safety is a culture of rewarded vulnerability, the enabling precondition for productive human interaction.
- **One lever, many gains:** Raising psychological safety reliably improves ten outcomes:
    1. Inclusion
    2. Team performance
    3. Resilience
    4. Physical safety
    5. Wellness
    6. Engagement
    7. Retention
    8. Learning agility
    9. Productivity
    10. Innovation
- **Why it works:** It lets people satisfy their non-economic workplace needs.
- **Workplace Hierarchy of Needs:**
    1. Inclusion and belonging
    2. Learning and growth
    3. Choice and contribution
    4. Challenge and improvement
- **Four stages, same condition:** Each stage advances through a combination of respect and permission that rewards vulnerability.
- **Not binary, contextual:** Every team has a level of psychological safety. It can shift with behavior and context.
- **Early rule:** The need to be accepted precedes the need to be heard.
- **Human cost:** Being ignored can wound like rejection, leading to compounding unintended consequences.

- **Vulnerability is universal, but risk is personal:** People experience the same act of vulnerability with different perceived risk.
- **Cultural mechanism:** Consistently modeling and rewarding vulnerability is the central mechanism of positive culture formation.
- **Leadership pitfalls:** Respect without permission creates paternalism. Permission without respect creates exploitation.
- **Talent reality:** Psychological safety is fast becoming a term of employment. Without it, organizations bleed out their best people.
- **Leadership mandate:** In creating psychological safety, you either lead the way or get in the way. There is no neutral.

—PART I—

Research and Theory

Before we can build psychological safety, we need to understand what it is, what it does, and why it matters. Part I establishes the conceptual foundation and answers these questions.

In the introduction, I defined psychological safety as a culture of rewarded vulnerability, traced its intellectual history from Kierkegaard to Google's Project Aristotle, and presented the evidence that it correlates significantly with ten organizational outcomes: inclusion, team performance, resilience, physical safety, wellness, engagement, retention, learning agility, productivity, and innovation. I also introduced the Workplace Hierarchy of Needs—the dominant sequence through which people seek to satisfy their non-economic needs at work.

The four chapters that follow unpack each stage of psychological safety in depth:

Stage 1, Inclusion Safety, satisfies the basic human need to feel *included and to belong*. We examine why inclusion is owed rather than earned, how threat detection shapes behavior, and why the need to be accepted precedes the need to be heard.

Stage 2, Learner Safety, satisfies the need to *learn and grow*. We explore why learning is both intellectual and emotional, how fear disconnects cognition, and why encouragement for engagement is the leader's first-mover obligation.

Stage 3, Contributor Safety, satisfies the need to *choose and contribute*. We examine the transition from preparation to performance, the three levels of accountability, and the social exchange of autonomy for results.

Stage 4, Challenger Safety, satisfies the need to *challenge and improve the status quo*. We explore why innovation requires deviation, the social exchange of candor for cover, and why the quality of interaction regulates the speed of discovery.

Part I answers the question: *What is psychological safety and why does it matter?* Part II will answer: *How do I create it?*

STAGE 1

Inclusion Safety

Our ability to reach unity in diversity will be the beauty and the test of our civilization.

—Mahatma Gandhi

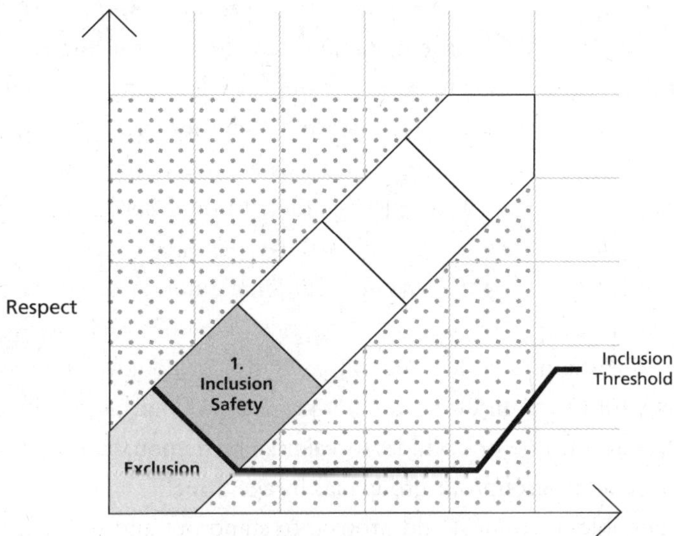

Figure 9. Stage 1: Inclusion safety

I see uncritical celebrations of diversity everywhere. Yes, diversity is a virtue, but it produces nothing and blesses no one unless its value can be drawn out. Many organizations have made great strides to diversify their employee populations, but they are no more inclusive as a consequence. These organizations haven't finished the job. In fact, they have only started the job. Creating a deeply inclusive environment is the consequence of creating stage 1, inclusion safety (figure 9). Without it, employees can't satisfy the first need category in the Workplace Hierarchy of Needs: inclusion and belonging.

As an example, my sardonic teenage daughter once went to a high school basketball game and held up a poster that read "I'm just here so I don't lose friends!" It's true: *We long to belong.*

Stage 1, inclusion safety, introduces two human paradoxes. First, consider that humans crave *connection and protection*. Connection requires more vulnerability, protection less. There's natural tension between the two. Second, consider that humans want to *stand out and fit in*. Standing out requires more vulnerability, while fitting in requires less. Another natural tension. These competing needs motivate us to seek inclusion and a secure basis of attachment. They also motivate us to exclude others through social rejection, which is how we inflict attachment and connection injuries on others.

We can debate forever if it's in our evolutionary biology to naturally exclude and engage in us-versus-them dichotomizing. Whether we're predisposed to be more tribal than relational, it's still a choice. Although they interact and exert powerful forces on us, we are not prisoners of our biology or culture.[64] We are free to include or exclude, to valorize or demonize, even though we may develop an in-group/out-group bias by age three![65]

Is it possible to connect and protect, to stand out and fit in, at the same time? It is, but it takes humility and a willingness to abandon beliefs, values, assumptions, stereotypes, traditions, customs, and biases that are harmful or untrue. Inclusion safety is grounded in the principle of universal human dignity.

Definition: Inclusion safety satisfies the basic human need to be included, to feel accepted, and to belong. It means it's not expensive to be yourself. You are accepted for who you are, including your unique attributes and defining characteristics.

With high levels of psychological safety, team members won't waste precious time worrying about personal worthiness. They'll know that they belong, and can move forward with confidence that they have a purpose. They'll feel a sense of equality as hierarchy and status are softened to remove barriers of connection. Bias will have a lesser effect on the organization as a whole, because every team member will be granted irrevocable participation rights. Cultural differences will enhance, not segment, your teams. The single most important question you can ask yourself and others to reveal the level of inclusion safety on your team is this: *Is it expensive to be yourself?* I call this the inclusion question.

I had a conversation with an executive from a large technology company who had been part of a leadership team that was breaking up. When I asked her the inclusion question, even on Zoom, I could see her eyes roll.

"My job," she said, "was to take orders and execute. They didn't want my opinion."

"But you're an executive," I protested.

"I know," she said. "And now that the old guard is gone, I can finally breathe. I can finally be myself. I can finally weigh in."

"But how did you survive under that regime for three years?" I asked.

"I had to be someone else," she said.

When talking to another woman who had just been promoted to management at a financial services company, I asked her the inclusion question.

"Wow," she said. "I'd have to say no. My boss is tough. Super high expectations. But he lets me be me. He respects me and listens. He's a validating human being and he holds me accountable."

The inclusion question penetrates to the first category of non-economic human need. But keep in mind that while being yourself is a basic human need, self-preservation is a deeper need. *Humans will always default to the deeper need. Thus, survival precedes self-expression.*

Remember, survival isn't just physical, it's social and emotional—and it requires inclusion safety. As Oxford's Robin Dunbar notes, "You can eat as much as you like, drink as much alcohol as you want, slob about as much as you fancy, fail to do your exercises and live in as polluted an atmosphere as you can find, and you will barely notice the difference. But having no friends or not being involved in community activities will dramatically affect how long you live."[66]

Threat Detection Is Innate in Humans

Have you ever raised your hand to ask a question and then put it down abruptly? You did that because your last-second risk/reward calculation convinced you that the risk of negative consequences was too high.

When human beings interact in social settings, they subconsciously engage in threat detection. We observe, monitor, listen, and perceive. We take in group dynamics—not just once, but continuously.[67] What are we looking for? We go in with "belonging uncertainty" and we want to know if we can gain that sense of belonging.[68] And yet the threat detection never ends, because belonging has to be created over and over. We're looking for social proof, evidence that we can be ourselves. If the environment offers you inclusion safety, you will feel and know that it's *not* expensive to be yourself.

As adaptable creatures, we have two modes of performance—offense and defense. If we sense that the setting is safe, we play offense. We offer a performance response and bring our honest, authentic selves to work (or whatever the setting may be). Because it's not expensive to be ourselves, we engage as ourselves. We release our discretionary effort and go headlong into what we're doing. Without reservation, we contribute our skills, knowledge, and experience. We want to make a difference.

On the other hand, if we sense that the setting is unsafe, we shift to defense. We offer a survival response (figure 10). We withdraw, retreat, and recoil. We're not playing to win; we're playing not to lose. We know instinctively that our first priority is to manage personal risk, so we toggle to a mindset of self-preservation and loss avoidance. We reduce vulnerability and use our creative and productive capacities to protect ourselves. We say less, do less, and try less. We ask fewer questions, make fewer suggestions, and make fewer attempts to

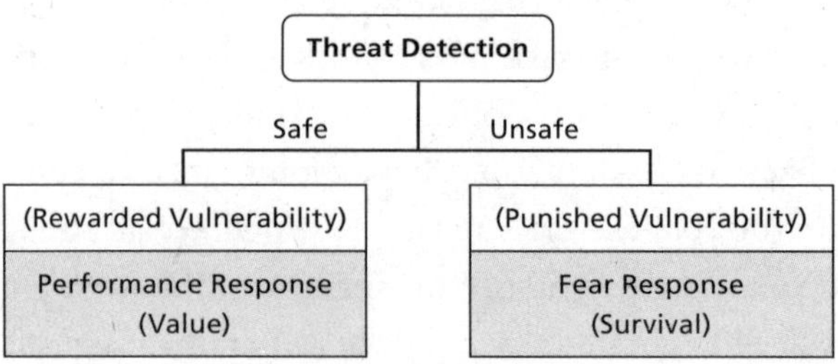

Figure 10. Threat detection

avoid fewer mistakes. *When it's expensive to be yourself, you will be tempted to mask, armor, modulate, or code switch.*

Triggering the Self-Censoring Instinct

Threat detection is hardwired. You don't need to be taught the concept or take a class on how to do it more skillfully. You do it naturally and instinctively. Which brings us to this: We all have a self-censoring instinct. It's standard equipment. When we sense danger in the environment, it triggers that self-censoring instinct and an adaptive response. Even healthy environments with high psychological safety can change in an instant if there's a violation of respect or an act of incivility.

Here's a quick self-assessment that includes twelve common breaches of psychological safety that routinely occur in human interaction. Read the twelve questions and ask yourself if you've experienced any of these breaches in the last week:

1. Have you felt excluded in a social setting?
2. Have you been afraid to ask a question?
3. Have you remained silent when you knew the answer to a problem?
4. Have you had someone else steal credit for something you did?
5. Have you given a suggestion that was ignored?
6. Have you been rudely interrupted in a meeting?
7. Have you felt that you were the target of a negative stereotype?
8. Have you faced retaliation for challenging the status quo?
9. Have you had a boss who asked for feedback but didn't really want it?
10. Have you been publicly shamed or made fun of?
11. Have you been punished for making an honest mistake?
12. Have you been made to feel inferior?

Is there a human being who hasn't experienced at least one of these breaches of psychological safety? Unfortunately not, but the more important point is the frequency with which they occur. These acts of incivility are far too common. They happen every day. In our survey research, my team has discovered that fully 60 percent of employees can say yes to one of these questions every twenty-four hours. That finding is not just explanatory; it's also predictive. We can predict with a high degree of certainty that you will experience some kind of microaggression or adverse interpersonal event that will activate your self-censoring instinct and thrust you into a defensive routine in the next twenty-four hours.

Let's bring gender into it. Gendered norms of participation—in which women tend toward accommodation, cooperation, inclusiveness, and interdependence, while men tend toward assertiveness—can be complementary. They can also be signs of significant self-censoring.[69] Fear, incivility, and a lack of psychological safety disproportionately silence women.[70] Teams perform better when women speak up more agentically as well as communally, meaning when they speak more assertively and confidently.[71] And yet when they do, they still face the risk of a gender backlash, because some perceive them violating the norms of "feminine niceness."[72]

No wonder most teams don't perform at capacity. Fear and incivility diminish performance.[73] I like the phrase "the strain of being watchful," coined by Ta-Nehisi Coates to describe the chronic activation of the body's threat system, which reduces access to safety and connection.[74]

Note to Leaders: Ask and Then Listen

Every team registers a different level of psychological safety. Clearly, the leader's behavior has the most profound impact on that. When we ask leaders if they're aware of the way their behavior affects others, 90 percent say yes. But if we probe and ask them to explain *how* their behavior affects others, they often can't offer a coherent response. How, then, do you shed layers of insulation to gain greater self-awareness?

Rather than spending hours in deep introspection, go talk to your people. Pull them aside one-on-one and ask them the inclusion question: "As a member of this team, is it expensive to be yourself?" Even in the face of fear and positional power, most employees will answer that question honestly, because it's far safer to talk about your own experience than to criticize someone else, even if you are indirectly indicting the person asking. And not least, you're giving the individual a chance to be heard. It's an act of interpersonal risk most people are willing to take. They want to talk about their experience and how they feel. As they answer the inclusion question, they will answer your question. Their response will be a mirror of your impact. Listen carefully. You might be amazed at what you learn.

Inclusion Is a Choice

As the first stage of psychological safety, inclusion safety is, in its purest sense, nothing more than species-based acceptance. If you have flesh and blood, we include you. *The choice to include another human being signals respect and permission, acknowledges a common bond, and activates our humanity.* Profoundly simple in concept, devilishly difficult in practice, we learn it in kindergarten and unlearn it later. A mere 36 percent of business professionals today believe their companies foster an inclusive culture.[75]

I remember talking to my son, Ben, after his first day of kindergarten:

"How did you like your first day of kindergarten, Ben?" I asked.

"It was fun, Dad."

"Are you excited to go to school tomorrow?"

"Yeah, I'm excited."

"Is Mom going to take you to school again tomorrow?"

"No, I'm going to walk."

"Do you have anyone to walk with?"

"No, Dad, I'll just walk by myself, but if anyone wants to walk with me, they can."

I'll never forget that tender exchange. It's a reflection of the uncorrupted, inclusive nature of children. *We include naturally in childhood and exclude unnaturally in adulthood.*

The basic decision to include or exclude is not about skill or personality, although those things can enhance your ability to include. You can't mandate inclusion safety, because granting it is about intent rather than technique. You can't legislate it, regulate it, train it, measure it, or gimmick it into existence. It doesn't respond to those forces. It's an act of will that flows from the empire of the heart. If there's no psychological safety, there's no inclusion. *Including another human being should be an act of prejudgment based on that person's worth, not an act of judgment based on that person's worthiness.*

Our children memorized passages from Martin Luther King Jr.'s "I Have a Dream" speech in school. I can still hear them recite the line "I look to a day when people will not be judged by the color of their skin, but by the content of their character."[76] The theologian Reinhold Niebuhr made a similar observation when he said, "We are admonished in scripture to judge men by their fruits, not by their roots."[77]

Before we judge others as less exalted, note that the Reverend King and Pastor Niebuhr are talking about judgment based on worthiness of character. That comes later. Inclusion safety is not about worthiness. It's about treating people like people. It's the act of extending fellowship, membership, association, and connection—regardless of rank, status, gender, race, appearance, intelligence, education, beliefs, values, politics, habits, traditions, language, customs, history, or any other defining characteristic. Inclusion marks passage into civilization. If we can't do that as a starting point, we're not being true to what Abraham Lincoln called "the better angels of our nature."[78] Withholding inclusion safety is a sign that we're engaged in a fight with our own willful blindness. We're self-medicating with enchanting tales about our distinctiveness and superiority. If it's a mild case of snobbery, that's easy to dismiss. But if it's a more severe case of narcissistic supremacy, that's a bigger problem. And then there's everything in between.

In our social units, we should create an environment of inclusion before we begin to think about judgments at all. Worth precedes worthiness. There's a time and a place to judge worthiness, but when you allow someone to cross the threshold of inclusion, there's no litmus test. We're not weighing your character in the balance to see if you're found wanting. To be deserving of inclusion has nothing to do with your personality, virtues, or abilities; nothing to do with your gender, race, ethnicity, education, or any other demographic variable that defines you. There are, at this level, no disqualifications except the threat of harm.

The only reciprocation requirement in this unwritten social contract is the mutual exchange of respect and permission to belong. That exchange is largely unenforceable by law and defines the circular interdependence of humanity. There are laws against discrimination, but in a thousand ways we can still informally persecute each other.

Let me give you an example of A/B testing for inclusion safety. I have two cars. One is old and rusty, with 315,000 miles on the odometer and a resale value of –$375. I would probably have to pay someone to take it away. The other is a black sports sedan. When I take in my sedan for service, the attendant is solicitous. When I take my rust bucket, the attendant is mildly disdainful. In both cases, the car is the lead indicator of my social status, and people grant or withhold inclusion safety based on my car, the artifact in which I sit. Some days I'm politely ignored, some days solicitously attended to. That's how sensitive people are to these indicators, because we scramble for status like apes for nuts.

What should it take to qualify for inclusion safety? Two things: Be human and be harmless. If you meet both criteria, you qualify. If you meet only one, you don't. The great African American abolitionist Frederick Douglass made the definitive statement about inclusion safety when he said, "I know of no rights of race superior to the rights of humanity." That statement can apply to any characteristic. When we extend inclusion to each other, we subordinate our differences to invoke a more important binding characteristic—our common humanity. And by the way, what was Douglass doing when he gave this speech in Boston in 1869? Advocating for the citizenship rights of Chinese immigrants![79]

Table 2 defines respect and permission in the first stage of psychological safety. The definition of *respect* in this stage is simply respect for the individual's humanity. *Permission* in this stage is the permission you give another to feel, be their authentic self, and enter your society. Finally, the social exchange is one in which we trade inclusion for human status, provided we don't threaten each other with harm.

Deep down, we know we should extend inclusion safety to everyone, but we have become very skilled at chasing each other to the margins and patrolling the boundaries. We splinter, segment, and stratify the human family. Sometimes we extend partial or conditional inclusion safety. Sometimes we revoke or withhold it. *Instead of granting inclusion safety based on*

Table 2. Stage 1: Inclusion safety

Stage	Definition of respect	Definition of permission	Social exchange
1. Inclusion safety	Respect for the individual's innate need to be included, accepted, and gain a sense of belonging	Permission for the individual to feel, be their authentic self, and enter your society	Inclusion in exchange for human status and the absence of harm

human status, we tend to judge another person's worth based on indicators like appearance, social status, or material possessions, when those indicators have nothing to do with worth.

Kimchi and Our Common Humanity

In the arc of every life are times when inclusion safety makes all the difference. When I was in graduate school, I had the opportunity to do research at the Seoul National University in Korea as a Fulbright scholar. The university offered me a place at its Social Science Research Center. The day I arrived, Professor Ahn Chung Si greeted me warmly and took me around the center to meet the staff and other researchers. My initial apprehension was replaced with a sense of inclusion when two Korean graduate students asked me to go to lunch. I was the different one, the stranger, the alien, the one who didn't fit in. But I was not the odd person out. Holding my bowl of rice dumpling soup, I sat down at one of the tables in the cafeteria and was soon greeting other students and faculty. With some hesitation, a student sitting next to me handed me a bowl of kimchi. That was the beginning of an extraordinary experience with inclusion safety.

True, I was a novelty, but I hasten to say that inclusion safety is not simply the expression of hospitality. You can be polite and not mean it. That kind of surface acting is a disingenuous way of abiding by common rules of decency and decorum. But these students were not only kind and helpful on my first day, which is easy to do. They were also kind and helpful on my thirtieth day and my sixtieth day and so on. I was clearly outside their social group and overstayed the normal expiration date for standard-protocol, obligatory, respectful treatment. But after weeks and weeks of long days at the center, they never revoked the inclusion safety they first extended. It was real.

Let's put this in historical context. South Korea is considered the world's most neo-Confucian society, historically embracing status hierarchy, inequality, and inherent discrimination as core values. Human rights have a short history. They have in recent years been acknowledged as a matter of political expediency, but not through some religious or philosophical sense of natural law, inalienability, or God-invested entitlement. In this society, rights are more instrumental than moral, more negotiated than inviolate, more legislated than guaranteed or absolute. Confucianism lacks rational, legal, or moral grounds for inclusion, instead emphasizing loyalty, devotion, allegiance, and compliance to authority in the promotion of group harmony and stability.

What does all of that mean? It means I'm an outsider. There's no natural place for me in Korean society or hierarchy. And yet my Korean friends included me in a way that superseded their neo-Confucian tradition. They suspended the normal terms of engagement, giving precedence to a higher principle of humanity. Rather than focus on differences, they emphasized common fellowship.[80] Was I now Korean? Did they grant me full social and cultural membership? No. They extended inclusion safety, but on what basis? Was it religious, ethnic, socioeconomic, geographic, cultural, political, legal? None of the above. It was based on a supernal, primordial human connection that overcame our separatism and penetrated to membership in a universal family.

Hardening the Concept of Equality

The philosopher John Rawls reminds us of this fundamental truth: "Institutions are just when no arbitrary distinctions are made between persons in the assigning of basic rights and duties."[81] To exclude a member of a social unit based on conscious or unconscious bias is exactly that—an arbitrary distinction. These must be removed, as Rawls says, to "build an enduring system of mutual cooperation."[82] There will always be differences, but there mustn't be barriers. There will always be majorities and minorities, but we should never attempt to deracinate each other until we melt into a homogenous lot. Our differences define us.

Some would object to this idea on grounds that we don't know each other. So how can we accept, include, tolerate, and connect with strangers? And in fact, research shows that the key drivers of psychological safety include familiarity among team members and the quality of those relationships based on prior interactions.[83] But extending inclusion safety doesn't require extending the mature, developed feelings of affection that come from knowing someone well. Our feelings toward someone, even when expectant and assumptive rather than informed by experience, can still be genuine and rooted in fundamental respect for their humanity. In contrast, xenophobic arguments are born of ignorance, fear, jealousy, or a dishonest desire for superiority. *God may have made us of different clay, but there are no grounds to say that your clay is better than mine.*

Inclusion safety is not earned but owed. Every human has title to it as a nonnegotiable right. In fact, we can't sustain civilization without it.[84] We hunger for and deserve dignity and esteem from each other and unavoidably practice morality when we extend or withhold inclusion safety. If there's no threat of harm, we should give it without a value judgment. As the basic glue of human society, psychological safety offers the comforting assurance that you matter. If you're a leader and you want your people to perform, you must internalize the universal truth that people want, need, and deserve validation. Inclusion safety requires that we condemn negative bias, arbitrary distinction, or destructive prejudice that refuses to acknowledge our equal worth and the obligation of equal treatment.

If everyone deserves inclusion—if we're all entitled to fellowship and connection, if we have the right to civil and respectful interactions, if the reciprocation of courtesy defines us as a species—then we have an obligation to demolish nativism and ethnocentrism. Nations, communities, and organizations aren't the only offenders.[85] We see alienation within families, as individuals shun, banish, and relegate each other to subordinate status. We see parents and children who neglect or harm each other. And then there are the glorious triumphs when we get it right, when we extend the hand of fellowship and are blessed in that moment with the nutrition of real human connection.

Granting, Withholding, and Revoking Inclusion Safety

After graduating high school, I took an athletic scholarship to play Division I football at Brigham Young University. Arriving on campus a month early to begin summer training camp, all freshmen players were assigned to live in the same dormitory near the practice facilities. Here was a group of ethnically and culturally diverse young men thrust into a highly structured environment, along the lines of a military boot camp, characterized by sudden and complete immersion.

We surrendered our personal freedom and space, and from that moment would eat, sleep, shower, and sweat together. The machinery of the football regimen dictated every aspect of our daily lives. My teammates represented three primary racial groups—black, white, and Polynesian. But this was nothing new. Despite our coming together from all parts of the country, our racial composition was familiar. We had been deeply socialized in the ethnically diverse subculture of American football and understood its norms and meritocracy.

The task was to form a new society, one that would organize itself on both Darwinian and communitarian principles. A football team competes with other teams, but its players compete with each other. While the external rivalry was institutional, the internal rivalry was personal. You might be competing with the guy sleeping in the bed next to you. We played a zero-sum, finite game. Introducing the element of competition changes the dynamics of a society and the terms of engagement for granting or withholding inclusion safety. The prevailing norms were at the same time collegial and adversarial, and that duality was maintained throughout the experience. Your teammate could be friend and foe.

The nature of the team-sport environment accelerates the development of familiarity, which is massively important in the formation of psychological safety. As sociometric research from the MIT Human Dynamics Lab attests, the faster and deeper you get to know each other, the more effectively you can work together.[86] More contact and context tend to create more empathy.

On the first day, we bonded slowly, knowing that we would begin practicing and competing the following day. That reality made the collegial and adversarial forces collide. As a result, our initial greetings were warm with fellow players who didn't play our same positions, and chilled with those who did. Every player arrived dripping with honors and recognition, so bluster and bravado were signs of insecurity and a clear signal that a player wasn't as good as advertised.

In what is akin to a modern-day blood sport, you can't carry on a rhetorical career for very long. Performance does the talking. Football was our common aspiration, but the internal competition was a divisive element. We were formally admitted members of the team, but extending inclusion safety to each other was an individual matter. Ironically, we admitted or refused to admit each other in the act of joining the society ourselves.

Instead of fusing into a cohesive group, we balkanized into smaller groups based on race or geography. And then of course there were the offensive linemen, who bonded into a unique fraternity of sensitive, industrial-size humans and shut the gates behind them. I, on the other hand, played defensive tackle, where that sort of bonding would violate our gladiator subculture. After a week of what MIT's Edgar Schein would call "spontaneous interaction," you could see norms starting to form.[87] But a week later, the upperclassmen arrived, and our organic society was swallowed up by the larger machine.

When you join an existing organization, as I came to the football team, you inherit a cultural legacy based on perpetuated norms. Unless you're forming a new social collective, you don't start clean. In our case, we freshmen started clean and erected a temporary society that was then abruptly dismantled. When the rest of the team arrived, it was as if the mothership had landed with its cargo of artifacts, habits, customs, and distribution of power. Here came the unyielding orthodoxy and way of doing things, all modeled and reinforced by the coaching staff. Punctuality rule? Enforced. Dress code rule? Not enforced. Respect rule? Enforced. No profanity rule? Not enforced. And so on. As we moved into the regular season, inclusion safety gradually emerged. The internal rivalries settled, and we came together.

Now came the inclusion safety lesson of a lifetime: Halfway into the season, I sustained a serious injury. When the diagnosis came back that I had severely damaged my ankle and needed surgery, I experienced a sudden and dramatic change in status. My position coach revoked inclusion safety through a silent campaign of neglect. I was injured and therefore unable to contribute to the team. To him, I was now invisible. He had extended conditional inclusion safety to me, based not on my worth as a human being, but rather on my worthiness as a player. The moment I got hurt and was no longer useful to the team, he withdrew his fellowship through subtle and unmistakable indifference. That indifference stung. As I quickly learned, inclusion safety, once built, is fragile, delicate, and impermanent. *In any social unit, inclusion safety can be granted, withheld, revoked, or partially or conditionally granted.*

Soothing Ourselves with Junk Theories of Superiority

Theories have consequences. Too often we have run our societies on intellectually unclean theories. Regardless of the society you live in, the historian's pen has shown that nearly every society has its origins in bigotry, discrimination, conquest, servitude, and exploitation. Governments and rulers have spent much of their time spinning theories of superiority to justify their grip on power. To make it respectable and give it the illusion of morality, they package privilege and power as political ideology.[88] Even though we know that every person is worthy of belonging, we do the same thing at a personal level as we marinate in notions of supremacy and award ourselves elevated status. *We like to tell ourselves soothing stories to justify our sense of superiority.*

Theories of superiority are attempts to show how, in the words of George Orwell, "All animals are equal, but some animals are more equal than others."[89] I remember reading Hitler's *Mein Kampf* as a student. I had to hold my nose, but I kept reading because I was fascinated that this clever work of eugenics-based grandiosity had influenced so many people. It's beguiling when someone tells you that you're better than everyone else, that you've been unjustly dealt with, and that you deserve more.

It's the same facile thesis we find in all theories of superiority and biological determinism, and all attempts at intellectual imperialism. It begins with a false claim of superiority, or election, on some grounds, and then moves to a call to action: You're in the minority, you're in danger, and you need to rise up and defend yourself. Unfortunately, absurd strains of social Darwinism have always been effective when presented with urgency and erudition. People fall for it. And it really doesn't matter whose theory of superiority you read; they're all meditations in hypocrisy, bathed in jingoism, resting on the same veiled attempts to preserve the vassalage of the past.

For example, the two most universal and pervasive forms of discrimination—sexism and racism—persist across civilizations, appearing in ancient, medieval, and modern societies. They are global in scope, affecting every inhabited region. Dislodging them is a wicked problem because they are institutionalized in law and religion, and deeply embedded in social systems and culture. We have always used junk theories as a patina of legitimacy.[90]

Shocking as it may sound, theories of supremacy and superiority have dominated human societies for millennia.[91] As one of the first power theorists, Aristotle declared, "It is clear that some men are by nature free and others by nature slaves, and that for these latter, slavery is both expedient and right."[92] We have libraries filled with theories of superiority, because we have an irrepressible desire to be just a little more special than the next person. John Adams wrote, "I believe there is no one principle which predominates in human nature so much in every stage of life, from the cradle to the grave, in males and females, old and young, black and white, rich and poor, high and low, as this passion for superiority."[93]

With history to ponder, how can we excuse ourselves on the premise that human nature is full of paradoxes, contradictions, and complexities, and we just can't help it? Haven't we graduated from our dangerous and nihilistic tendency to dismiss the natural-rights tradition as just one of many propaganda traditions? How many times have we dressed up vanity as moral philosophy? How many times have we disguised elitism as the naturally stratified order of heaven?

Thankfully, many people don't subscribe to these pretensions. But many do. In our modern society, we have long since repudiated the grand theories of bloodline aristocracy, but we continue to hatch, nurse, and perpetuate informal versions that do the same thing. They show up as stereotypes, resentment, bias, and prejudice, and linger in our values, assumptions, and behavior.

When I began my service as plant manager at Geneva Steel, I conducted a series of tours throughout the plant. I traveled from facility to facility, holding town hall meetings, greeting the managers and production and maintenance workers. I started at the coke plant and then moved to the blast furnaces, steelmaking operations, casting, rolling mills, finishing units, shipping and transportation, and central maintenance.

In the coke plant, two production workers cornered me. They removed their hard hats and safety goggles, revealing faces caked with sweat and soot. "Mr. Clark," they said deferentially, "thank you for coming to visit our department. I know you're new to your position as plant manager. I know you're going to visit all the departments, but we just wanted you to know that our department is a little different than the others. Our department is a little more complicated than the others, and it requires a little more expertise to do what we do. If we weren't here, the plant would shut down tomorrow." They made their case and stated their claim. I politely responded, "Thank you for sharing that with me. I appreciate your feedback."

That scene repeated itself in every department. The faces were different, but the script was the same. After my weeklong tour, I was illuminated with the revelation that every department was just a little more important than the others, occupied by a special class of people, doing what no one else could do. They all gently shunted their brothers and sisters in order to distinguish themselves. I have kept that little secret to myself all these years! I suppose we have all made, or been tempted to make, a similar claim and fallen prey to the grand illusion of superiority. Is the moral principle of inclusion a convenient or inconvenient truth for you? Do you think you're just a little more special than the next person? If so, why?

The Elite and the Great Unwashed

Why is it difficult to grant inclusion safety to each other when any justification for withholding it is patently false? Where does the illusion of superiority come from? Our marble cake society features streaks of equality and prejudice. The US Constitution includes an unequivocal declaration of human rights, but it's taken generations to unwind legalized discrimination and dismantle the edifice that sustains it.

In 1776, Abigail Adams wrote to her husband, John, "I desire you would Remember the Ladies. . . . [We] will not hold ourselves bound by any Laws in which we have no voice, or Representation."[94] Two years later, the original American colonies ratified the US Constitution. Although the document was the first government charter that acknowledged the equality of all human beings, it carved out exceptions and violated the ideals it espoused, allowing slavery, counting slaves as equal to a three-fifths of a "normal" human, and, not least, withholding voting rights from women. Nor could women own property, keep their own wages, or, in some states, even choose their own husbands. With lyrical language, the Constitution decreed inclusion, but too often we practiced exclusion. It would still take many generations to internalize the espoused values, because theories of superiority were deeply ingrained in the American psyche, as they were in every nation.[95] Consider the following official acts of exclusion:

- Congress passed the Naturalization Act of 1790, declaring that only white people could become citizens of the nation.
- Congress passed the Indian Removal Act of 1830 to drive out Native Americans from their tribal lands.
- Lincoln issued the Emancipation Proclamation in 1863, but states passed Jim Crow laws to enforce discrimination, and the Supreme Court piled on with its "separate but equal" legal doctrine.
- In 1882, Congress passed the Chinese Exclusion Act, barring Chinese immigration.
- In 1910, 1.6 million children aged ten to fifteen worked in factories. The Fair Labor Standards Act didn't ban child labor until 1938.
- Women did not win the right to vote until Congress passed the Nineteenth Amendment in 1920.

- In 1942, President Franklin D. Roosevelt authorized the evacuation and incarceration of 127,000 Japanese Americans from the West Coast to internment camps.
- Hispanic American workers didn't gain the right to unionize until the 1950s.
- Ultimately, the United States didn't purge deliberate and systematic prejudice out of our immigration laws until the Immigration Act of 1965.

But what about our culture? We continue to struggle to redress inequality and forsake notions of male and Anglo-Saxon supremacy. As my teenage daughter asks, "Dad, why is gender wage equity still a thing?" Why *is* it a thing?

We have purged most of our policies of discrimination, but have our hearts changed? Have we become a more inclusive society? A recent EY study reports that less than half of employees trust their bosses and employers.[96] Where there's no trust, there's exclusion. This number is troubling, because we know that trust is what binds us together. As the political scientist Robert Putnam reminds us, "trustworthiness lubricates social life. Frequent interaction among a diverse set of people tends to produce a norm of generalized reciprocity."[97] If this is true, if familiarity based on the frequency of interaction has this amazing ability to eliminate bias and distrust, why are trust numbers so low?

This is the "society versus community" dichotomy.[98] We would expect to see a trusting community within a more distrustful society. There should be proportionately more trust as we move to smaller social units. Organizations should have more trust than governments. Teams should have more than organizations. Families should have more than teams, and marriages should have the most. There should be more good faith and lower transaction costs in our interactions as we move from big to small.[99] If this is true, and I think it is, we get nowhere until we grant each other inclusion safety.

Who's getting in the way? The psychologist Carol Dweck has said, "Your failures and misfortunes don't threaten other people. It's your assets and your successes that are problems for people who derive their self-esteem from being superior."[100] The irony is that because of our insecurity we refuse to validate each other, which is the very thing that heals the insecurity. That unmet need expresses itself in jealousy, resentment, and contempt. Meanwhile, society is filled to overflowing with incivility, and hate has become a growth industry. But if we just get to know each other, we like each other.

Excluding another person is more often the result of unmet needs than a genuine dislike of the person.

How many times have you been suspicious or critical of someone you didn't really know, and when you got to know that person, your entire attitude changed? Differences tend to repel us initially, but when we suspend judgment, we can bridge those differences. When I was in college, I took a class from a professor with radical views. I braced myself for combat. I went to class and learned that this gentleman did indeed hold views very different from my own, but we developed a wonderful friendship à la Ruth Bader Ginsberg and Antonin Scalia. We had marvelous disagreements but maintained a deep respect for each other. If we don't watch ourselves, there's a thousand ways to show hostility and withhold inclusion safety. And if we dehumanize each other, we give ourselves permission to harm each other.

I once worked with an executive team whose members had withdrawn inclusion safety from each other. They were legal officers of a corporation but had revoked each other's cultural passports. The team was dysfunctional. They would verbally bruise and bludgeon each other and could barely stand to be in the same room. In an interview, one member told me, "We don't have to like each other; we just have to work together, so I guess it doesn't really matter. I'm all about getting the job done. I don't care too much about the relationships anyway."

I worked with another leader who asserted dominance through an arbitrary pattern of giving and revoking inclusion safety. You were in his good graces one day, out the next, respected then neglected, heard then ignored, fawned over then forgotten, coached then coerced, healed then hurt. Let's be clear: Head games are a form of abuse in which one human toys with another. That pattern of interaction is moral cowardice at its finest.

Family as the Realm of Thick Trust

The word *accept* means to consent to receive. The word *inclusion* means having the status of association or connection to a group. Now think about these two words as they relate to the family unit. The relationship between husband and wife is based on the consent to receive the other. The family unit that is created from that union is a new entity to which both are parties. If one spouse denies membership to the other, the social unit doesn't function. The legal tie that binds them together may be intact, but the reality of their union has evaporated.

The interdependence of the marriage relationship is more fundamental than in any other social collective. It is fragile and yet designed to be the realm of the thickest trust. At any moment, one party may withdraw inclusion safety from the other. The respect and permission to participate that each gives the other is the very basis of their interdependency, their success, and their happiness. That inclusion safety is dynamic and perishable. It must be replenished every day. Particularly in marriage, respect must be translated into acts of kindness, service, and sacrifice. Without a consistent investment in gestures of respect, the relationship will wither from neglect. But in a coequal partnership, in which both spouses participate and permit the other equal power and participation rights, the relationship is likely to produce sustainable, high levels of inclusion safety and a deeply fulfilling experience for both.

The relationship between parents and children is somewhat different. Children begin life in a stage of dependence and hopefully move to a stage of interdependence as they learn and grow. *A stage of pure independence is of course a fiction.* How many times have you heard parental advice to raise your children to be independent? Amend that: Raise your children to be interdependent, to give and take, share and sacrifice, concentrate and collaborate. In that development process, the intersection of love and accountability is all important. Parents shouldn't condone poor behavior, but neither should they condemn the child for it. The child is much more able to learn both rights and responsibility in a nurturing environment of sustained inclusion safety. It's over the elusive combination of love and accountability that so many of us stumble. I've stumbled many times, often to my children's dismay. I've learned to say, "I love you and I'm going to hold you accountable." I've also learned to say, "I'm sorry and I'm going to hold myself accountable." *The basic social unit of the family is the primary laboratory for gaining a true civic education in inclusion safety.*

Behave Until You Believe

What if you can't find the conviction to include someone? What if you have a deep-seated bias or prejudice that you can't dislodge from your heart? How do you overcome it? Where do we find, to use Kafka's phrase, "the ax for the frozen sea within us"?[101] One thing that doesn't work very well is to sit back and wait for your heart to change.

There's not a person alive without at least some trace elements of negative bias against some human characteristic. But some of us are more blameworthy than others. We need to be honest about the acquisition of bias and prejudice and work hard to remove it. We don't get to make choices about diversity; diversity simply is. It's our job to embrace it.

Learn to love yourself first. People with low self-regard have a hard time being inclusive. Whatever your level of self-regard, it spills into your interpersonal behavior. As Nathaniel Branden observes, "Research shows that a well-developed sense of personal value and autonomy correlates significantly with kindness, generosity, social cooperation, and a spirit of mutual aid."[102] The best and quickest way to develop self-regard is to develop your own capacity and confidence and to perform acts of service for others, especially for those whom you struggle to include. In the very act of reaching out to include others, your self-regard grows.

Think about the traditional approach most organizations take to diversity and inclusion. They train their employees to be inclusive by teaching them awareness, understanding, and appreciation for differences. That's nice, but it's a coat of paint.[103] We simply get defensive and then go back to taking counsel from our fears, vanity, and deeply grooved beliefs. A better way is to practice inclusion. Make it experiential. *You learn inclusion when you practice inclusion. Behave until you believe.*

Inclusive behavior produces its own confirming evidence.[104] The call to action is simple: Affirm the individual worth of other human beings. Do I mean fake it until you feel it? Lease your kindness? Pretend? Mask, armor, code switch, or modulate? No, I mean earnest striving with real intent. Remember, there are two sides to stage 1, inclusion safety: While you must be permitted to be yourself, you must also be willing to be yourself if others are doing their part. As Carl Rogers said, "Only real people have real relationships."[105]

As you love people with action, you come to love them with emotion. The feeling of love is the reward of the action of love. In fact, if we fail to serve others, our relationships remain superficial, and even suspicious, until we close the distance. In that closeness, in living, working, eating, and breathing together, regard and affection finally arrive. If you don't feel the way you want to feel or know you should feel toward an individual or group, the passage of time won't change that, but your actions will. Act yourself into the emotion of love.

I've lived and worked with people from all parts of the world. I love them all and yet I realize that every nation, society, and family thinks it's special. If we take *special* to mean singular or unique, I wholeheartedly agree. But if we take it to mean that we are better than our neighbors, I know where that comes from. We all want to count. We all want to matter. Unfortunately, we often convince ourselves that subordinating others will allow us to count and matter more. The sense of superiority we feel when we put others down is pure self-deception. *No person living in a prison of prejudice can be truly happy or free.*[106]

Conclusion

Creating inclusion safety is a moral responsibility, because an objective moral order exists. And yet creating and maintaining a moral community, which is an inclusive community by definition, is delicate and fragile.[107] The moral obligation runs in both directions—from the community to the individual, and from the individual to the community. Both bear responsibility.

Inclusion requires effort and investment. It requires that we give each other attention, which is a moral act. I recently observed a group of teenagers at a social activity. Even the quiet, shy, inhibited, and less confident ones seemed to forget about their insecurities for a few minutes. They moved to active participation and lit up in the process. That act of agency gave fuller expression to their personalities. It released their energy and excitement. In that process, they reached out to each other, and paradoxically, left with a greater sense of belonging.

Let's also acknowledge that maintaining inclusion safety requires that we be slow to take offense and quick to forgive in an environment that is prone to weaponize offense-taking. In some cases, the fragility that we have created in society has become ridiculous. Remember, inclusion safety heals. It does restorative work. *But you can't passively belong. You belong when you help others belong.*

Chapter Summary

- **Definition:** Stage 1, inclusion safety, satisfies the basic human need to be included, to feel accepted, and to belong. It means it's not expensive to be yourself.
- **Foundation:** Grounded in universal human dignity, inclusion is owed, not earned.
- **Human paradox:** We crave both connection and protection, to stand out and fit in. We step into vulnerability to connect and step out of it to protect.
- **Survival versus self-expression:** People prioritize self-preservation over authenticity; survival precedes self-expression.
- **Threat detection:** Humans continually scan for psychological safety cues; when unsafe, we retreat, self-censor, and mask identity.
- **Leadership imperative:** Leaders shape inclusion most powerfully by modeling and rewarding vulnerability.
- **Moral principle:** Inclusion safety should be granted based on shared humanity, not worthiness, status, or similarity.
- **Childhood versus adulthood:** We include naturally as children but unlearn inclusion as adults through bias, hierarchy, and the interpretation of difference.
- **Fragility of inclusion safety:** Inclusion can be granted, withheld, revoked, or made conditional.
- **Roots of exclusion:** Fear, insecurity, and unmet needs, not genuine dislike, drive exclusion and junk theories of superiority to justify it.
- **Family and community:** The family is the primary school of inclusion safety, which must be replenished continuously.
- **Behavioral change:** Inclusion grows through practice, not policy. Behave until you believe.
- **Emotion follows action:** The emotion of love follows the action of love.
- **Shared obligation:** Inclusion safety is everyone's moral responsibility—to make the world safe for differences.

STAGE 2

Learner Safety

Real learning comes about when the competitive spirit has ceased.

—Jiddu Krishnamurti

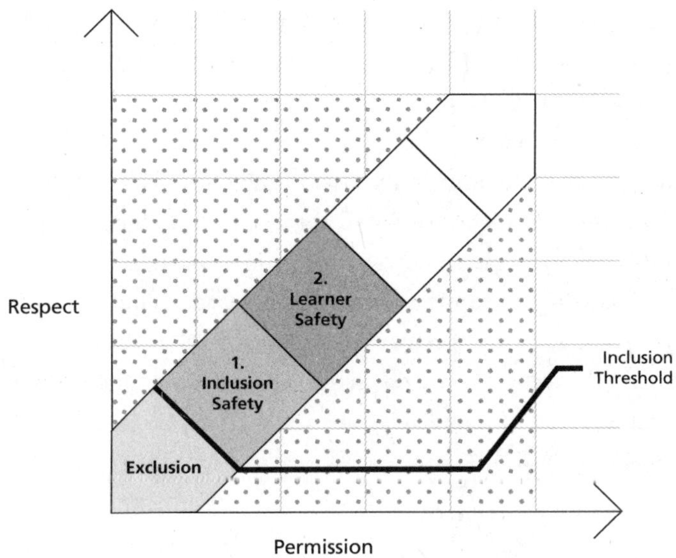

Figure 11. Stage 2: Learner safety

The Need to Learn and Grow

In the second stage of psychological safety (figure 11), we shift from the innate need to be included to the innate need to learn and grow.

> **Definition:** Learner safety satisfies the basic human need to learn and grow. Rather than being embarrassed, marginalized, or punished in some way, you feel encouraged, rewarded, and safe when you engage in acts of learning vulnerability, such as asking questions, giving and receiving feedback, saying you don't know, trying something new, or making a mistake.

The premise of stage 2, learner safety (figure 11), is that learning is both intellectual and emotional, that the thinking brain and feeling brain are interwoven and can't be separated in the learning process (figure 12). As philosopher Martha Nussbaum explains, "Emotions are not just the fuel that powers the psychological mechanism of a reasoning creature, they are parts, highly complex and messy parts, of this creature's reasoning itself."[108] Research shows unequivocally that an individual's learning environment has a profound impact on their motivation and ability to learn. The simple cause and effect chain goes like this: Environment influences affect. Affect regulates cognitive processing, expands attention, and sharpens judgment.[109] No one expressed this better than the marine biologist Rachel Carson: "If facts are the seeds that later produce knowledge and wisdom, then the emotions and the impressions of the senses are the fertile soil in which the seeds must grow."[110]

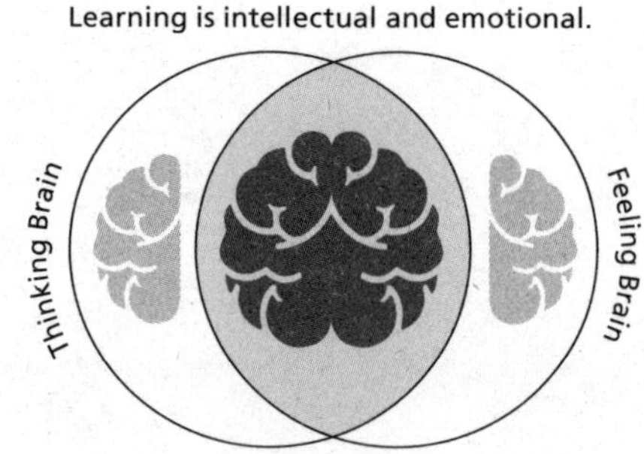

Figure 12. Thinking brain + feeling brain

But those delicate emotions that surround learning must be nurtured and protected, because they will fail along the way. Emerson said, "What if you do fail, and get fairly rolled in the dirt once or twice. Up again, you shall never be so afraid of a tumble."[111] But what if you are afraid to tumble for fear of punished vulnerability? *An emotionally empowered learner becomes a cognitively enabled learner, while an emotionally punished learner becomes a cognitively impaired learner.*

Consider the evidence that social pain limits cognitive performance. In the United States, a student drops out of high school every twenty-six seconds.[112] Do we seriously believe most of these students are dropping out because they don't have the mental bandwidth to do the work? Except for those who may suffer from a legitimate learning disability, the majority have ample ability to learn, graduate, and succeed in all aspects of personal and professional life. Most drop out because they fall behind, lack parental support at home, and find an apathetic learning environment at school.[113] In other words, we aid or block each other's exploration. Restrictive surroundings and stultifying environments hinder gene expression and cognitive development.[114] *The true definition of devastation is no one caring when you fail.*

Researchers have called the nearly two thousand high schools in America that suffer from chronically high dropout rates "dropout factories."[115] When we take a closer look at these schools, we see a pattern of neglect. More than anything, these failing students become emotionally estranged. Over time they lose confidence, feel defeated, and then call it quits. The indifference and lack of validation hijack their sense of identity. The fear that overtakes them grows from the inside out until they literally believe that they can't do it. In their forsaken condition, no one comes to their rescue. *In most cases, parents and schools fail students before the students fail themselves.*

There are three patterns of fear-inducing emotional danger that remove learner safety and create a state of risk: (1) neglect, (2) manipulation, and (3) coercion. Failing schools and classrooms tend to exhibit the first pattern of neglect. How about the workplace? When employees disengage and retreat into silence, they are often responding to a hostile and abusive environment. Fear comes as a result of ridicule, bullying, harassment, threats, and intimidation. These fear-inducing behaviors tend to conform to a pattern of manipulation and coercion.

I recently spent a day with a silent team. I've worked with thousands of teams and have come to learn that unnatural silence is usually an indication that a team has been neutralized by its leader. In this case, we were doing some long-range planning, but no one would speak up. The self-censoring instinct dominated the room, which is a sign that people are managing personal risk out of fear. The team had just failed on a big project, and its members were suffering the period effects of that experience. But it wasn't the failure that stung, it was the leader's scorn that iced the team. Going silent is a normal response to being rejected, humiliated, or punished in some way. Silent team members disengage because they have no voice.

The alarming thing is when the abuse is tolerated. The leader of this team was emotionally disfiguring people, and no one would unmask the fiction that this guy's behavior was acceptable. He was nothing short of an equal opportunity harasser. I had a sidebar conversation with one of the team members after the meeting and asked her if the leader always acted this way. She confirmed that he did. Seeing an opportunity to discuss power dynamics, I asked, "Why do you put up with it?" Then came the reply, "We've just gotten used to it."

While the unsafe school is most likely a nursery of neglect, the unsafe workplace is most likely a refuge of ridicule. When it comes to low psychological safety, the failing school doesn't care about individuals or their performance. The failing workplace doesn't care about individuals either but does have a stake in their performance. Both are harmful, but in different ways. Finally, emotionally unsafe families demonstrate behaviors across the spectrum. We see neglect in some, manipulation in others, and raw coercion in the most unhappy cases. A hostile learning environment, whether at home, school, or work, is a place where fear elicits the self-censoring instinct and shuts down the learning process.

In a fear-based classroom, defeated students drop out and confident students keep their heads down. Same story in the workplace: Top talent leaves because they have options. Mediocre talent stays because they don't. Meanwhile, productivity suffers. Finally, in an emotionally dysfunctional family, regardless of the pattern of that dysfunction, children wilt emotionally as they crumble academically. *When the environment punishes rather than teaches, whether through neglect, manipulation, or coercion, individuals become more defensive, less reflective, and less able to self-diagnose, self-coach, and self-correct. That introduces the risk of real failure—the failure to keep trying.*

Where learner safety exists, the leader creates a learning process with low social friction and low emotional expense. That requires levels of respect and permission that go beyond inclusion safety, because the learning process itself introduces more risk, more vulnerability, and more potential exposure to social and emotional harm.

With inclusion safety, there's no active participation requirement other than to be humane and courteous, but with learner safety you must put yourself out there to ask questions, solicit feedback, float ideas, take risks, reflect openly, experiment, make mistakes, admit errors, and even fail. You naturally look around and do a risk/reward calculation in your head: *If I ask that question, or request help, or make a suggestion, or admit I don't know, or make a mistake, what will it cost me? Can I be myself? Will I look stupid? Am I on trial? Will people laugh? Will they ignore me? Will I hurt my prospects? Will I damage my reputation?* In every learning context, consciously or not, we assess the level of interpersonal risk around us.

Table 3 adds the definition of respect and permission, as well as the social exchange requirement, for learner safety.

To the universal need to belong, we add the universal need to learn and grow. Permission in this case is permission for the individual to engage in all aspects of the learning process. Inclusion safety requires that we show courtesy to each other, but with learner safety, we add another social exchange. If I'm giving learner safety to an individual, I want and expect the individual to make an effort to learn. If I'm the learner, I expect the leader, teacher, coach,

Table 3. Stage 2: Learner safety

Stage	Definition of respect	Definition of permission	Social exchange
1. Inclusion safety	Respect for the individual's innate need to be included, accepted, and gain a sense of belonging	Permission for the individual to feel, be their authentic self, and enter your society	Inclusion in exchange for human status and the absence of harm
2. Learner safety	Respect for the individual's innate need to learn and grow	Permission for the individual to engage in the learning process and make mistakes	Encouragement to learn in exchange for engagement in the learning process

or parent to support me in the learning process. It's encouragement to learn in exchange for engagement to learn. *The moral imperative to grant learner safety is to act first by encouraging the learner to learn. Be the first mover.*

Yes, learners must do their part to engage in the learning process, but sometimes they don't know how or have the confidence to try. Individuals are often unprepared or unable to give the effort that learning requires. They don't believe they can learn and may be paralyzed from previous failures or embarrassments. In this case, we can't expect the learners to initiate the effort to learn when experience may have taught them that the risk is too great.

If you were put in charge of a class in a struggling high school, what would you expect of the students? Engagement, energy, focus, confidence, self-efficacy? No, you would start with hope and no expectations! If education is "not the filling of a pail, but the lighting of a fire," you have a fire to light.[116] We need to remind ourselves that we don't command learning, we invite it. The climate we create feeds the desire and motivation to learn. In an ideal setting, learner safety is a mutual giving and receiving of ideas, observations, questions, and discussion. If leaders are to meet learners where they are, you may need to back up and begin by supplying the inclusion safety that's been absent. I have yet to see learner safety where inclusion safety is absent. One builds on the other.

Let me emphasize that granting learner safety is not a passive act. When we grant it, we make a commitment to create a supportive and encouraging environment. We commit to be patient with learners. We commit to model effective learning, and we commit to share power, credit, and resources to enable others to learn. We commit to empower learners to think independently, resist conformity, and engage actively with an ever-changing world.[117]

The learner's side of the social contract is different. The learner hopes, if not expects, to find a supportive and encouraging environment but commits to nothing up front, because learning is a process fraught with personal risk. Learners rarely put forth the effort to learn unless learner safety is in place. It's a "build it and they will come" principle. If you don't build it, they may still come, but they won't learn.

Disconnecting Fear from Mistakes and Failure

If you walk into the high school gym at Lone Peak High School in Highland, Utah, on the second Saturday in May, you will see an ocean of chairs. The gym has been transformed into a giant classroom and more than three hundred students are sitting for the national Advanced Placement (AP) Calculus exam. Consider the irony: If you scan the high school academic landscape, the tallest peak—the Everest of them all—is calculus. And yet despite the fear factor, student demand for calculus has soared at this school. Why is there such an appetite for this challenging course?

The culprit is Craig B. Smith, a reformed electrical engineer who found his way to the classroom in 2007 after a highly successful career with ExxonMobil and other commercial organizations.[118] Craig teaches seven straight periods of calculus, with an average class size of thirty-four. I have spent several hours interviewing Craig and his students and observing his classroom. Instead of meeting a jaded educator, surrendered to the woes of American secondary education, you will find a man brimming with enthusiasm for his students and his craft. Officially, Craig teaches calculus. Unofficially, he presides over a leadership laboratory as a coach, grief counselor, and triage nurse. A true outlier, Craig is widely regarded as one of the best secondary math teachers in the nation. Judging from normalized data taken from the Utah State Office of Education, he may be the best.

In 2006, the year before Craig began teaching calculus, 46 students per thousand took the AP Calculus AB test at Lone Peak High School. Eight years later in 2016, 160 students per thousand took the AB test (a nearly 250 percent jump), compared to 34 students per thousand statewide. The current participation rate is 800 percent higher than the national average. What about performance? In 2006, 13 students per thousand at Lone Peak passed the standardized AP Calculus AB exam administered by the College Board, compared to a slightly higher rate of 22 per thousand among students throughout the state. In 2014, the state pass rate per thousand was still stuck at 22, whereas the pass rate for Craig's students rocketed to 114 per thousand, a stunning 777 percent increase. It's one thing to make steady incremental improvement. It's quite another to engineer a radical transformation. In an era when American teenagers don't even crack the global top 20 among developed nations in math performance, Craig's achievements are stunning.

He begins with one all-important preconception, one rigid bias, one unyielding prejudice: that every student can learn calculus. His math dojo is a personal development center that rejects the idea that learning ability is fixed or implanted at birth.[119] "I try never to judge a student's aptitude or effort."

Craig maintains that slow students are not less intelligent students. They simply assimilate at a slower pace, so his focus is on student effort and pace rather than aptitude. That ability to resist making discriminating judgments of students' abilities is a skill, but it's also a moral capacity, and one that many teachers don't have the discipline to develop. Many teachers make aptitude judgments and begin sorting and assigning value to their students immediately. As the Nobel Prize–winning researcher Daniel Kahneman observes, "You tend to form a global impression unless you make a special effort not to form a global impression."[120] Craig began suppressing that natural impulse years ago. Ask yourself, when you start working with new people, do you judge their aptitude immediately or do you suppress that impulse? Harvard Business School's legendary C. Roland Christensen echoed this conclusion:

> I believe in the unlimited potential of every student. At first glance they range, like instructors, from mediocre to magnificent. But potential is invisible to the superficial gaze. It takes faith to discern it, but I have witnessed too many academic miracles to doubt its existence. I now view each student as "material for a work of art." If I have faith, deep faith, in students' capacities for creativity and growth, how very much we can accomplish together. If, on the other hand, I fail to believe in that potential, my failure sows seeds of doubt. Students read our negative signals, however carefully cloaked, and retreat from creative risk to the "just possible." When this happens, everyone loses.[121]

In social psychology, there's a vein of research devoted to *stereotype threat theory*, which says that when we are subjected to a negative stereotype, we tend to conform to it. In other words, labels limit. They can also enlarge and magnify. With negative stereotypes, simply being aware that you may be the target of one can motivate us to conform to the invisible limitation. Stereotypes about race, gender, age, body image, and learning ability can exert significant emotional damage on their targets. As Claude Steele notes, stereotype threat can result in "low self-esteem, low expectations, low motivation, self-doubt."[122] *Expectations shape behavior in both directions. When you set the bar high or low, people tend to jump high or low.*

Stereotypes can also influence individuals to stretch to higher levels of performance. Craig helps students shed any psychic damage a harmful stereotype may be inflicting. Every year students arrive with the conviction that they are poor at math, and every year those same students pass the national AP Calculus exam.

To the belief that everyone can learn calculus, Craig adds the precondition of learner safety. As he explains it, "I can't teach students unless I like them. I can't like them unless I know them, and I can't know them unless I talk to them." That's why he spends the first class period every term doing nothing but learning his students' names and a little about their lives. After that, everyone gets down to work, but he continues to punctuate his class time with short, personal touch points with each student. He begins each class by checking in with each student to acknowledge them individually and to check on homework completion.

In my classroom observations, I notice that Craig toggles back and forth between lecture and discussion.[123] The choreography seems effortless, creating a feeling of relaxed intensity and a total absence of fear, inhibition, or formality. Craig teaches a concept in lecture style and then asks a series of questions in discussion style to test understanding. He uses a participation point system that reinforces questions as the students navigate through an emotional and intellectual journey of small victories and defeats. "A wrong answer is as good as a right answer, as long as you know why," he maintains. *Failure isn't the exception, it's the expectation and the way forward. Don't be surprised if discouragement precedes discovery.*

Indeed, if you're really trying, there should be no stigma, no shame, and no embarrassment associated with failure. It's simply a stepping stone. We should reward failure, because it's not failure—it's progress. The examination of failure is often more valuable than the examination of success. Consistent with this principle, Craig has debunked the conventional wisdom that retesting—the practice of allowing students to retake a test if they do poorly—doesn't work. "It's a little more work for the teacher," Craig observes. "Retesting clearly works, so I give endless chances. If you're willing to work, there's always mercy. You can try again."

Craig invites students to learn without adding fear to a subject that already creates its own. He recognizes that students who are emotionally distressed—anxious, angry, or depressed—are cognitively impaired and don't learn well, so he fosters a challenging and yet nurturing climate of learner safety to dramatically reduce learning risk. "There's no embarrassment in Mr. Smith's class," one student said. "You never feel dumb even if you don't understand something."

Learner safety requires low ego and uncommonly high emotional intelligence, traits that Craig possesses in abundance. He's a man of great warmth who clearly seeks to bless rather than impress his students. He's not competitive, combative, or punitive. He's not there to pontificate, display brilliance, or duel with his students. Instead, he shows patience and intellectual humility. Perhaps what is most invisible of all is the way he monitors both content and context. He has developed an acute social sensitivity to interpret the nonverbal cues of the students. He is fluent in this language, which allows him to stay in sync with the students' cognitive and emotional progress so that he never runs past them.[124]

"He never acts bothered or irritated when you ask a question," another student said. "He'll kneel down by your desk, find out what you know, and help you from there. But he doesn't give you the answer. You have to explain where and why you're stuck."

"Calculus is not an easy subject," Craig says. "I also recognize that many of my students will never use calculus again. What we're trying to do is build confident, self-reliant, mentally tenacious, and unafraid students who are prepared for life. The journey makes you accountable. It makes you stretch. It makes you feel good about yourself. Yes, I teach calculus. More importantly, I teach students."

Does Craig understand calculus better than other calculus teachers? Is this the source of his competitive advantage? Clearly not. Based on his extraordinary perceptive capacity and ability to ward off compassion fatigue, he has mastered the art of shaping the social, emotional, and cognitive context, in creating a figuratively "clean, well-lighted place" where the whole student can flourish.[125] This is learner safety.

The Intellectual and the Emotional

A person's ability to learn requires staying focused, managing impulses, and avoiding distractions. Researchers use terms such as *flow state*, *metacognition*, *executive function*, *effective effort*, and *high engagement* to describe what good learners do. These terms refer to the supervisory attentional or cognitive control system.

If we've learned anything about learning, it's that it's not an isolated, rational process that is cold, dry, and mechanistic. Emotion is nested in reason, and reason in emotion. Cognition and affect are inseparably connected. Before I went to Oxford, I earned a master's degree at the University of Utah. My adviser was an internationally respected social scientist named John Francis. He helped prepare me academically for Oxford by spilling red ink all over my papers. He pushed me, stretched me, and roughed me up. In one class, I became absolutely exasperated because I could never earn an A on a paper. I'd sit down with John in his office and go over his corrections, and every time I'd walk away with lingering frustration, yet loving this man. There was a beautiful weirdness about the process that motivated me to redouble my efforts. He was driving me crazy, but I wasn't disengaging. As he connected with me personally, I gave him permission to push me.

And what did he do in the classroom? He shared power through discussion. He's a brilliant man, but there was little didactic and zero pedantic time in his courses. A traditional lecture is authoritarian. John opted for a more democratic and collaborative approach where we learned together. This of course created more risk for the students because we bore more responsibility to teach each other—but out of that joint ownership came a deeper emotional investment and a greater willingness to take risks in the learning process.

A leader maintains a culture of learning only by minimizing vulnerability through a consistent pattern of positive emotional response.[126] People want to see how you react to dissent and bad news. If you listen intently, respond constructively, and convey appreciation, participants absorb these cues and calculate their participation accordingly. *The most important signal in granting or withholding learner safety is the leader's emotional response to dissent and bad news.*

As a teacher, John had mastered the integration of cognitive and affective systems. If you lose emotional engagement, intellectual engagement slows down or may not happen at all. People learn from the people they love more than from the people they don't.

Learning is not the operation of a detached, dispassionate data center; it's an interplay of the head and the heart. Humans process socially, emotionally, and intellectually at the same time. Another witness, and perhaps our biggest proof of the need for learner safety, is artificial intelligence and the democratization of learning. The barriers to learning that have stood resolutely for millennia are coming down. The scalability of the internet and the personalization of AI allow anyone to access the best content and the best teachers in the world. All you need is a smart device and an internet connection.

As the traditional barriers of access, cost, and quality fall, we should theoretically see a surge in learning across all populations. My daughter can be tutored by Khanmigo on Khan Academy, which adapts in real time to her pace in linear algebra, diagnosing gaps and adjusting lessons as she learns. My son can explore the history of cheese through an AI-curated blend of a TED-Ed video, interactive quiz, and virtual field trip that deepens his understanding through multiple modes of engagement. After I finish Harvard professor Michael Sandel's course on justice, an AI Socratic coach can extend my learning through conversation, asking probing questions that test my reasoning and apply ethical principles to real-world dilemmas. Not least, a student in Nairobi can translate Sandel's lecture into Swahili or a learner with hearing loss can access AI-generated transcripts and adaptive captions.

With AI, you can learn anything you want, anytime you want, anyplace you want. It's the great equalizer, except for one thing: you need focus and motivation, and therein lies the problem. We have entered a time of unprecedented opportunity for human improvement, when the challenge is no longer time and access, but desire and discipline. AI has created a learning renaissance, but it's leaving behind millions who lack the interest, confidence, and drive to participate, largely because they've been deprived of learner safety.

Humans learn in context, not in isolation, and they are continuously influenced by that context. When the learning context is encouraging, it taps the drive to be curious. Add to that the fact that the level of learner safety directly shapes the way learners interact. "The degree and quality of learner participation in interprofessional simulation courses," writes the Dutch social scientist Babette Bronkhorst, "is influenced by self-efficacy as well as perceptions of the psychological safety of the learning environment. Learners who feel safe are far more willing to practice at the edge of their expertise to experiment, solve difficult problems, and to reflect on their performance."[127]

Learner safety is an enabling precondition that creates the curiosity and willingness to be brave in personal learning. Bill Gates said, "People who are as curious as I am will be fine in any system. For the self-motivated student, these are the golden days. I wish I was growing up now. I envy my son. If he and I are talking about something that we don't understand, we just watch videos and click on articles, and that feeds our discussion. Unfortunately, the highly curious student is a small percentage of the kids."[128]

Gates says that only a small percentage of kids are highly curious, but notice what he does with his own son. He gets knee to knee and shoulder to shoulder and they learn together. He makes an emotional connection with his son to fuel discovery. It's amazing how quickly the curiosity and motivation to learn can be kindled when someone creates the nurturing environment of learner safety.

Remember that humans instinctively look for learner safety before they engage in the learning process. If you know you're going to be ridiculed if you ask a question, the self-censoring instinct will hush that impulse and transition you to a defensive routine. Trusted leaders have security clearance. Distrusted leaders are barred entry. When it comes to learner safety, the learner has the final say.

"There is *no* relation," Stanford's Carol Dweck maintains, "between students' abilities or intelligence and the development of mastery-oriented qualities. Some of the very brightest students avoid challenges, dislike effort, and wilt in the face of difficulty. And some of the less bright students are real go-getters, thriving on challenge, persisting intensely when things get difficult, and accomplishing more than you expected."[129] What Dweck doesn't mention is the crucial role the environment plays in all of this. *We guard our social and emotional selves with sophisticated personal surveillance systems.* Grit alone will not close the learning gap. Learner safety is essential.

Decommoditizing People in Organizations

The management ranks of many organizations are still populated by immobilized baby boomers who are barely hanging on, trying to avoid career misfortune until retirement, clinging to old skills from another time, publicly acknowledging the new world but privately unwilling to learn in it.

Why are they doing this? They fell behind and now they're caught between two worlds. They grew up in a world obsessed with the machines that provided automation, mass production, and economies of scale and didn't pay much attention to human capital, especially their own.

Human capital is everything. And yet Steve Kerr, the first person to bear the title of chief learning officer, was appointed to that position at General Electric by then-CEO Jack Welch in 1994. The acknowledgment of the individual as the source of productive capacity was a slow, evolutionary process.

The prevailing mindset held that only a small part of an organization's population could learn and contribute as knowledge workers. Leaders operated on the assumption that there were thinking and nonthinking parts of the organization. Influenced by the work of Frederick Winslow Taylor, organizations restricted and compartmentalized human labor as measured in terms of raw, task-based productivity. The larger nonthinking part of the organization was not even considered for its creative output, a mindset mired in centuries of prejudice that made us blind to people's potential. *The prejudiced mind is willfully blind.*

Even within the thinking part of the organization, the mindset emphasized onetime learning for permanent qualification. This inherited model from the industrial age rested on a basic tenet that valued assets and commoditized people. Despite organizational behaviorists appearing on the scene in the latter part of the twentieth century, the legacy of hierarchy and the rules-based emphasis on accountability and internal control remained the focus.

Think about that legacy in today's context. The natural rise and fall of competitive advantage is nothing new. What is new is the average length of that rise and fall. It's much shorter. As that trend continues, learning becomes more important to success, because the half-life of an organization's knowledge mirrors its competitive strategy. An overall compression of time frames naturally shifts the source of ongoing competitiveness to learning. A competitive cycle is a learning cycle. Either learn and retool to maintain competitiveness, or face the grave risk of irrelevance.

We used to think of learning as discrete and event-based, something that was triggered by a problem or question. Now it's continuous and embedded in the workflow. As a result, it's becoming increasingly difficult to separate learning from production because of the interwoven nature of acquiring knowledge and creating value. The boundary between the two processes is thinner than ever as individuals toggle back and forth in real time. Process technologies will eventually integrate with learning and talent management systems to facilitate a more seamless integration of workflow and learning.

The danger is to believe that technology is the secret sauce that can set you free in your quest to be a learning organization. This overabundant faith in the power of technology is what Richard Florida refers to as "techno-utopianism."[130] As impressive as the advances in collaborative technology are, they can't overcome the formidable barrier of fear that autocratic leadership always plants.

And yet we continue to hear evangelists proclaiming the limitless potential of the latest technology advances, such as mashup web applications, virtual learning worlds, hackathons, and performance support tools. The technology hype cycle, romanticism, and offers of salvation never go away.

It's helpful to reflect on what an organization really is. There are many definitions, but perhaps the best one for our time was put forward by the education theorist Malcolm Knowles, who invites us to think of an organization as a "system of learning as well as production."[131] In our day, organizations literally compete based on their ability to learn. In an unforgiving, hypercompetitive environment, creating an organization that learns at or above the speed of change—the very definition of learning agility—is the central organizational challenge of our time.

Peter Drucker coined the term *knowledge worker* in 1959, and yet we're still trying to break down industrial age orthodoxies.[132] We continue to elevate hardcore authoritarian bosses, conditioned in another time and place, to lead organizations. The only reason they survive is that their organizations have sources of competitive advantage that compensate for and conceal their liabilities. The increasing demands of a protean organization require a leader to be direction setter, servant, coach, enabler, and facilitator. We see the predominant patterns of leadership continuing their migration from bureaucratic and autocratic to democratic and egalitarian, from task oriented to people oriented, and from directive to facilitative.

Not only is this a fundamental change from the leader-as-oracle model, but it also requires leaders to assume a very different emotional and social posture. Leaders must become comfortable portraying themselves as competent through their ability to learn and adapt rather than through their expertise. To foster learner safety, leaders must model a level of humility and curiosity that is simply alien to most traditional conceptions of leadership. Ironically, leaders are being challenged to develop confidence in the very act of not knowing. They must be submissive to the fact that they will pass through periods of temporary incompetence as they move through learning cycles.

As one who has worked with some very difficult teams, let me offer three final suggestions to cultivate and preserve learner safety. First, manage those who learn with their mouths—the vocally aggressive members of your team who are prone to menace their colleagues with verbal firestorms and shafts of criticism. Second, never let hierarchy relieve anyone of the responsibility to learn. When I do training sessions with executive teams, about half the CEOs don't attend. The others come eager to learn. Who has the advantage? Ask yourself if you model the "leader as learner" or "the leader as oracle." Third, use psychological safety to help your team adopt AI in their roles. A recent study shows that AI implementation causes employees to fear job displacement, loss of competence, or reduced human value. This results in heightened employee anxiety and uncertainty, which erodes a willingness to speak up, ask questions, or acknowledge mistakes. Lower psychological safety accentuates these negative effects, but ethical leadership and high psychological safety create the opposite outcomes, resulting in fewer depressive symptoms and greater well-being. Recognize that we are in the midst of the AI transformation, and the mediating effects that can come from psychological safety can ultimately be the factor that leads to a positive AI adoption experience.[133]

Conclusion

Leaders committed to safeguarding learner safety understand that learning is where competitive advantage comes from, that it represents the highest form of enterprise risk management, and that the biggest risk a firm can take is to cease to learn. It seems increasingly clear that leaders who do not demonstrate deep patterns of agile and self-directed learning in their own lives are almost certain to fail, whereas the ones who do are almost certain to succeed—provided they combine those learning patterns with the ability to engage people with high levels of learner safety. Ultimately, learner safety doesn't happen unless it is modeled, communicated, taught, measured, recognized, and rewarded. Here's the standard: *Remove all barriers to learning anxiety to the point that the most inhibited and fearful member of the team will come forward and engage.*

Your team may be exquisitely endowed with brilliant people and abundant resources, but if individuals don't feel free to probe, prod, poke, pilot, and prototype, to ask silly questions, to stretch and stumble, they won't venture.[134] Learner safety is important because it encourages these specific learning behaviors. What's even more impressive is that it can act as an invisible leveling agent to remove the hesitation and reduce the anxiety employees often feel in asking for help from those who could literally terminate their employment.[135] In the end, we each have a choice to cultivate or crush, nurture or neglect, stimulate or stifle learner safety.

Chapter Summary

- **Definition:** Stage 2, learner safety, satisfies the basic human need to learn and grow. It means feeling safe to ask, try, iterate, and make mistakes.
- **Emotion drives cognition:** Fear narrows attention, and learner safety expands it. An emotionally empowered learner becomes cognitively enabled, while an emotionally punished learner becomes cognitively impaired.
- **Primary blockers:** Loss of learner safety follows neglect, manipulation, or coercion.
- **Default human behavior:** In unsafe settings, people self-censor and switch from offense (learning) to defense (risk management).
- **Social exchange:** Encouragement for engagement is the deal. The leader is the first mover.
- **Expectation effect:** Standards shape outcomes. Set the bar high or low, and people will jump high or low.
- **Failure reframed:** Disconnect fear from mistakes. Failure isn't the exception, it's the expectation.
- **Leader response:** The leader's emotional reaction to dissent and bad news signals whether it's safe to learn.
- **Constant scanning:** People run personal surveillance for cues to see if it's safe to engage in the learning process.
- **Prerequisite chain:** Learner safety rarely exists without inclusion safety. Stage 1 enables stage 2.
- **Grit is not sufficient:** Effort converts to growth only in a climate of safety; grit alone won't close the gap.
- **Delabeling:** Pace ≠ aptitude. Labels limit; respect pace and build confidence. The prejudiced mind is willfully blind.
- **Operating standard:** Remove learning anxiety until even the most inhibited learner will participate.
- **Enterprise stakes:** Organizations compete on learning agility. Culture outperforms tools because technology can't fix fear.
- **Leader identity:** Be the leader-as-learner (humble, curious, collaborator) rather than the leader-as-oracle (self-appointed repository of answers).

STAGE 3

Contributor Safety

I look upon ourselves as partners in all of this, and that each of us contributes and does what he can do best. And so I see not a top rung and a bottom rung—I see all this horizontally—and I see this as part of a matrix.

—Jonas Salk

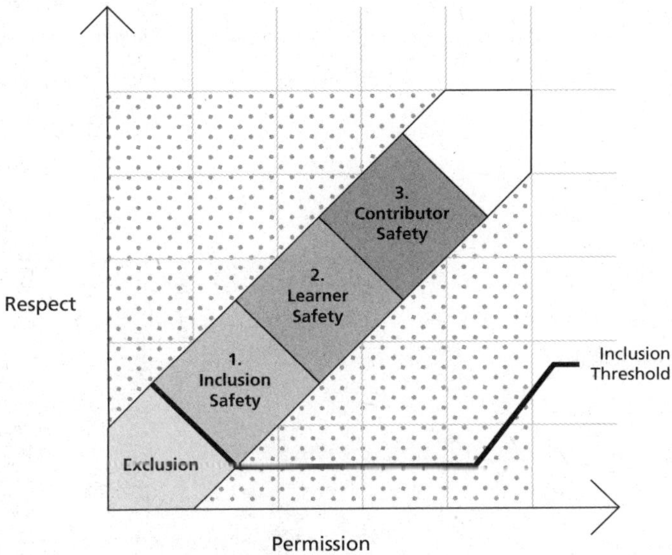

Figure 13. Stage 3: Contributor safety

A Signal That It's Go Time

In January of 1542, during his work on *The Last Judgment*, the fresco covering the altar wall of the Sistine Chapel, Michelangelo wrote a letter to his friend Luigi del Riccio, saying, "I am not allowed to follow my own judgment in the work I do."[136] That was not the first time he had expressed frustration with a lack of artistic autonomy. It was a theme that ran through his correspondence. He lamented working "against my own will" or "under the orders of others."

Notice the spectacular absurdity of the world's greatest artist being micromanaged. He felt bound to the demands of his powerful patrons because they were the ones who put food on his table. And yet here he was saying, "Give me some space. I kind of have a track record!"

You may not have the towering reputation of Michelangelo, but you have probably felt the same feelings. Why? Because human beings yearn to be agents and to do something meaningful in the world. If stage 2, learner safety, is the stage of preparation, then stage 3, contributor safety (figure 13), is the stage of performance. Indeed, preparation precedes performance. Now we transition from the human need category to learn, grow, and develop mastery to the need category of autonomy and contribution.

> **Definition:** Contributor safety satisfies the basic human need for choice and contribution. You feel safe and are given the opportunity and role clarity to use your skills and abilities to make a difference.

Have you ever been on an athletic team but didn't get to play in the games? Instead, you sat the bench. What does it feel like to ride the pine? If your teammates accepted you, you had inclusion safety. If you practiced hard, you had learner safety. But if you never played in the games, you were denied contributor safety.

Sitting the bench is a state of suspension between preparation and performance. It's socially and emotionally painful. Then one day the coach taps you on the shoulder and says, "Get in the game." In an instant, you're on the field. You're not spectating anymore, you're contributing. In that moment, satisfaction replaces suspension. You're no longer preparing for something that never comes. *Except for those who may be paralyzed by fear or anxiety, human beings have a deep and unrelenting drive to play in the game.*

Carl Jung said human beings "cannot stand a meaningless life."[137] He was right. We crave autonomy.[138] We hunger for meaning. We are built for purpose. In stage 1, inclusion safety, we accept the individual on human grounds. In stage 2, learner safety, we encourage the individual's learning on human grounds as well, and then encourage that individual to engage in the learning process. But this stage of psychological safety—contributor safety—is not a natural right. Rather, it's an earned privilege based on demonstrated performance. With contributor safety, we provide autonomy in exchange for performance. We will empower you if you can deliver results. Contributor safety marks the end of the apprenticeship and the beginning of solid, self-directed performance. It's time to put something meaningful on the table. The leader grants contributor safety when the individual has the chops to do the job. In business terms, it means the individual is an asset rather than a liability, a net contributor delivering a positive return on investment. The organization grants more autonomy to the individual in exchange for the demonstrated ability to take personal accountability.

Contributor safety makes greater demands on both parties. This is a mutual investment in which the individual invests effort and skill, and the team invests support, guidance, and direction. When the progression to contributor safety works, the team empowers the individual and says, "Go do it!" Similarly, the individual at this point is now prepared and has developed a greater desire to contribute, and says, "Let me do it." This is the current situation with my son, who recently received his driver's license. He passed the written test and the road test. His mother and I logged forty hours of daytime driving practice and eight hours of nighttime driving practice with him to meet the licensing requirements.

At this point, it would be quite unnatural for him to say to me, "Dad, can you drive me to my friend's house?" He wants to take the wheel. And that's as it should be. *The preparation to perform creates the desire to perform.*

That's why you can't be content sitting on the bench. The reciprocity requirement in this third stage is autonomy for performance. But if the individual doesn't perform, the organization retrenches to learner safety. Once you get in the game, you've got to carry your weight, or you'll soon be on the bench again. On the other hand, if you can contribute but never get the chance, you'll either decide to live with that reality or find another team.

Contributor safety is therefore the full activation of the social contract. Once the individual graduates from trainee status, they expect to be treated like a full-fledged member of the team, and the organization expects a meaningful contribution. If learner safety is the stage of preparation, contributor safety is the stage of performance. Crossing over to contributor safety is the signal that it's go time, that the team is trusting you to perform in the role it has given you. The organization is expecting you to carry your load and perform competently.

The basic unit of performance in the twenty-first century is the team. Chances are that you will participate as a member of numerous intact and cross-functional teams during your professional lifetime. You will colocate with some and span the globe with others. In fact, as organizations get flatter, it's becoming more common to be a member of several teams at the same time.[139] Regardless of the nature of work you do and the team you're a part of, this third stage of psychological safety will always be the foundation of performance.

Execution Versus Innovation

If learner safety fosters preparation and contributor safety fosters performance, what exactly do we mean by *performance*? Execution and innovation—the only two processes in which organizations engage. *Execution is the creation and delivery of value today, while innovation is the creation and delivery of value tomorrow.*

The differences in those two processes are fundamental. Execution is about economizing work and scaling processes. It's about control and driving out variability to achieve efficiency. Innovation is the opposite: It's about freedom, imagination, creativity, and the introduction of variability. Because execution is more about standardization, and innovation is more about deviation, there's a natural tension and trade-off between the two.[140] The fundamental distinction between execution and innovation is true whether you're a multinational corporation or the local chapter of the shiitake mushroom growers' association. Does this mean that contributor safety is solely about execution and not innovation? Not quite. This is where the progression of psychological safety gets even more interesting.

Innovation can be further divided into offensive and defensive types. Offensive innovation is proactive, while defensive innovation is reactive. Both are responses to adaptive challenges, just different kinds. *Offensive innovation is a response to an opportunity, while defensive innovation is a response to a threat or crisis.*[141]

Offensive innovation is you choosing change. Defensive innovation is change choosing you. This distinction matters because defensive innovation is a natural part of contributor safety, while offensive innovation is not (see figure 14).

When I was the plant manager at Geneva Steel, we sold plate steel to Caterpillar, which made parts for the large equipment they manufactured. At one point, they informed us that the surface quality of our plate steel was no longer acceptable. They were tightening their quality parameters, and either we could figure out a way to meet the new standards or they would find another supplier. So here we were, confronted with a new adaptive challenge. In this case, it was a threat quickly bordering on a crisis. I still remember calling our team together for the first emergency meeting. It was all hands on deck—the operators; the process, chemical, metallurgical, and quality engineers; the maintenance folks—trying to figure out how to remove small surface-level defects that had previously been acceptable. Suddenly, that was history. We needed not only good root-cause analysis and corrective action but also defensive innovation—and we needed it fast.

This example is typical of what happens in just about every organization. Stakeholder demands change, consumer preferences evolve, new competitors emerge, demographics shift, technology accelerates. We either engage in defensive innovation to stay in the game, or bow out because we don't have

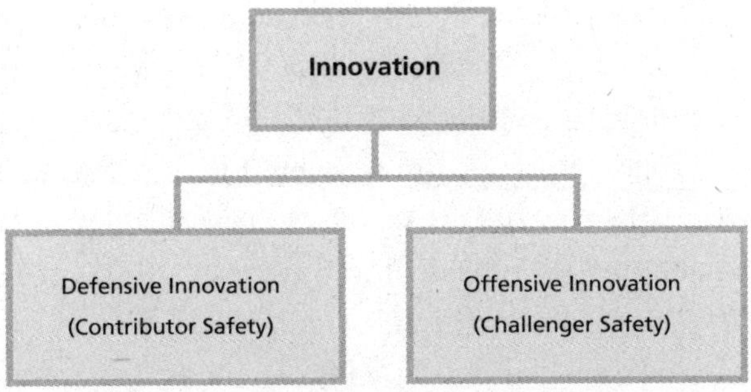

Figure 14. Defensive versus offensive innovation

enough contributor safety to frankly discuss mistakes or improvements. The reason defensive innovation is part of contributor safety is that it's riskier to do nothing than to formulate a response. *When an external threat challenges the status quo, the natural fear of challenging the status quo is replaced with the survival instinct.*

At this point, we want and expect defensive innovation. You're no longer taking a personal risk to challenge the status quo. You can thank an outside force for performing that task for you. In this case, it was Caterpillar, and once they issued the challenge, there was no fear associated with challenging the status quo. Survival was now at stake.

For nearly every team or organization that I've observed, this pattern holds true. Engaging in defensive innovation to survive is within the realm of normal expectations. You seldom feel threatened internally when you're threatened externally.

In fact, external threats bind you together. They act as an agent of alignment, providing the clear and present danger of a common enemy. Proactive innovation, however, is another matter. It involves far more personal risk and thus a higher level of psychological safety based on higher levels of respect and permission. That, of course, is the preserve of challenger safety, which we will discuss in the next chapter. To summarize: Contributor safety fosters execution and defensive innovation but falls short of addressing the higher level of risk and vulnerability that is usually needed for offensive innovation.

Autonomy in Exchange for Results

The social contract for contributor safety, outlined in table 4, trades autonomy for performance. The social unit grants the individual increased independence and ownership as they demonstrate the ability to contribute based not only on acquired knowledge and skills but also on good work habits and disciplined follow-through—both know-how and reliability. In short, when we move to the contributor stage, we move to a higher level of individual accountability. Any individual who moves to the contributor stage is responsible for a work product, results, and deliverables. My teenage children have daily and weekly chores to complete, musical instruments to practice, homework to do, and dogs to feed. The better the performance, the greater the autonomy.

Table 4. Stage 3: Contributor safety

Stage	Definition of respect	Definition of permission	Social exchange
1. Inclusion safety	Respect for the individual's innate need to be included, accepted, and gain a sense of belonging	Permission for the individual to feel, be their authentic self, and enter your society	Inclusion in exchange for human status and the absence of harm
2. Learner safety	Respect for the individual's innate need to learn and grow	Permission for the individual to engage in all aspects of the learning process	Encouragement in exchange for engagement
3. Contributor safety	Respect for the individual's innate need for choice and contribution	Permission for the individual to work with appropriate autonomy and independence	Autonomy with guidance in exchange for performance and results

Regardless of the individual's performance, we retain the moral responsibility to grant inclusion safety and learner safety, provided the individual is courteous and willing to learn. The morality of contributor safety, however, is different because the individual bears a higher responsibility. Contributor safety is a mutual investment by the individual and the social unit, not a natural right, and not something human beings are entitled to by virtue of their human status. You must earn it, and it's an instinct for leaders to let up on the reins as another human being under their charge becomes more self-directed and delivers the expected results. My wife and I frequently remind our children that parenting is the gradual transfer of responsibility, and the sooner our children are willing to take it on, the sooner we are willing to give it. When you're willing to hold yourself accountable, you earn more autonomy.

With contributor safety, the organization assumes risk on behalf of the individual, who is expected to contribute. When something goes wrong, the liability associated with the risk of failure normally falls back on the organization rather than the individual. If my company's software development team delivers a bug-ridden solution to one of our customers, we all feel the pain. Not surprisingly, the higher the risk associated with performance, the less autonomy we grant, even if we have enormous trust in the individual, their skills, and their reliability. When I managed the steel plant, we had no fewer than ten thousand written standard operating procedures, governing every stage of the steel-making process to guide, manage, direct, and contain autonomy.

If the organization grants contributor safety as it should, you can expect it when you earn it. This also means you will be denied it if you're not ready or fall seriously short. That's why we wait to see a track record of consistent performance before granting full contributor safety. In fact, if the individual isn't prepared to do a job, it would be foolish to offer contributor safety. We do it gradually based on performance to manage risk along the way.

Making the Transition to Contribution

In many organizations, the transition to contributor safety corresponds with the completion of formal training and the earning of a credential certifying that the individual is ready to perform a specific job, role, or function. For example, doctors, lawyers, teachers, engineers, airline pilots, brick masons, accountants, and sometimes even floral designers must pass certifying exams to demonstrate competence and be admitted as members of their professional societies. But there are even more roles that don't rely on formal credentialing and admittance—the golf pro, the TV news anchor, the Little League coach, the barista, and the surfing instructor. And then there are some roles where credentials are optional—the chef, the river guide, the landscaper, or the personal trainer. The transition from preparation to performance can be formal or informal, and it may come gradually or immediately (table 5).

FORMAL IMMEDIATE Becoming a lawyer requires three years of law school or apprenticeship, but you are authorized to practice law in a state only after you pass its bar exam. The transition to the stage of contribution is formal and immediate once you pass the exam. You're certainly not an experienced lawyer, but you have the minimum knowledge and skills to perform the role in that state.

Table 5. Transitioning from preparation to performance

Formal/immediate (Lawyer)	Formal/gradual (Reporter)
Informal/immediate (Athlete)	Informal/gradual (Parent)

FORMAL GRADUAL Examples of formal gradual transitions to performance are common because although you are given a formal role, you can't perform it competently at first. A gradual time-to-competency development process must follow. A formal gradual transition usually involves a qualitative rather than quantitative judgment of the individual's capacity to do a job. For instance, I worked with a newspaper that hired a new journalist to write stories. The person's hiring and appointment to the reporter role was formal, but they were initially considered a cub reporter in the learning stage. Their transition to becoming a feature writer who took on in-depth stories was a gradual process supervised by the managing editor. There was no test or certification, but rather a slow transition based on the individual's maturing reporting ability. Many jobs in the business world are like this: You are appointed to a job, but you still have a big skills gap to close before you can contribute competently in the role.

INFORMAL IMMEDIATE An informal immediate move to performance is one in which there is no formal credentialing or appointment to accompany the transition. This often happens when needs arise in real time because of a shortage or a surge in demand. Someone needs to step in and fill the need. For example, an athlete gets injured and a replacement is called into the game immediately. An employee unexpectedly leaves an organization, and you're asked to lead the team.

INFORMAL GRADUAL Finally, an informal and gradual transition to contribution is perhaps the most common pattern of all. It represents the natural process of maturing into higher performance. The most important roles that I have in life are that of husband and father. Ironically, in these most crucial responsibilities, I'm not formally credentialed, licensed, or certified. Now it's true that the day of my marriage marked the day I became a husband, but it didn't qualify me to become one. Similarly, I formally became a father the moment my son was born, but again, his birth did not coincide with my competent performance as a father. Having the role doesn't mean you can perform in the role. In both cases, I had much to learn. I assumed these roles before I was adequately prepared for them. But isn't that true with most roles, positions, and assignments in life? Don't we often have to grow into them?

Three Levels of Accountability

The autonomy-for-results exchange that defines contributor safety increases in scale and scope as the individual learns to contribute more. The granting of contributor safety follows a consistent pattern in which the social unit gives autonomy based on three levels of accountability:

3. Outcome

2. Process

1. Task

If we consistently perform well at one level, the organization is inclined to advance us to the next. Consider an example from my own illustrious career when I was a teenager. My first job was to pick apricots in a large orchard in Cupertino, California. I would carry two metal pails to the trees, fill them up with apricots, and then bring them back to the foreman, who would pour the apricots into wood crates. Two full pails would fill a one-bushel crate. I was confined to task work in this job and never graduated to process work.

In high school, I found a summer job on a grounds crew. We spent each day manicuring the grounds of homes and businesses. As soon as I learned the tasks, my boss elevated me to process-level accountability. He would drop me off at a customer site and then pick me up later in the day, expecting to see the project completed. I remember when he dropped me off at an office building with several flats of petunias to plant. At other times, he would assign us to complete the grounds of a particular property. We would mow, trim, and edge the grass; weed; and turn up the flower beds. He delegated more responsibility as we demonstrated the skill and willingness to perform the work at the process level. First, it was, "Cut the grass." Then it was, "Weed the flower beds." Finally, he would drop us off at a nice commercial property and say, "Make it look great. I'll be back to pick you up in two hours."

As we move to outcome accountability, how we get our work done, how we accomplish our tasks, and how we manage projects and processes doesn't matter so much. It's about the outcome. When I enrolled in graduate school, the new doctoral students were invited to a meeting the first week. I can still remember sitting in the Rhodes House at Oxford, listening to the vice chancellor hold forth about the mysteries of this ancient institution. I can't remember anything he said except one thing that is forever emblazoned in my memory. After his long speech, he said, "Please understand that only one in three of you will successfully complete the doctorate. The rest of you will either quit or fail. Welcome to Oxford University!"

At that moment, I seriously considered taking a bus to Heathrow and getting on a plane back to the States. Fortunately, I did stay and learned that he had not exaggerated. I also learned that the Oxford model of accountability was a pure outcome model. They granted complete autonomy with the expectation that you would make an original contribution to knowledge in your field. They were very serious about this, and my academic adviser was the embodiment of this model. He was quite willing to help me but would agree to meet only if I had a respectable work product to show him. There was no handholding, no coddling, and, most importantly, no shortcuts. *The exchange of autonomy for results is the basis of human performance.*

This has been the consistent expectation of my entire professional life. When I became a young CEO of a consulting company based in San Francisco, my boss was in Boston, and I saw him four times a year. He seldom asked me "how" questions, but always asked me "what" and "why" questions. Every quarter he would ask, "What is your vision? What is your strategy? What are your goals and why?" If my answers were acceptable, he would say, "Great, see you next quarter." If I had a problem, he would do a deeper dive with me, but he was paying me for outcomes, and I understood that. As you can see, contributor safety is built on trust, which is a predictive understanding about the way a person will behave. My boss gave me incredible autonomy if I delivered predictable results.

Blue Zone and Red Zone

Every person possesses five uniquely human characteristics:

- **Motivation:** Our desire to act. Motivation is the fuel to get up and go.
- **Volition:** Our power to choose and act for ourselves. For example, right now you can continue reading or listening to this book. Please continue.
- **Cognition:** The mental process of learning and the capacity for moral and rational thought. We process information through our thoughts and the five senses.

- **Emotion:** Our state of feeling. For example, we can feel joy, love, fear, surprise, or anger, which can be caused by our own thoughts and the circumstances we're in.
- **Apprehension:** The state of being conscious or aware of ourselves, our thoughts and feelings, and the world around us. This includes the ability to be aware of our own awareness.

Everyone is in charge of their attention, activity, and exertions. It's a matter of personal discretion to contribute or slack off. You have *discretionary effort*, the portion of effort you choose to give beyond simple compliance. When a person restricts contributor safety in a way that causes us to freeze our discretionary efforts due to fear and the potential of social and emotional harm, we call that a red zone. Conversely, when a person grants contributor safety in a way that tends to release discretionary effort, we call that a blue zone (see table 6).

One summer when I was a college student, I accepted an invitation from my friend Joe Huston to work on a table grape ranch in California's San Joaquin Valley. I didn't realize that I was entering a blue zone. We worked ten hours a day in the hot sun outside the small town of Arvin, under the supervision of Joe's father, Boom Huston. Boom was the general manager of El Rancho Farms, a big operation that included packing and cold storage. The college kids worked alongside the migrant workers in an integrated crew. There were no arbitrary distinctions between us. We worked the same jobs, had the same hours, and earned the same pay. The only real difference was lunch. Their carne asada, tortillas, and salsa were better than anything I pulled out of my brown bag.

Table 6. Blue zone/red zone descriptors

Blue zone	Red zone
Collaboration	Competition
Alignment	Fractures
Engagement	Silence
Confidence	Fearfulness
Risk taking	Risk aversion
Fast feedback	Slow and filtered feedback
Renewal and resilience	Burnout
Manageable stress	Debilitating stress
Self-efficacy	Self-sabotage
Initiative and resourcefulness	Learned helplessness
Creativity	Compliance

At first, I thought it was simply a matter of professional obligation that Boom treated all of us with equal respect, but it went beyond that. He hosted a barbecue for the workers at his home and all were invited, again without arbitrary distinctions of any kind.[142] There was no preferential treatment, just equal regard. The result of the egalitarian ethos that Boom created was highly engaged workers who were willing to release their full discretionary efforts. Ask yourself: Do you respect only high achievers and the highly educated, or do you recognize that insight and answers can come from some of the most unlikely people?

I never saw people work so hard and smile so much. The work environment Boom created affirmed their coequal status with the other workers regardless of socioeconomic background. It offered patient encouragement for them to learn the skills to do a job without fear of a belittling response. And finally, it granted autonomy for results. Boom exacted high standards and ran a clean and organized operation, but he didn't needlessly micromanage. The contributor safety he created fueled our performance. The college kids lost their attitude, and the migrant workers had a very real sense that they were not second-class citizens. Our working relationship was on equal footing.[143]

Now you might say to yourself at this point, "That's nice. Everyone worked hard and performed well because Boom made them feel good about themselves." If that were the takeaway, you would have missed the other half of the equation. Boom elevated performance in terms of raw output, but he did more than that. He planted a postindustrial mindset into a preindustrial agricultural setting. Boom was a son of the Dust Bowl, with parents who had never finished the eighth grade, migrated to California in a Model A, and settled in Salinas. Having grown up as a cantaloupe laborer and joined the United Packinghouse Workers union at age thirteen, Boom had created a blue zone from a deeply internalized sense of justice and equity.

The blue zone he created rooted out fear, allowing people to give and receive constructive feedback, to collaborate by thinking out loud rather than competing in silence.[144] It emboldened people to speak up, ask for clarification, and even talk about mistakes.[145]

You see, it only takes a little fear to create a fear-stricken team. *Fear-stricken teams give you their hands, some of their head, and none of their heart.* They become dutiful yes-men and women. The past lingers so powerfully in the present that the "despotism of custom" hinders human achievement, as John

Stuart Mill observed during England's Industrial Revolution.[146] If I'm overstating the case, why, then, does Gallup continue to report that 85 percent of employees worldwide are "not engaged or [are] actively disengaged at work," resulting in a global downward trend in workplace productivity?[147] Why do we constantly launch anti-harassment campaigns in our corporations? We have some work to do.

I walked away from my experience in California's Central Valley with the very real conviction that most people will release their discretionary efforts if they are working in a climate of contributor safety. If given the chance, they will produce outstanding results in exchange for autonomy, guidance, and support.

Every person regulates their own discretionary effort, and the internal regulator we use to freeze or release that effort is very sensitive to the way others treat us. On one occasion, I took my son to the doctor, a well-respected specialist. He came into the room, didn't make eye contact with us, didn't say hello, didn't even raise his eyes above his clipboard. "Okay, what seems to be the problem?" he asked. He quickly examined my son and wrote a prescription. And then he was gone. As we walked out of the office, my son turned to me and said, "Dad, he's a terrible doctor and I don't ever want to come back." As it turns out, the doctor's diagnosis and treatment were correct. He was a competent physician. But that's not the whole job, is it? The doctor's skills were first-rate, but his demeanor was either aloof or indifferent. My son, observing human interaction, reacted accordingly.

In case you're tempted to dismiss this example as simply a matter of an introverted personality, which we sometimes use as an excuse for ourselves, consider two US presidents: George Washington and Abraham Lincoln. By anyone's estimation, they were both incredible leaders who changed the history of the world. But if we take a closer look, we realize that they were miles apart in basic temperament and disposition. Washington had a commanding presence and yet was an awkward speaker. Lincoln, on the other hand, had an awkward presence and was a commanding speaker. Washington was stately, dignified, formal, detached, quiet, and reserved. Lincoln was informal and personable and would lighten the mood with jokes, humor, and storytelling. Yet, despite their big differences in personality, they nurtured contributor safety. They both had the ability to recruit the best people and enlist their highest service even when those very people were filled with envy and resentment toward them.

Don't excuse yourself from the obligation of creating contributor safety because you think you may not possess certain gifts of personality. I had an English teacher in high school, Mr. Westergard, who I thought was a rather austere man. He never said much, and yet I could sense that he respected me. If you lack a sparkly, bubbly personality and are more Spock-like in demeanor, people might not know you care. If you're effusive, the emotional display can be tiresome. In any situation, we must exercise emotional intelligence by governing our interactions with appropriate balance and composure. In the fourth century BC, Aristotle wrote about the need for this poise and moderation: "Emotions may be felt both too much and too little, and in both cases not well; but to feel them at the right times, with reference to the right objects, towards the right people, with the right motive, and in the right way."[148] Be yourself. Just be your best self.

Are You Prepared to Create Contributor Safety?

On one occasion, I made what I call a charisma hire: I confused rhetorical talent and showmanship for leadership, and paid the price. It stung so bad that I made sure it was the first and last time I made this mistake. Here's how it went down: I had to let a sales manager go and was looking for a replacement. In walked a very experienced, polished, and highly impressive candidate. She was a superstar. She had the education, drive, and track record—everything that would normally indicate certain success. On top of it all, she had charisma—that ineffable quality that can be so dangerous because it is more stylistic than substantive. It can blind even experienced leaders from asking tough questions about a person's background, experience, and qualifications, turning due diligence into negligence. On this occasion, I became willfully blind. This individual had such a commanding presence, and was so utterly convincing in her claim that she could double sales in two years, that I got sucked in and spent the next eighteen months regretting it.

The month after I promoted her, I returned to the office where she worked with her team. The office registered a subzero temperature. My employees were silent, moved in slow motion, and wore painted smiles. What on earth had happened in the space of thirty days? I started pulling people aside to find out. As one of the employees put it, "The reign of terror has begun." Regrettably, while this new executive was incredibly talented, she was not emotionally prepared to create contributor safety. Whether you're in a leadership role or an individual contributor role, you have the responsibility to help create contributor safety for the team. Ask yourself if you are emotionally prepared to do it.

I've seen cases in which a cruel environment extracted a great deal of labor from people. Yes, but what kind? Mindless labor, resentful labor, low-productivity labor. And for how long? *I've never seen a toxic work environment produce high performance and sustain it over time.* A toxic environment is one in which employees are motivated by personal gain to the point that they engage in mean-spirited comments, unethical behavior, abuse, and bullying. *A toxic environment shuts down performance because it thrusts people into a chronic fear response.* If we are prudently managing risk, and the individual is capable and doing their part, we should grant as much autonomy as we can. But sometimes we don't. Why would someone withhold contributor safety?

Remember, contributor safety is an earned privilege, but it requires preparation on both sides. Sometimes an individual is ready to contribute, but the leader isn't. Arrogance or insecurity of the leader, personal or institutional bias, prejudice or discrimination, prevailing team norms that reinforce insensitivity, a lack of empathy, or aloofness block the way.

Increase Your Powers of Observation

To foster the high level of contributor safety needed for a blue zone, you must get to know the members of your team. That means spending time with them, studying their individual dispositions, and then listening intently to what they say. In fact, if you listen long enough, people will often reveal what they would otherwise conceal.

Finally, watch them in action and pay attention to the way they contribute. Some of your people are natural collaborators. They thrive on dialogue. They relish problem-solving as a social process. They love banter and the repartee of hard-hitting give-and-take. But others can't stand it. They love problem-solving as an internal process. They love to deconstruct problems and think through solutions but wouldn't think of fighting for airtime in a discussion. They may be more reflective and solitary, and yet they possess first-rate critical thinking skills.

If you as the leader don't develop higher powers of observation, if you don't watch the way everyone responds to social cues, if you think leadership is a performance and you're the show, your tone deafness could deal a fatal blow to your team. When you're engaged in inquiry, when you're trying to figure something out, when you're in discovery mode, what are you doing as you participate in dialogue or discussion? That's right, you're asking questions. On the other hand, if you're engaged in advocacy, trying to influence others toward your point of view, what are you doing? Right again—you're telling. Figure 15 shows the tell-to-ask continuum.

Telling and Asking

What's your tell-to-ask ratio? Track yourself for a day or so and figure out how much of the time you're telling versus asking. I've sat in way too many meetings in which the boss is telling everyone what to do and everyone nods politely. Telling is efficient, but it quickly moves the listener into a passive mode and can slow down learning. The entire culture of major college football is steeped in an industrial model of tell. Just watch coach-to-player interactions: The coach is talking, talking, talking, and the players stand there and nod their heads at the end of each exchange. No wonder it takes so long to develop football IQ.

Over a period of four years, I spent endless hours in practice and team meetings, listening to coaches and watching film. Was it collaborative? Was it true dialogue? Was it active intellectual engagement? Not remotely. The signal-to-noise ratio (the amount of signal compared to the amount of background noise) gets so low that as a player you simply stop listening. The coach's incessant telling voice eventually becomes part of the noise.

Here's how it would go: "Clark, look at your body angle. You came off the line too slow. I don't know why your hand placement is that way. You've got

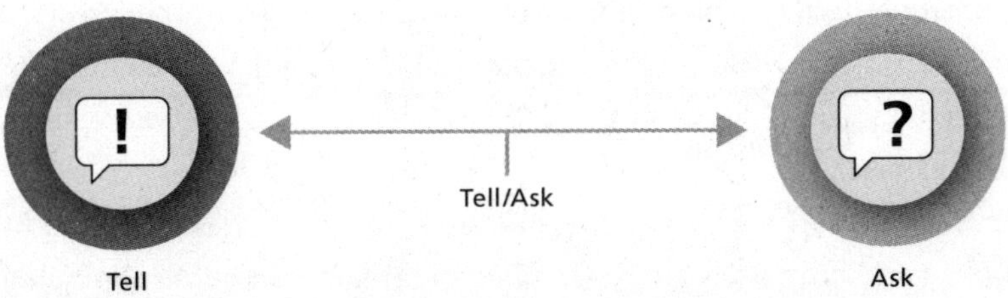

Figure 15. The tell-to-ask continuum

to get lower and stop your man's momentum. Read the linemen's stance. Look at how much weight they put on their hands. That will tell you if it's a run play. Look at the tackle's first step. What's he doing? He's trying to draw you inside. You know they run this draw-trap play almost every series." And it goes on and on. Can you imagine how our progress would have accelerated if my coaches had shifted from tell to ask, if they had handed me the remote control and said, "Clark, here's the next play. Please take us through it. Break it down"? It would have transformed culture and performance.

A leader's tell-to-ask ratio shapes the signal-to-noise ratio for the team. If the leader is telling all the time, that telling becomes noise. Can you see the risk? Some of the most wonderful, kind-hearted people I know are stuck at the "tell" end of the coaching continuum, and that is the root of their problem. They lead teams of talented people but are unable to draw them out because they are in chronic and perpetual advocacy mode, which lowers the signal-to-noise ratio. Their voices become noise to their listeners. As I said, some team members are willing to take this on and jump into the fray, and it's all good fun to them. But the quiet, contemplative, introverted, and often brilliant ones take a pass because it's not their natural habitat.

Listen Carefully, Speak Last

I once worked with a group of high-potential leaders at a technology company in Silicon Valley. They had been nominated to participate in a six-month leadership program to accelerate their development and prepare them for further responsibility. The team had to work virtually with each other because it consisted of members from nearly every continent. As a capstone to their cohort experience, they were tasked with making a major strategic recommendation to the company's executives. The day before their presentation, the members of the team flew in from their respective office locations to rehearse. They had worked weekends and made tremendous personal sacrifices to get to this point, and now they were ready to make their pitch.

They used every second of the allocated thirty minutes to make a well-researched and beautifully choreographed presentation. The agenda called for thirty minutes of Q&A to follow. Visibly exhausted and yet satisfied with their performance, they turned eagerly to the executives for feedback. To everyone's amazement, the CEO spoke first. In a monotone voice and with no visible display of emotion, he matter-of-factly said he thought the proposal was good but would cost too much money to pursue. He droned on for ten minutes about the company's strategy and priorities. Can you guess what happened next? That's right: nothing. The other executives didn't make a peep. The meeting disbanded after the CEO's sermonic performance, and the crestfallen team moved to a neighboring conference room, where I spent the next hour helping them de-escalate their anger and frustration.

The next week, I debriefed with several of the executives and asked that they tell the CEO that the next time it would be better for him to speak last, after the other executives had asked their questions and expressed their views. *Speaking first when you hold positional power softly censors your team.*

Not long after, I got confirmation that the feedback had been delivered to the CEO. But the story doesn't end there. We ran the same program the following year. The new team was given the same assignment. They invested comparable time and effort and arrived at the appointed day to make their presentation. Following a similarly well-vetted and well-crafted presentation, the CEO did the very same thing. He shut them down in the first five minutes of Q&A. He wasn't rude or mean in what he said or the way he said it. But by virtue of his position, he brought the process to a swift and ignominious end. He was obtuse, insensitive, and self-indulgent. Ask yourself: Are you emotionally advanced beyond needing to hear yourself talk?

Help Others Think Beyond Their Roles

One of the most powerful things you can do to engender contributor safety is help the members of your team think beyond their individual roles. Surely, you've seen how the boundaries of a person's role tend to confine thinking to the role. We become small and siloed in our perspectives instead of getting up in our hot-air balloon to see the whole and how the parts fit together.

When people join an organization, they normally join a team that is part of a function or department. And the first thing they do is learn to perform basic tasks that relate to their specific role. If they're in marketing, they may learn how to launch a Google ad word campaign; if they're in accounting, they may learn how to reconcile the inventory; if they're in purchasing, they may learn how to review a new potential vendor—you get the picture. The point is that most of us grow up in organizations with a task-based, tactical mindset. We perform our roles and we get good at what we do.

But increasingly, especially in highly dynamic environments, the team needs us to contribute in our roles *and* think beyond them. Doing so requires that we have both the skill and the will to make that bigger contribution. Here's how the skill side of it normally plays out: One day the organization taps you on the shoulder and says, "Hey, I need you to think strategically. Go and be strategic!" And you say, "That sounds great. How do I do that?"

"I'm not sure, but go do it," comes the reply.

Sound familiar? This scenario repeats itself over and over in organizations. So let's back up. To think beyond your role, you need both skill and will. I should have said will and skill, because the sequence matters. Do you find people attempting to think and contribute beyond their roles if they don't feel confident to at least try? *Before people can get out of their tactical and functional siloes to think strategically, they must be liberated by the contributor safety you give them.*

I once worked with the vice president of procurement for a Fortune 500 organization. He lorded over his people as if he were the hereditary monarch and they were peasants. In one meeting, he chided them for not thinking more strategically about the company's overall purchasing strategy and the need to squeeze the list of approved suppliers. In effect, he was asking them to think and contribute beyond their roles without supplying support. He had some people with incredible potential. When I came back a year later, he still had the same *unrealized* incredible potential.

Helping others think beyond their roles starts with an opportunity and a direct invitation. In our company, we invite the software development team to think about our marketing strategy. We invite sales to think about software development. It's not something we spend time on every day, but we deliberately ask each employee to think beyond their role. *The invitation to think beyond one's role expresses greater respect for the individual and grants greater permission to contribute.*

The way you do it makes all the difference. You still need people to stay focused on their primary roles. I've seen some leaders get carried away with an unbounded sense of collaboration that resulted in chaos. Be deliberate about the topics or challenges you want to address and make specific invitations to address those issues. Then issue a standing invitation for ideas and suggestions on any aspect of performance, with the understanding that everyone will be heard but not always heeded.

Finally, to prevent a team's descent into chaos, the leader must know when constructive dissent is giving way to destructive derailment. It's the leader's job to recognize the difference between dissenting and derailing behavior and to manage the boundary between the two.

It's one thing to disagree or to offer an alternative point of view with an intention to contribute based on a sense of where the team is and whether the alternative is viable. It's quite another to dissent in a way that is disruptive to team morale and not helpful to overall progress. Those who dissent constructively are guided by a sense of self-awareness and pure intent. Those who dissent destructively are misguided by a personal agenda and a lack of self-awareness. *In short, it's the intent behind the dissent that separates the innovator from the agitator.*

INTROSPECTION QUESTIONS:

1. Do you collaborate effectively with other members of your team?
2. Do you respect only the high achievers and highly educated?
3. Do you recognize that insights can come from some of the most unlikely people?
4. Can you be genuinely happy for the success of others?
5. Do you empower others without micromanaging them?
6. Have you ever withheld contributor safety from someone when they have earned it?
7. Do you freely share your experience, knowledge, and skills?
8. Are you emotionally advanced beyond needing to hear yourself talk?
9. Do you see the potential of others on your team?

If you find that you struggle to let everyone participate, focus your efforts on including everyone in meaningful contribution. Do you tend to keep your talents to yourself? Make an effort to share them. Are you willing to keep quiet in a meeting that's going well, even if that means that no one hears your voice? If not, take steps to become a better listener.

One of the hardest components of contributor safety is knowing when to stop talking and when to intervene. For leaders especially, managing the contributions of others is a delicate dance on the tightrope of autonomy. Too much autonomy with little guidance will leave your team with more questions than they know what to do with. Too much guidance with zero autonomy will turn your teams into robots with no space to innovate. Remind yourself that contributor safety satisfies the basic human need to do meaningful work, to make a difference in the world.

Conclusion

If you want to foster a blue zone of contributor safety, create a democracy of contribution. If your style is heavy-handed, your communication didactic, and your ego fragile, you will scorch any seedling of contributor safety that's beginning to shoot up. Remember, you set the tone for your team's mode of execution. If you're not a leader by position and must lead by influence only, which is the case for most of us, create contributor safety in the same way. There should be no difference in approach.

The level of contributor safety on your team is expressed by the invitation to contribute that you extend to each person to jump into action. It's your culture on display and your DNA in action. It's how you give and take, push and pull, talk and listen, question and answer, act and react, analyze and solve. Remember, people want to play in the game!

Chapter Summary

- **Definition:** Contributor safety satisfies the basic human need for choice and meaningful contribution.
- **Preparation to performance:** Preparation creates the desire to perform. Contributor safety enables the individual to deliver real value.
- **Earned privilege:** Unlike inclusion and learner safety, contributor safety is earned through competence, performance, and accountability.
- **Social exchange:** The deal is autonomy with guidance for results. Independence is granted in proportion to performance.
- **Bench effect:** Being denied the chance to contribute creates emotional suspension. Active contribution fosters identity, confidence, and motivation.

- **Three-level accountability:** Autonomy expands with predictable performance at three levels:
  - Task
  - Process
  - Outcome
- **Defensive innovation:** Threat-driven adaptation requires contributor safety.
- **Offensive innovation:** Opportunity-driven innovation requires challenger safety. Contributor safety alone is insufficient.
- **Blue zone versus red zone:** Blue zones of rewarded vulnerability release discretionary effort. Red zones of punished vulnerability suppress it through fear, ego, and micromanagement.
- **Discretionary effort regulator:** People give or withhold their best efforts based on whether their vulnerability is rewarded or punished.
- **Tell/ask ratio:** Chronic telling becomes noise, while asking activates thinking, ownership, and contribution.
- **Speak last:** Leaders with positional power must speak last to avoid softly censoring the team and collapsing dialogue.
- **Think beyond roles:** Contributor safety enables people to think beyond their tasks and silos toward broader, cross-functional contribution.
- **Intent behind dissent:** Constructive dissent propels progress. Destructive dissent derails it. Intent is the dividing line.
- **Ego management:** Contributor safety expands when leaders regulate ego and grant autonomy responsibly.
- **Pathway to mastery:** Repeated autonomy-for-results cycles build capability and confidence until performance is defined by outcomes, not tasks or processes.

STAGE 4

Challenger Safety

Every society has its protectors of status quo and its fraternities of the indifferent who are notorious for sleeping through revolutions. Today, our very survival depends on our ability to stay awake, to adjust to new ideas, to remain vigilant and to face the challenge of change.

—Martin Luther King Jr.

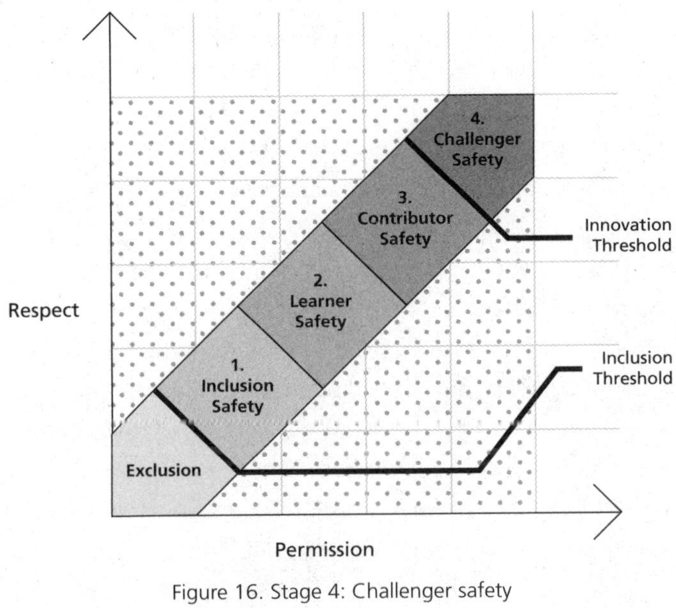

Figure 16. Stage 4: Challenger safety

Let me paint a picture of an organization for you: First, each department is a thought silo, intellectual gated community, and conceptual island. Second, most employees are loyal. Loyalty means conformity. The desire for unanimity overrides the motivation to objectively evaluate alternative courses of action.[149] Third, the authoritarian leader of the team interprets challenge as subversion.

This is what you might call a state of emotional and intellectual agony. Everything that confounds innovation is present. Think about the nature of innovation. Innovation disrupts the status quo. The process produces conflict, confrontation, and a measure of chaos. These things are dangerous, yet necessary. If organizational conflict turns into interpersonal conflict, if fear becomes a motivator, if there is censure or punishment, the process collapses and people go silent. As Margaret Atwood said, "Powerlessness and silence go together."[150]

That was the state of affairs when Satya Nadella took the helm as CEO of Microsoft in 2014. Since then, he has led one of the most remarkable corporate transformations in modern history. How did he achieve this? By embedding psychological safety into Microsoft's culture and creating a nonpunishing environment that encourages creative friction through challenger safety (figure 16).

Nadella shifted the prevailing norms and changed the terms of engagement. He helped the organization understand that either too much conflict or too much conformity was dangerous—dangerous to humans and dangerous to the business (figure 17).

When Nadella stepped into the role, Microsoft had just endured what historians and analysts call its "lost decade," a period in which the company missed major market shifts and inflection points—so many, in fact, that it became a chronic pattern and threatened the company's future. It was miss after miss after miss. These failures stemmed from a fear-based culture that stifled candor and discouraged people from challenging the status quo. Leaders made decisions based on power and hierarchy, not merit. In short, Microsoft lost its capacity to productively harness conflict (table 7).

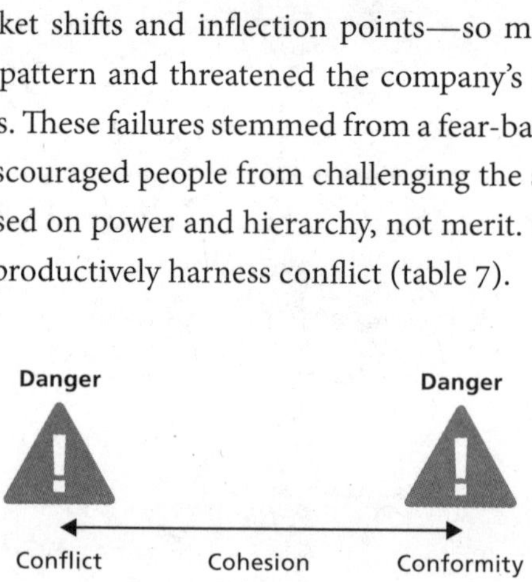

Figure 17. Danger of conflict and conformity

Table 7. Microsoft's misses

#	Domain	Missed shift	Key competitors who capitalized
1	Cloud infrastructure	Public cloud and SaaS	Amazon, Google
2	Open source ecosystems	Developer platforms	Linux, Apache, Red Hat
3	App economics	Mobile developer ecosystems	Apple, Google
4	Consumer hardware	Integrated design	Apple
5	Collaboration tools	Cloud productivity	Google, Slack
6	User experience	Design simplicity	Apple, Google
7	Advertising	Data monetization	Google, Facebook
8	Streaming	Video and entertainment	Netflix, YouTube
9	Social messaging	Mobile-first communication	WhatsApp, Instagram
10	AI foundations	Early applied machine learning	Google, Facebook

Performance before and since Nadella confirms what is perhaps my single most important research finding when it comes to innovation: *The quality of interaction regulates the speed of discovery.*

Nadella changed the way Microsoft interacts. And that has made all the difference. He exemplifies the leadership principle: "If you could understand impermanence deeply, you would develop more equanimity."[151] Equanimity—a calmness of mind and ego—is a vital leadership quality that allows one to benefit from productive conflict. Research shows that equanimity leads to psychological safety: the ability to function in a group without fear of negative consequences. This, in turn, fosters innovation. That cycle—equanimity leading to psychological safety, leading to innovation—describes Microsoft's transformation under Nadella, who helped make it the most valuable company in the world.

Let's reduce the relationship between psychological safety and innovation into one statement: Innovation requires deviation. Are there any exceptions? None! Even the smallest marginal gain requires some departure from the status quo (figure 18).

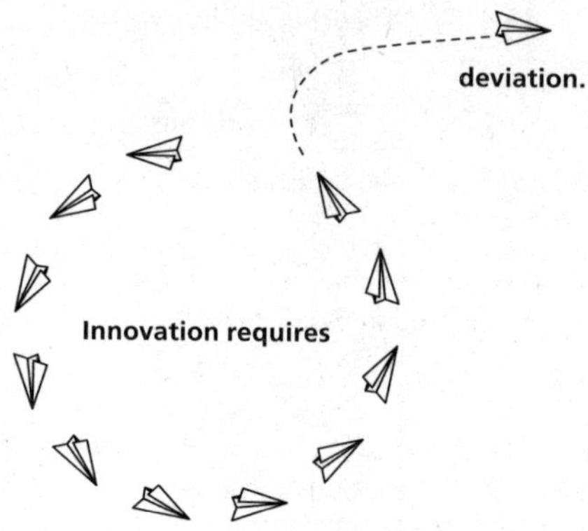

Figure 18. Innovation requires deviation

Observing your team like a cultural anthropologist, ask: What does innovation look like? What enables it? What blocks it? At its core, innovation is a social process driven by human interaction. The right kind of interaction fosters innovation and competitive advantage. The wrong kind shuts it down.

This brings us to stage 4, challenger safety, the culminating stage of psychological safety that enables the fourth human need category to challenge and improve.

Definition: Challenger safety satisfies the basic human need to challenge and improve. You feel safe to speak up and challenge the status quo when you think there is a need or opportunity to improve.

The Neural Plasticity of Teams

Brain researchers used to think that the circuitry of the brain was fixed. They have since learned that the hundred billion neurons and hundred trillion connections among those neurons operate in an incredibly flexible way. The brain has plasticity and can rewire itself. A team is nothing less than a great brain. But the synapses take place between people rather than between neurons. Similarly, there is nothing fixed or hardwired about the speed or patterns of these connections. Teams are astonishingly plastic, so we really don't know the natural capacity of any team to perform. We simply know they can surprise us, because the human ingenuity of a given group of people is unknown and unknowable.

More than anything else, team plasticity reflects the leader's modeling behavior. If the leader suppresses dissent, people recoil as predictably as deer react to sudden movements. If the leader accommodates dissent, it builds the team's innovation-surge capacity. Collectively, the team has sensory organs that react to the environment, adapting a weave of social, emotional, and intellectual processing to the conditions that surround it.

I once worked with a CEO whose team was struggling to adapt in a rapidly changing industry. He said his team was not smart enough, curious enough, or entrepreneurial enough. When his amygdala overpowered his prefrontal cortex and he acted out of frustration, the tenor of the team changed. No surprise there. His efforts to "drive" innovation would always result in a blowback of crippling silence. As fear extinguished curiosity, the team became sluggish, stubborn, and slow. *Challenger safety invites the courage necessary to democratize innovation.*

After posting lackluster results for a couple of years, this feudal lord was fired. Fortunately, I had the pleasure of working with his successor. The anatomy of the executive team didn't change, but the environment did. The new leader introduced a new social technology—none other than challenger safety. He nurtured respect and permission to astonishing levels. He brought down the cultural barriers to entry. The team was a little skittish at first, but then came a wave of unprecedented productivity. You see, humans are designed to respond to kindness and empathy.[152] They responded with improvement after improvement, innovation after innovation. The new CEO regenerated the neurological system of the team. The velocity of information increased. The cocreative process came alive. The adaptive capacity emerged. He took the team to intellectual depths they had never known. As a unit, they became more artistic and more athletic, more disciplined and more demanding, and ultimately, much more confident and aware of themselves.

The changes in inputs brought changes in outputs. *Connectivity increases productivity*. Here came the flow of insights, connections, associations, ideations, unexpected leaps, and aha moments. This is the promise of challenger safety. You can do the same thing this leader did if you encourage dialogue and emotionally tolerate dissent along the way. Because people are creative within a cultural context, it's the leader's job to liberate the creative impulse in that context.[153]

Now here's the other side of it: Although the brain is plastic, it defaults to rigidity. Teams do too, which means that the past lingers in the present. The early socialization patterns and original norms tend to be incredibly stubborn and hard to replace. *To socialize a team with challenger safety from the start is always easier than to resocialize a team later.*

Organizational change is a process that moves through three separate layers—technical, behavioral, and cultural. We often start by changing all three layers at the same time, but each one changes at a different pace. First is the technical or nonhuman layer, or what we call artifacts. They include systems, processes, structures, roles, responsibilities, policies, procedures, and tools and technology. These things represent configurable parts and can be changed relatively quickly with money and authority. In the behavioral layer, we change the way people behave as they interact with the technical layer and each other in new ways. But simply because people are behaving differently doesn't mean that they want to or that they would continue in the new patterns if given the choice. When artifacts hold up behavior, they act as scaffolding, and once the scaffolding is removed, behavior reverts to past patterns—unless there are changes in the cultural layer. That tendency to snap back is what we call a regression to the mean. The third layer of change is the invisible layer, consisting of values, beliefs, and assumptions.

In all social units, the cultural layer is the single most difficult thing to change and the layer that changes last. It's your lag indicator. You can impose change and get people to comply. If the chief medical officer at a hospital is watching, the doctors and nurses will wash their hands to decrease the risk of nosocomial infection. But if the chief steps away, their level of compliance immediately falls. Why? Because they lack intrinsic motivation. Behavioral patterns calcify. Team behavior is much the same. What compounds the problem in challenger safety is that you are asking people not only to change their behavior but to do it in an environment of greater personal risk.

The Stage of Brave

The culminating stage of psychological safety is the place where respect and permission intersect at the highest level—a super-enriched zone dedicated to exploration and experimentation. To advance from contributor safety to challenger safety requires crossing the "innovation threshold"—a place where the highest possible level of psychological safety replaces what would normally be a place inhabited with the greatest fear. But creating challenger safety is far more difficult than understanding it, especially if the culture is already toxic. As Celia Swanson, a former executive vice president at Walmart, said, "Making the decision to speak up against a toxic culture is one of the most difficult decisions employees may face in their careers."[154]

Challenger safety is a level of psychological safety so high that people feel empowered to challenge the status quo, leaving their comfort zones to put a creative or disruptive idea on the table, which, by definition, is a threat to the way things are done and therefore a risk to themselves personally. To invite people to challenge the status quo is both natural and unnatural. It's natural in the sense that human beings are innately creative. The biologist Edward O. Wilson said creativity is "the unique and defining trait of our species."[155] The creative instinct propels us to challenge the status quo out of a desire to create and improve things, but doing so is unnatural in an environment that we perceive is unsafe. If the environment is a pocket of thick trust, we will go forward with our challenge. If it's a pocket of thin trust, our self-censoring instinct is triggered, and we will remove ourselves from participation. The atmosphere either draws out or shuts down the creative impulse to challenge. It's scary enough to speak truth to power. It's even scarier to speak opinion to power, because there's a bigger personal risk of rejection and embarrassment.

I recently interviewed a vice president at one of the largest health-care systems in the nation. He said the organization was more militaristic than the military. He challenged the status quo on a staffing issue early on and barely lived to tell about it. "I thought I had a brain, but I guess I don't," he said. "In this organization, you do exactly what you're told, with no commentary." I interviewed another woman who worked at a large media company in South America. "We are not allowed to be creative," she said. "If you're not in senior leadership, you don't challenge anything. If you do, you're out."

Clearly, not all leaders are convinced that psychological safety is necessary for innovation. Some believe that psychological safety is nothing more than asking people to be polite, on the assumption that they need to be coddled before they can be expected to engage. Two Australian scholars, Ben Farr-Wharton and Ace Simpson, share this insight: "Through a systems management perspective, the very human concept of compassion seems wasteful. This is because noticing, empathizing with, making sense of and responding to a colleague's suffering (how we define the process of organizational compassion) may be considered an indulgent and time-consuming process that detracts from immediate work duties."[156]

Those who say that psychological safety is nothing more than sympathetic and sentimental slush offered by leaders who are unwilling to hold others accountable are in denial themselves. They refuse to acknowledge that you can't coerce or manipulate innovation. The process is surrounded by interpersonal risk. Unless you lower or remove the barriers to entry and violations of human interaction, people simply will not engage at full capacity. This is exactly the norm Stephen A. Schwarzman, chairman and CEO of private equity firm Blackstone, has tried to model and reinforce. "If there's any genius at Blackstone, it's coming up with that structure where you can say anything that is fact-based to get to a logical answer without it being personal."[157]

This final stage of psychological safety governs what are clearly the most sensitive, charged, pressurized, politicized, stressful, and high-stakes situations of all. Because the fear and the potential risk to the individual are highest, the level of psychological safety must be deepest. With inclusion safety, you're asking to be included; with learner safety, you're asking to be encouraged; with contributor safety, you're asking for autonomy; but with challenger safety, the social exchange has now gone to another level: The team is asking you to challenge the status quo. That's a mighty ask! Thus, the only reasonable condition is that the organization protects you in the process. If the organization wants candor, you need cover—you need real and sustained air cover to be brave enough to take what is almost always a substantial personal risk. *The greatest enemy to innovation is the homogenization of thought.*

In case it still hasn't sunk in, let me sketch the emotional landscape of innovation in an organization. It's one thing to use your talents in creative pursuits or be curious about something on your own. It's quite another to take aim at the status quo in an organization when the entire system and culture preserve it. If challenger safety doesn't exist in the organization, there's a high cost to that curiosity and creativity. It tends to be an arena of shame, pain, and embarrassment in addition to the normal uncertainty, ambiguity, and chaos. Innovation is hard enough, because there's no safety from failure. No one can give you that. But what the leader can do is take the social sting and emotional bite out of the process. De-bottleneck the flow of information that allows collaboration to happen.

For organizations trying to create a thriving environment for neurodivergent talent—including employees who demonstrate variations in learning, attention, mood, and sociability due to autism, dyslexia, attention deficit and/or hyperactivity disorder, depression, or other atypical neurological conditions—challenger safety becomes a precondition for basic productivity. It's my personal experience that neurodivergent employees are more acutely sensitive to indicators of fear, react faster to them, and require more time to reemerge out of defensive routines.

When I teach leaders the concept of challenger safety and the social exchange of candor for cover, they often nod and say, "I got it." That's when I stare back at them and say, "Please consider that you may not yet fully grasp what you are asking people to do. If you want your people to innovate, you need to do some soul-searching and deep introspection about what you're asking. Innovation is not some kind of frictionless, comfortable process. No, innovation is always about disassembling the current regime. It's willfully knocking yourself out of orbit. It's trading certainty for ambiguity. Most of the time, it's asking for failure. That's just the organizational side of it. What about the personal side? *You're asking your people to expose themselves to criticism, risk failure, take chances, be vulnerable, not fit in, and feel pain.* And you're asking them to do all of this without any real control over the outcome.

Now do you see what you're asking? If you're going to ask that, your employees are going to make a reasonable request of you. They know you can't promise zero loss. They know you can't remove all risk, and they know you can't eliminate the pain. Everybody gets that, so at a minimum, they're asking you to protect them socially and emotionally as they engage in this free-ranging process. "At least protect me from embarrassment and rejection" comes the petition. Now that's a reasonable request. And don't forget that not everyone craves creative contribution over comfort.

Which now brings us to the question of who goes first. I was training a group of employees at a university once and sat down at one of the tables to join a discussion. One of the participants said, "I get the cover-for-candor concept. Would you please tell the executives that the air cover must come first? Do they really expect me to give the candor when I haven't seen evidence of the cover? I may be dumb, but I'm not stupid." There you have it.

Cover for candor means that you as the leader protect each person's right to speak candidly about any topic, provided they don't make personal attacks or have malicious intent. When people feel protected in that right, they tend to exercise it (see table 8). *The social exchange for challenger safety is air cover for candor.*

The definition of *respect* in the fourth stage of psychological safety is "respect for the individual's innate need to challenge and improve the status quo." Like the definitions of respect for learner safety and contributor safety, respect at this level is an earned privilege rather than a right. Thus, you earn the right to innovate as you demonstrate competent skills and accountable performance. If you lack a track record based on these things, don't expect people to take you seriously. Am I saying you shouldn't have a voice until you become an expert? Not remotely. Everyone should have a voice, but you will naturally find that people will take you seriously if that voice has a track record behind it.

Table 8. Stage 4: Challenger safety

Stage	**Definition of respect**	**Definition of permission**	**Social exchange**
1. Inclusion safety	Respect for the individual's innate need to be included, accepted, and gain a sense of belonging	Permission for the individual to feel, be their authentic self, and enter your society	Inclusion in exchange for human status and the absence of harm
2. Learner safety	Respect for the individual's innate need to learn and grow	Permission for the individual to engage in all aspects of the learning process and make mistakes	Encouragement to learn in exchange for engagement to learn
3. Contributor safety	Respect for the individual's innate need for choice and contribution	Permission for the individual to work with appropriate autonomy and independence	Autonomy with guidance in exchange for performance and results
4. Challenger safety	Respect for the individual's innate need to challenge and improve the status quo	Permission for the individual to challenge and improve the status quo in good faith	Air cover in exchange for candor

In addition to respect, the nature of permission changes as well when we transition to challenger safety. In the fourth stage, implicitly or explicitly, we are giving the individual permission to challenge the status quo in good faith. That means we assume the individual is acting with pure motive to help improve things. Sometimes people challenge the status quo with ideas for incremental improvement. Sometimes they take moon shots and propose a wholesale transformation to the way we do things. Sometimes they come with fully baked ideas and plans, and sometimes they come with nothing but an unsupported hunch or gut instinct. In an atmosphere of challenger safety, we take all comers and all contributions. We may take some challenges more seriously than others as we consider the source, but we honor each person's offering regardless of hierarchy. We make it safe to collaborate.

If you have challenged the status quo without challenger safety, you no doubt remember that painful experience, and you're very careful not to repeat it. Your brave attempt was met with retribution. You thought you had the air cover, but you were wrong, which left you naked to rejection. Those experiences are neurobiological encounters that create stress, scars, and vivid memories that cause us to err on the side of caution the next time.

On one occasion, I was training a large law enforcement agency. I sensed right away that the culture was toxic and vindictive. Sure enough, as soon as we moved into the first discussion, you could plainly see that the members of this organization were not healthy enough to hold even a basic dialogue. By imposing the constant fear of criticism, the leaders had successfully created an atmosphere of jaded cynicism. The group dynamic was silence interspersed with sarcasm, an occasional wisecrack, and cutting humor. No one would dare challenge the status quo in good faith. That would be tantamount to a request for verbal and emotional abuse, which would come swiftly.

If you're encouraging your people to challenge the status quo but haven't prepared the climate by cultivating the necessary challenger safety, what can you reasonably expect? Are your people going to be brave and wander into enemy territory when they know their bravery will be met with punishment? Do people volunteer opinions when opinions are suppressed?[158] Only fools rush in when it's not safe. If there's no air cover to back them up, it's unwise of them to try and disingenuous of you to ask. Even if you frame challenging the status quo as expressing healthy dissatisfaction, it's still subversive and always a personal risk. No cover, no candor. People will come up with defensive routines to save themselves from the risk of embarrassment.[159] And if they make mistakes, they will be sorely tempted to cover them up.

Let me illustrate from my own professional experience. For three years I had a Japanese boss based in Tokyo. When I was given the assignment to report to him, I braced myself because of what I had read about the rigid hierarchical nature of Japanese business culture. I read a book about Japanese society that issued this warning: "An expression of a contradictory opinion to that of the head was considered a sign of misbehavior."[160] *I'm in trouble*, I thought, because I don't know how to do my job without giving my opinions, and sometimes they are bound to be contrary. But then came the pleasant surprise: My boss turned out to be a collaborative, trustworthy man who allowed me to be brave. He used psychological safety to level the power dynamics and drain anxiety out of the process of seeking help or feedback.[161] In the twilight of his career, this man had worked for several multinational corporations and had learned that diverse, multidisciplinary teams don't innovate unless they are lubricated with the oil of challenger safety. He understood that innovation requires exploring the unknown and always involves tension and stress. He asked me to be brave, but first created the organization's accommodation for that bravery, which of course would mean that I would sometimes offer up bad ideas, make poor suggestions, and go down dead-end roads. But then there were times when I would come up with a meaningful innovation.

As a last step to set the table for challenger safety, he demonstrated transparency. He shared all the information he could, and he did it consistently. Here's the principle: *As the leader eliminates unknowns through transparency, they lower the barriers of entry to participate.*

I accepted the invitation. I ventured out slowly, observing my boss carefully for any signs of emotional defensiveness. Eventually, I quit fearing failure or judgment, because it was, as Abraham Maslow put it, "safe enough to dare."[162] It was never a career ender to challenge something, because I knew the culture tolerated and even expected it. It's the leader that creates that organizational laboratory of experimentation, and that lab requires conditions that differ from a pure execution mode of operations. Think about the inherent constraints under which we must innovate. Typically, we have less data, more ambiguity, more unknowns, and more failures, so we need more exploratory inquiry, more tolerance for unreasonable ideas, and more capacity to absorb failure.[163]

Clearly, innovation most often happens under conditions of stress, when you're feeling the pressure of competition, when you're trying to figure out a solution surrounded by constraints and limitations. There's nothing relaxed or carefree about it. *And yet there is no necessary relationship between stress and fear.*

The stress and pressure we feel doesn't automatically create fear. I remember feeling enormous pressure and exhilaration many times while working for my Japanese boss. The pressure was imposed by our competitive circumstances, but he didn't add a layer of fear to the mix as a perverse way to motivate us. By creating challenger safety, he helped convert stress into positive energy. I had been put in charge of an organization that was hemorrhaging cash. The market tanked and we were in a free fall. Instead of escalating interpersonal tension to accompany the crisis, my boss increased the frequency of his touch points with me, but they were always calm and focused encounters. Even when others showed up with spiked emotion, the boss was a de-escalating influence. Eventually, we came through the crisis with a stronger, faster, and more engaged organization.

It's possible to unlock creativity in a crisis if the leader welcomes dissent and doesn't add a layer of manufactured fear to the existing level of natural stress. Many employees already feel they are living and working in the age of overwhelm. Just look at the World Uncertainty Index's long-term upward trend (WorldUncertaintyIndex.com). Even if current conditions are well beyond the normal range of uncertainty, whatever that might be, learner safety shifts the paradigm. Inflections, disruptions, and dislocations all become learning opportunities. Learner safety pumps motivation into the veins of employees. It summons even more energy out of the organizational system. It propels people to "go forth to meet the shadowy future without fear," as Longfellow put it.[164]

The Social Origins of Innovation

Innovation means looking into the foggy future and trying to make something better by connecting things that are not normally connected using divergent, lateral, associative, or nonlinear thinking. You basically have three options. You can connect:

- Existing knowledge with existing knowledge
- Existing knowledge with new knowledge
- New knowledge with new knowledge

Remember when Netflix knocked Blockbuster out of the market? How did they do it? They connected snail mail with DVDs! Those two ordinary things became the source of an unlikely, disruptive innovation. That's the pattern most of the time. We build on what we know, using the tools, technology, and ideas we already have.[165] How do you think chocolate and peanut butter came together? But here's the irony of innovation: Even though it's built on knowledge assets, it's the learning process that brings them together to create value in new ways.

In the process of innovation, learning is more important than knowing. Learning is the process of combining knowledge assets, but those assets are constantly becoming obsolete. In the long run, an enduring and adaptable learning process is more valuable than the perishable knowledge assets themselves. If we look at innovation further, we can see that there are two basic types:

TYPE 1

- Incremental
- Derivative

TYPE 2

- Radical
- Disruptive

As you might expect, type 1 is much more common because it's natural to start with what we know and connect it with something else that we know. If that doesn't work, we try new combinations of things (figure 19). We combine and recombine. That recombination is the essence of innovation. That's why

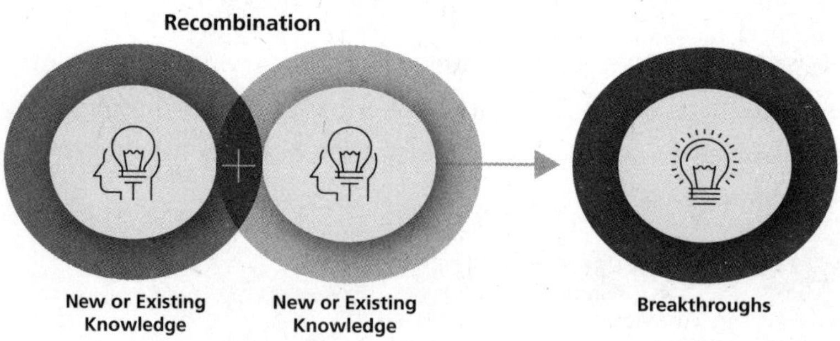

Figure 19. Process of innovation

Steve Jobs said, "Creativity is just connecting things."[166] But I'd like to amend that statement. *Innovation is the process of connected people connecting things.*

We all know that simply putting a bunch of virtuosos together doesn't automatically create beautiful music. They must learn to play together. They must connect first, and out of that connection comes the magic.

People can, of course, experience a light bulb moment of lone genius, a burst of inspiration, a eureka moment, but those are the exceptions. The more common pattern is for innovation to spring out of social interaction. In a Q&A session at Facebook, Mark Zuckerberg said, "Ideas typically do not just come to you. They happen because you've been talking about something and talking to a lot of people about it for a long period of time."[167] Brian Wilson, the musical genius behind the Beach Boys, expressed the same sentiment: "The key to our success was respecting one another's ideas and opinions."[168] Yes, you need talented people to innovate, but the magic is in the way they blend and merge ideas as they work together in what often seems a chaotic and spontaneous process. It doesn't matter if you are writing software or writing music, innovation usually has a social origin.

Are Questions Welcome?

I invite you to be a cultural anthropologist for a day and watch the way innovation happens on your team. If you look carefully, you'll notice that innovation ultimately emerges from the process of inquiry. That process comprises five steps, as shown in figure 20.

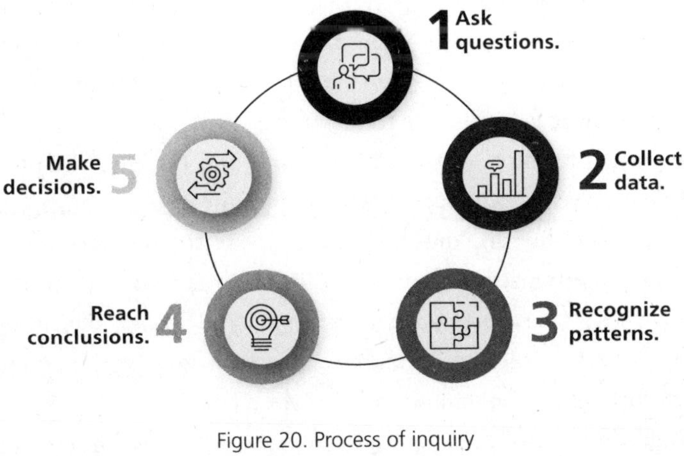

Figure 20. Process of inquiry

The first step is to ask questions. Questions act as the catalyst. They activate the process. Without questions, nothing happens. And yet we must acknowledge that asking questions introduces personal risk.

And if we're talking about questions that point to innovation, they almost always introduce more personal risk because they challenge the status quo. They attack the way things are done. From a career standpoint, this is the high-risk, high-reward zone. Ask yourself: Are questions really welcome on my team—not soft, easy, nonthreatening questions, but courageous and disruptive questions?

Have you cultivated a culture of inquiry that is hospitable to tough, uncomfortable questions, and do people really feel that? If you want a surge of ideas, you first need a surge of questions. If you want a surge of questions, you need to nurture the highest level of psychological safety based on the respect and permission that you give people.

We see very quickly that the entire process of innovation depends on a willingness to activate the inquiry process with questions. All organizations traffic in information and ideas, but not all organizations innovate. What makes the difference? If you haven't noticed, the natural consequence of analysis is friction. People see things differently and draw different conclusions. Now comes the hard part. How do you lubricate the gears of collaboration to reduce friction? If you can do it, you'll create new value. But if the friction increases, sand becomes the lubricant and your gears will grind to a halt.

My Japanese boss was a master at nurturing a culture of inquiry. From the tone he set, I knew two things: First, there were no dumb questions. I think he had learned from experience, as many of us do, that the line between brilliance and ignorance can be very thin. Second, there were no questions that were off limits, no topics that we couldn't talk about. Those were the ground rules he established, reinforced by his own modeling behavior and a talk-to-listen ratio that hovered at fifty-fifty. Without his example and the cover he provided, I would have been reluctant to activate the inquiry process and engage in innovation. In the end, inviting questions is the spigot that turns innovation on. Discouraging questions, and punishing those who ask them, turns the spigot off. *If you deprive your team of challenger safety, you unknowingly relegate the team to the status quo.* Rather than protecting your team against groupthink, you're reinforcing it. You're conditioning your people not to think and not to challenge, and teams learn very quickly not to think and not to challenge.

They learn very quickly how to "lock themselves inside an echo chamber of like-minded friends."[169]

Whether and how fast your team innovates is up to you. You regulate the velocity of information and the speed of discovery. You accelerate problem-solving. You create a climate of discipline and agility. You engender the patterns and prevailing norms that allow the team to manage itself.[170]

I worked with another CEO who needed a lot of oxygen in any room and would always commandeer meetings. He couldn't get off the stage. At the request of a distraught vice president of human resources, I attended an executive meeting with this CEO and his team to observe the dynamic. In this case, the CEO wasn't outwardly insulting, just subtly demeaning. He began the meeting and drove the agenda. He would ask yes/no questions and would become visibly agitated if his direct reports gave more than a few words of explanation beyond a simple yes or no. At one point, and I'll never forget this, the group started discussing a topic and getting into some productive dialogue. About two or three minutes in, the CEO literally opened his laptop and began doing email—in the middle of the meeting! I looked at the vice president of human resources in disbelief, and she gave me a knowing look of resignation. This is the way he would censure and censor. Eventually, the CEO lost his job, dying of self-inflicted wounds: He failed because his team functioned as vertical and independent blocks of knowledge that never came together.

It's important to remember that innovation is interdisciplinary. Your success will depend not on independent action, but on your dependent interaction. If the team can't gel and productively work through the five steps of inquiry, you'll never get there—regardless of the talent you have. You can only win as a team. It may seem unspectacular, but when you're watching innovation happen, you're watching people talk, interact, discuss, and debate. Only through that interplay and synthesis of ideas does constructive dissent, creative abrasion, and the process of combination and recombination happen.

When I was the plant manager at Geneva Steel, I learned the lifelong lesson that every system has a constraint. The constraint not only limits but also dictates the output of the entire system. The constraint is the bottleneck, and other parts of the system can't compensate for it. Consider the 4×400-meter relay event. Each of the four members of the team runs one lap around the track. If you're the slowest member, your slowness will dictate the team's overall performance. Everyone depends on each other. If the three other members of the team run their stages in forty-eight seconds and it takes you seventy-five, the team must still include your time in the total. Regardless of how fast they run, you're the drag.

Innovation works the same way. Your job as a leader is to reduce social friction without decreasing intellectual friction. This is the primary way to de-bottleneck the innovation constraint. If you can do this, people will invest deeply in the process, because we become attached to what we create through the fusion of the rational and the emotional. I see team after team exquisitely blessed with every resource it needs to innovate, except one—psychological safety, which is the constraint in the system.

It's one thing to collaborate for execution, which normally preserves the status quo. It's quite another to collaborate for innovation. Whereas execution is about creating value today, innovation is about creating value for tomorrow. It's an insurgent mission, a Skunk Works within the mothership. You're acting as disrupters in residence. That's what the great brain project is all about. The process is not tidy, clean, or linear. It's messy and iterative. Innovation is the marriage of gnarly problems and creative chaos with only a possibility that you'll produce something better. *The pattern of innovation is to try a lot and triumph a little.*

Seek Out Differences and Reduce the Risk of Ridicule

Let's dig a little deeper into the process of de-bottlenecking the organization to release its innovative potential. How do you get that innovation to flow? First, seek out differences. Second, reduce the risk of ridicule.

Remember that innovation is the process of connected people connecting things. By *connecting things*, I mean things that are not normally connected. For example, James Dyson, the inventor of the Dyson vacuum cleaner, said he went to a lumberyard one day and noticed giant cyclones on top of the roof that were collecting dust. Immediately, he started connecting those cyclones to his idea of a bagless vacuum. If innovation comes from connecting different things, the leader's job is to stimulate differences in the first place. Those differences become the raw material that results in innovation.[171]

You're not looking for compliance or consensus. In fact, you're looking for the opposite. You want to create and bring out differences. *You want people to make new, strange, and non-obvious connections*. How do you do that? Create differences in composition. That means assembling a diverse team. Diversity in composition can lead to diversity in thought. Because diversity creates dissent, diverse teams are less susceptible to groupthink.[172] Now bring out those differences by encouraging divergent thinking. Peter Drucker said, "Disagreement is needed to stimulate the imagination."[173] Again, the natural consequence of analysis is friction because people see things differently and draw different conclusions. Do you see the delicate balance? You're trying to reduce social friction, but not intellectual friction. You need to nurture differences and create a theater of conflict that carries natural pressure and stress, but not fear.

When differences come out, do everything in your power as a leader to reduce the risk of ridicule. Eliminate any ridiculing behavior in yourself and create a norm that frowns on all forms of ridicule and installs peer-based accountability to maintain that norm. When it comes to innovation, challenger safety is the enabler, while fear and ridicule are the inhibitors. People are born curious, so the goal is to help them stay curious. Any form of ridicule shuts innovation down.

I remember being in a meeting with my team in which our chief financial officer openly ridiculed our chief marketing officer for some of his marketing ideas and the way he wanted to allocate his budget. Rather than intercede and call out the CFO right then and there, I let it go. I tolerated the ridicule in front of the entire team, and my inaction that day sent a cowardly message that I spent the next month trying to undo. Because I didn't walk the talk, I opened the door for more ridicule and closed the door on more innovation. My failure of nerve compromised challenger safety.

A team of Israeli and European social psychologists recently verified the link between psychological safety and creativity. Simply knowing that your vulnerability will not be exploited encourages you to be brave and contribute to the generative process.[174]

As the psychologist Mihaly Csikszentmihalyi argues, "Each of us is born with two contradictory sets of instructions: a conservative tendency, made up of instincts for self-preservation, self-aggrandizement, and saving energy, and an expansive tendency made up of instincts for exploring, for enjoying novelty and risk—the curiosity that leads to creativity belongs to this set."[175]

Nothing can shut down curiosity and exploratory inquiry faster than a small dose of ridicule administered at just the right time. I've known leaders who thought it was acceptable to use ridicule for effect, perhaps reasoning that all the times they didn't use it would compensate for the few times they did. It doesn't work that way. If you scoff at an idea once for every ten times you don't, it's the scoff your team will remember. *Challenger safety takes time to create and no time to destroy.*

Are You Emotionally Prepared to Be Wrong?

Don't rush in and tell yourself that you're prepared to be wrong. It's a lot harder than it seems. Just look at the social psychology of scientists for a clue. How does science progress? It's a slow and often painful process. Scientists lock on to theories so tightly, they can't let go. The theoretical physicist Max Planck said, "A new scientific truth does not triumph by convincing its opponents and making them see the light, but rather because its opponents eventually die, and a new generation grows up that is familiar with it."[176] Are you prepared to accept the next "accident of investigation"? Can you tolerate those who subvert existing traditions?

Remember the social exchange for challenger safety: cover for candor. If your organization relies on innovation, you'll be serious about providing the needed air cover to others as they venture into the territory of challenging the status quo. You'll be more motivated to demonstrate a fundamental receptivity to both people and ideas, a cognitive and emotional openness that others clearly perceive. Not least, you'll develop the capacity to be wrong. That openness activates and facilitates the innovation process. Yes, you're a player-coach and you can participate in challenging the status quo as yourself, but your primary role is to sponsor and protect rather than snare and disinfect ideas coming from every direction.

Some leaders can't get out of their own way in this process. They net the good ideas and either cast them out or adopt them as their own. If you have an unappeasable need for status, if you crave credit and relish the trappings of power, if you need to be right, creating challenger safety may well be your biggest leadership challenge. As former United Airlines CEO Oscar Munoz said, "It's the saddest thing when people haven't figured out the emotional intelligence side of things. You have to make yourself the kind of person that people are willing to come up to and provide advice."[177]

I once had a boss who wasn't very good at being wrong. He was a brazen leader with a deep sense of his own entitlement. He had a "those who think they know everything are very offensive to those of us who do" attitude. He was dogmatic, didactic, and pedantic. It was not only tiresome to be around him, but risky. His dripping ego shut challenger safety down wherever he went. Not surprisingly, people adapted to his style quickly. One of the first adjustments his team made was to turn a real meeting into a charade. They venerated the boss with nervous respect in the official meeting but then held the real meeting later in the form of sidebar discussions and kangaroo courts. *When a leader personally replaces the search for innovation with rivalry for prominence, the team can't achieve the social cohesion necessary for the cocreative process of innovation.*

My boss was practicing territoriality by controlling the airtime—the modern version of an antiquated model of dominance that eventually sealed his fate. He was fired. The great irony about this boss was that although he was highly intelligent, he acted this way because he felt vulnerable. He didn't want to expose himself to threat or embarrassment, but in the very act of trying to give himself challenger safety, he was taking it away from us. This is exactly the pattern with a lot of smart people.[178]

You must be humble and open, and you must listen, and if you don't, the people around you will eventually have nothing to say. The world-famous cellist Yo-Yo Ma was once asked in an interview, "What's the key to fruitful collaboration, especially across cultures or disciplines?" His response: "Ego management."[179] In small organizations and the lower levels of large organizations, I see the pattern of hubris less often, but as you climb to the C-suite, it appears more frequently. The leadership scholar Manfred Kets de Vries asserts, "The dysfunction most frequently found at senior levels is pathological narcissism. Narcissism is not something a person either has or hasn't. We all possess narcissistic characteristics to a degree."[180]

The speed of change outside an organization now favors the leader who explores, monitors the periphery, and extends the field of vision for the entire organization. Increasingly, we will not look upon our leaders as those who have the answers, but as those who can draw out the answers by tapping the creative potential of the organization.

Neutralize the Liability of Hierarchy

If you're in a management position, your relationship with each of your direct reports is asymmetrical. By virtue of your position, there is a measure of power distance between you based on hierarchy.[181] But whether you have a steep or soft authority gradient between you and them is up to you. Risk and fear are closely associated with formal authority. Your direct reports are often incentivized to flatter you and filter what they feed you. Even a thin layer of fear becomes a tax. If a team is healthy, the pattern of exchange will be free-flowing, candid, and energized. If it's unhealthy, the team will retreat into silence, superficial niceness, or some combination of the two. You have the ability to lower that status hierarchy gap by making your team *culturally flat* even though it's not structurally flat. When you do this, *you shape an egalitarian norm and make status an artificial constraint.*

Much of the know-how required for innovation comes from the bottom of the organization—in other words, from *local knowledge*. Yet many non-management employees consider innovation outside the scope of their jobs. Even when they want to participate, they don't, because the organization's tacit norms discourage it. *The pressure to execute and remove variance overwhelms the motivation to innovate and introduce variance.*

For example, an employee at a large health-care organization said to me, "If you're new in this organization, you have to listen for a year before the organization will listen to you." That's a cultural barrier to entry that silences a team and hobbles creative output. That barrier is *authority bias*—the tendency to overvalue opinions from the top of the hierarchy and undervalue opinions from the bottom—and it eventually turns into exaggerated deference to the chain of command. Organizations tend to give the most credibility to ideas, suggestions, or points of view based on source rather than substance. In fact, source becomes a proxy for substance, because we reasonably expect more competency as we move up the hierarchy. But this creates natural disincentives for those at the bottom to raise their voices. The greater the power distance, the higher the perceived risk of speaking up. *Thus, the grander the perch, the rarer the feedback.*

Conclusion

The ultimate source of adaptive capacity, competitiveness, and self-preservation—indeed, the key to resilience and renewal—is the ongoing ability of an organization to learn and adapt. It allows you to engage in innovation and give an adaptive or preemptive response. Though it may appear personally threatening, leaders must stand first in line to model this pattern. Not only is it a fundamental change from the expert model of leadership, but it also requires you to assume a very different emotional and social posture.

You are the curator of culture. You set the tone. At all costs, protect the team's right to speak up. Call out anyone who tries to silence others. Help the team understand that sometimes you will see something they can't. Sometimes they will see something you can't. If you jealously guard your own ideas, they will do the same thing. So display no pride of authorship. Give every member of your team a license to disagree. Then brace yourself. Remember that a negative response to bad news or dissent will re-silence the team and seal your fate as a hapless leader. Finally, keep in mind that a team often becomes lost and temporarily fails before it finds its way and eventually succeeds. This is a normal journey. The process is messy, iterative, and nonlinear, and there may be some pivots along the way. Remember, you're in uncharted territory.

Chapter Summary

- **Definition:** Challenger safety satisfies the basic human need to challenge and improve the status quo without fear of embarrassment or retribution.
- **Innovation imperative:** Innovation requires deviation. Deviation requires challenge. Challenge requires challenger safety. Fear or conformity collapses the process.
- **Social exchange:** The deal is air cover for candor. Leaders protect people's right to challenge in good faith.
- **Status quo danger:** Without challenger safety, teams default to silence, groupthink, echo chambers, and preservation of the current state.
- **Fragility:** Challenger safety is slow to build and fast to destroy. Ridicule, defensiveness, or punishment instantly closes inquiry.
- **Leader equanimity:** Calm ego under pressure keeps innovation alive.
- **Team plasticity:** Teams expand or contract their innovation capacity based on the leader's modeling behavior. The quality of interaction regulates the speed of discovery.
- **Stress versus fear:** Innovation often occurs under pressure, but leaders must remove fear so pressure becomes energy, not a threat.

- **Learning > knowing:** Innovation is recombining ideas. Progress depends on humility, exploration, and willingness to be wrong.
- **Interdisciplinary creativity:** Innovation is connected people connecting things. Diversity of perspective fuels recombination.
- **Questions as catalysts:** Innovation begins with questions, but questions carry personal risk.
- **Increase intellectual friction, reduce social friction:** Increase intellectual friction while lowering social friction. Lower ego, fear, hierarchy, and politics. Be hard on ideas, soft on people.
- **Reduce the risk of ridicule:** Even small doses of ridicule shut down curiosity, creativity, and exploratory inquiry.
- **Be prepared to be wrong:** Arrest your ego and show cognitive and emotional openness.
- **Neutralize the liability of hierarchy:** Create cultural flatness to reduce authority bias.
- **Innovation bottleneck:** Psychological safety, rather than talent or resources, is the constraint that limits or releases innovation velocity.
- **Try a lot, triumph a little:** Innovation is messy, nonlinear, exploratory work that relies on challenger safety to sustain the cycle.
- **Leader identity:** Leaders must embody humility, openness, transparency, and emotional maturity. Be the kind of person others can safely challenge.

— PART II —
Practice and Application

Part I was about understanding psychological safety. Part II is about creating it. These chapters move from research and theory to practice and application, equipping you to become a cultural architect and lead your team successfully through all 4 Stages of Psychological Safety.

Chapter 5, What Psychological Safety Is Not, clears the conceptual air by confronting ten common misconceptions—that psychological safety is a shield from accountability; mere niceness; coddling; consensus decision-making; unearned autonomy; political correctness; rhetorical reassurance; wellness programs; a white-collar luxury; and someone else's job. Each misconception, if left unchallenged, will send your efforts astray.

Chapter 6, The Catastrophic Consequences of a Nice Culture, exposes a specific and dangerous trap: Organizations confuse civility with candor. We examine how niceness chokes innovation, activates crisis, bleeds talent, slows decisions, and induces learned helplessness. We discuss how to combat these consequences.

Chapter 7, How the Leader Warms or Chills the Air, addresses the leader's disproportionate influence on psychological safety. I present fourteen concrete practices for neutralizing the liability of hierarchy and creating conditions where people bring their authentic selves to work.

Chapter 8, How to Create a Sanctuary of Inclusion, explains how to make the journey from awareness to action with active, cross-affinity, bridge-then-bond connection. I introduce the L.I.V.E. model to make rewarding vulnerability a conscious habit.

Chapter 9, How to Challenge the Status Quo, equips individuals at every level to voice dissent skillfully. I offer ten practices for challenging entrenched paradigms without triggering defensiveness or career damage.

Chapter 10, The Behavioral Guide, translates all four stages into specific, observable behaviors you can model and reward. Each behavior is coded for relevance to teams, individuals, or managers, with instructions for focused practice.

Part II ends with a conclusion that addresses the gutters of paternalism and exploitation, the failure patterns that emerge when either respect or permission is dangerously deficient. I conclude with a call to action: Abandon the imperial model of leadership and cultivate psychological safety to unlock human potential.

CHAPTER 5

What Psychological Safety Is Not

When you misdefine psychological safety, you misapply it and your efforts go astray. Many leaders have twisted psychological safety into something it was never meant to be. To set the record straight, this chapter debunks the most common myths and misconceptions.

A Shield from Accountability

Myth: If we prioritize psychological safety, we can't hold people accountable for results or mistakes.

Reality: Psychological safety strengthens accountability.

In a psychologically safe team, people are more, not less, accountable. They admit mistakes and learn from them, instead of being punished or fearing blame. Psychological safety enables accountability by creating an environment where team members feel secure enough to own their performance and confront tough issues before they spiral out of control.

A high-profile example of this occurred in June 2021, when an HBO Max intern mistakenly sent out a blank test email to millions of subscribers. The company publicly acknowledged the error and added, "Yes, it was the intern . . . and we're helping them through it."[182] Rather than excoriating the individual, they made it a coaching moment. This illustrates how a psychologically safe culture handles mistakes: not with immunity from consequences, but with respectful accountability. The intern's error was not ignored. It was visible to everyone, but the response focused on learning and support rather than shame. Psychological safety ensures that when people get it wrong, they can be held accountable in a constructive way: The team discusses what happened and why, and how to prevent it going forward, without fear of scapegoating.

Here's what to look for: If a team is increasing in psychological safety, you will see more ownership and accountability as a natural consequence. The highest-performing teams marry high psychological safety with high accountability. Research bears this out. A meta-analytic review found that psychological safety is positively associated with task performance and citizenship behaviors. Feeling safe to speak up improves accountability and outcomes rather than undermining them.[183]

When people know they won't be unfairly punished, they become more responsible. They take ownership of problems early, report issues promptly, and work to fix errors, because they trust that the team will address problems fairly. In contrast, in a low-psychological safety environment, individuals may hide mistakes or avoid difficult tasks to protect themselves, leading to larger failures and lower accountability. True psychological safety creates a culture of proactive accountability. Problems are identified and solved before they fester, and everyone holds themselves to a high standard because the team functions based on universal terms of engagement—respect and permission. People are accountable to each other not through coercion or fear, but through transparency, guidance, and encouragement.

A Mandate for Niceness

Myth: Psychological safety means everyone has to be nice and never disagree.

Reality: Psychological safety is about kindness and candor.

This misconception is so pervasive that I'm going to do a deeper dive into it in the next chapter. A "nice" environment where no one ever challenges or debates is, by definition, a superficial one. But forced pleasantness can create false harmony, where people smile and nod but withhold their true concerns. In fact, chronic niceness that suppresses disagreement is the enemy of growth. Niceness can lead to stagnation and become a euphemism for silent compliance.

Psychological safety, in contrast, welcomes respectful dissent. If an idea is flawed or a plan has risks, team members in a psychologically safe climate will surface those issues directly, because they know it's better to speak up than to maintain a polite façade. As a well-known fitness trainer explains, "Safety is not the same as comfort. . . . A good fitness trainer will help you to safely exercise and grow your muscles. And you will be uncomfortable. But you will be safe."[184]

In an organization, psychological safety tolerates tension. People feel secure enough to disagree and deliver tough feedback, knowing it's in service of better performance. Consider the alternative: Teams that prioritize "being nice" often avoid hard discussions. A notable example of false harmony is the Bay of Pigs fiasco in 1961. President Kennedy's advisors were so concerned with maintaining group harmony that they withheld objections to a flawed plan, leading to disaster.[185] Only after that failure did Kennedy change his team norms to encourage dissenting views, which later helped avert the Cuban Missile Crisis.[186] Take note if your team is too congenial and avoidant when it comes to discussing tough issues.

Encouraging open dialogue can feel less comfortable in the short term than keeping things "nice," but it pays off. Research finds that teams with higher psychological safety report more idea sharing and constructive conflict, which drive innovation and improvement.[187] In a psychologically safe team, people give real feedback, rather than passive-aggressive comments or silent acquiescence. The aim is to make it safe for *necessary conflict*.

A Form of Coddling

Myth: Psychological safety means rolling everyone in bubble wrap, so feelings never get hurt.

Reality: Psychological safety develops resilience, not fragility.

This misconception comes from the image of a "safety" culture as overly protective, with managers tiptoeing around feedback or shielding team members from consequences out of fear of upsetting them. That is a gross misinterpretation. In fact, genuine psychological safety enables us to have tough conversations and give hard feedback without causing distress or resentment. It's the very opposite of mollycoddling. It's about treating people as capable adults who can hear the truth, learn, and grow.

To clarify, psychological safety provides support, not indulgence. Leaders still hold their teams to high standards and enforce necessary discipline.

The difference is how they do it. Instead of barking at an employee or punishing them, a leader in a psychologically safe culture will address performance gaps with candor and care: "Here's where we fell short, and here's how we can improve. Let's figure this out together." No pampering, but also no belittling. This approach doesn't make things easier in the sense of eliminating challenges. Employees will still face demanding goals and frank critiques, but it makes things better by ensuring those challenges come with coaching rather than ridicule. Overprotecting people by never challenging them actually stunts their growth.

This means team members feel safe to take risks, and they are expected to deliver results. When mistakes happen, they aren't swept under the rug but addressed constructively. *Instead of a blame game after an error, a psychologically safe team will perform a blameless postmortem.*[188] What went wrong? How can we fix the process? Everyone is held accountable for contributing to solutions. They aren't coddled. If anything, they're challenged to improve continually, but in a way that harnesses their intrinsic motivation rather than triggering their defense mechanisms. We don't punish people for honest mistakes. Neither do we eliminate stretch goals or excuse subpar work. Instead, we say, "We believe you can meet this high bar, and we have your back as you try. If you stumble, we'll help you recover and learn."

A Requirement for Consensus

Myth: Psychological safety means everyone gets an equal say, and we can't make decisions unless everyone agrees.

Reality: Psychological safety gives you a voice, not necessarily a vote.

Psychological safety doesn't magically change the decision model. For example, most decisions in organizations use a consultative model. Yes, there are times for consensus, but that's up to the leaders who have decision-making authority. Consensus decision-making is inefficient, often impractical, and even counterproductive. The misconception that everyone gets a vote likely arises because people equate an inclusive environment with a redistribution of power. In a psychologically safe culture, everyone's voice should be heard, but that doesn't mean every opinion carries equal weight or that leadership abdicates its decision-making responsibility. As I often remind leaders: To be heard is not to be heeded. Just because you speak up doesn't mean your idea will be adopted. *Psychological safety ensures your input is considered, but it doesn't guarantee consensus or veto power.*

In practice, effective organizations balance participation with clear decision authority. During deliberation, a psychologically safe team encourages diverse viewpoints and candid debate. But when it's time to decide, the designated decision-maker must choose a course of action and move forward. Those who offered input understand that not every suggestion can be implemented, but if the process is fair and transparent, team members are more likely to accept the final decision even if it wasn't their preferred outcome. *To have a voice is not necessarily to have a vote.*

Contrast this with a fear-ridden environment, where people might outwardly comply with a top-down decision but inwardly resent or sabotage it because they never felt heard. In a psychologically safe climate, people will commit to the decision once made, because the pathway to get there was respectful and inclusive of all perspectives. Research on team dynamics suggests that clarity in decision-making roles actually enhances psychological safety, because ambiguity in authority can breed frustration or false expectations.[189] When leaders explicitly communicate, "I value all of your input; I will consider it seriously; and then I (or we) will make the decision based on the best available information," teams function best. People understand the rules of engagement and the decision model. Safe teams waste less time on politicking or second-guessing; they can debate vigorously and then unite behind a decision once it's made.

An Invitation to Chaos

Myth: If we have psychological safety, we can do whatever we want.

Reality: Psychological safety fosters ownership, not entitlement or anarchy.

Psychological safety doesn't automatically grant authority or autonomy that hasn't been earned. *In a workplace, autonomy is never free. We exchange it for performance.* This is the social exchange that defines stage 3, contributor safety. And yet some people perceive that it means throwing out the rules and letting employees run the show. Psychological safety may be a leveling device, as it encourages everyone to use their participation rights, but it doesn't redistribute authority or grant unlimited freedom. It doesn't mean the intern suddenly gets to override the manager's decisions, or that team members can unilaterally set their own goals in defiance of organizational priorities. This misconception might stem from conflating empowerment with entitlement. Let me be clear: *Empowerment is not entitlement.*

A psychologically safe culture certainly empowers individuals to speak up and take initiative. For instance, an assembly-line worker can halt production and pull the famous "andon cord" (a mechanism used to stop the production line) if they see a safety issue, or a junior developer can suggest a new approach to a coding problem. However, empowerment exists within a framework of accountability and role clarity.[190] If someone speaks up by saying, "I refuse to do task X because I don't feel like it," that's not exercising psychological safety, that's just insubordination or lack of accountability.

Real psychological safety asks leaders to listen to concerns and ideas from all levels, but it doesn't erase the fact that certain decisions and responsibilities still reside with certain roles.

Over time, team members who consistently contribute constructively and deliver results will naturally earn more autonomy as they progress through (1) task, (2) process, and (3) outcome levels of accountability. Organizational research emphasizes that clarity and psychological safety go together. A recent study on senior leadership teams found that teams function best when members share similar perceptions of psychological safety and understand their roles. Problems arise when perceptions (and by extension, expectations of autonomy) diverge widely within a team.[191]

Political Oversensitivity

Myth: Psychological safety means we have to walk on eggshells and be politically correct all the time.

Reality: Psychological safety allows minority, dissenting, and unpopular viewpoints.

Psychological safety does imply sensitivity for the views, feelings, and human attributes that define people. At its core, it is an apolitical, universal concept that unleashes human potential. Don't try to harness it to advance political ends. It's not a mandate for political correctness and ideologically sanitized language. In fact, a hallmark of a psychologically safe team is that members can speak candidly. They can use plain language about issues (even hot-button ones like quality problems, ethical concerns, or diversity challenges) without fear of being ostracized, because they have established respect and permission.

The term *political correctness* often implies suppressing thoughts that might be controversial. But psychological safety permits respectful candor. It is beholden to no political party, ideology, or policy stance. It creates a climate where speaking truth to power is possible. Far from enforcing a rigid orthodoxy of thought, it allows more perspectives to be voiced. The key is developing a respectful manner of discourse: Ideas can be criticized, but individuals are not demeaned. A team member in a psychologically safe environment might say, "I strongly disagree with this policy; here's why. . . ." This might be a candid, perhaps uncomfortable position, but it can happen without anyone attacking the person's character or questioning their right to speak. In contrast, in a politically charged environment, people might either stay silent or resort to passive-aggressive comments and side conversations.

There is a subtle but important distinction here: *Psychological safety requires civility, but it does not require oversensitivity*. Team members shouldn't deliberately cause offense. Derogatory remarks have no place. But neither should they be so hypersensitive that any critique or differing opinion is taken as a personal slight. Greg Lukianoff and Jonathan Haidt argue that confusing disagreement, or even mild offense, with actual harm can erode resilience and healthy debate.[192] It doesn't equate an uncomfortable feeling with a violation of psychological safety, let alone a form of violence. Instead, it differentiates between being unsafe (e.g., being bullied or punished for speaking) and simply being challenged (e.g., hearing an idea that contradicts yours or receiving blunt feedback). The former is unacceptable; the latter is normal and necessary.

Of course, respect remains a nonnegotiable. There's no license to be rude or drop basic courtesy under the banner of candor. You demonstrate respect by listening and by phrasing your points in a way that critiques the idea or behavior, not the person's worth. But you don't withhold important truths. If an employee is underperforming, psychological safety means you owe them honest feedback delivered humanely, rather than avoiding the topic until a crisis point. If a common practice feels unfair or outdated, psychological safety means raising that concern openly, not whispering about it in the hallway.

Rhetorical Cheerleading

Myth: We've told people the workplace is safe and that we value their input, so we have psychological safety now.

Reality: You can't speak psychological safety into existence with slogans, statements, or declarations from leadership.

I witnessed a CEO try to decree psychological safety into existence with mere words. He called an all-hands meeting and declared that the organization was now psychologically safe.

His pronouncements only made him appear culturally tone-deaf and hypocritical. Please don't make this mistake and confuse rhetoric with reality. If people speak up, then get ignored or subtly punished, no amount of cheerful messaging will convince them that psychological safety exists. The words mean nothing. Show, don't tell.

If employees hear the talk but don't see the walk, psychological safety erodes even further. They might conclude that management is either out-of-touch or disingenuous. In a way, false reassurance is more damaging than saying nothing, because it sets expectations that are then dramatically unmet. It's analogous to a safety sign in a factory that says "Zero accidents. You will not be hurt here," while workers every day see colleagues getting injured due to negligence. The dissonance creates anger, inflames resentment, and promotes disengagement.

To build real psychological safety, *leaders must align words and deeds*. This starts with modeling vulnerability at the top. For example, a manager might say in a meeting, "I may miss something, so I need all of you to speak up if you see a problem." It's the pattern of behavior in the leader (habit) that becomes a pattern of behavior in the team (norm).

Research finds that employees judge the safety of speaking up by watching what happens to those who do.[193] If a colleague challenges a plan and is subsequently excluded from meetings, everyone gets the message. If, however, that colleague is thanked and the plan is thoughtfully reconsidered, others feel safer to do the same thing. Thus, psychological safety develops through an ongoing loop of actions:

1. Leaders actively solicit input.
2. Employees take the interpersonal risk to speak.

3. Leaders respond constructively (not defensively).
4. Over time, this pattern becomes a norm.

In practical steps, avoiding the trap of "rhetorical reassurance" means leaders should be wary of overpromising. Instead of "You can tell me anything with no repercussions," practice small behaviors. Ask questions in meetings, reward candor by praising someone who has offered dissent, implement one suggestion from the front line, and visibly give credit.

A Substitute for Wellness Programs

Myth: We offer yoga classes, meditation apps, and free counseling, so our workplace is psychologically safe.

Reality: Offering wellness initiatives is commendable, but psychological safety is not the same as employee well-being or mindfulness programs.

There is a growing trend to confuse the two: Leaders assume that because they've provided stress-reduction perks or mental health resources, they have checked the psychological safety box. *But psychological safety is fundamentally about interpersonal climate and open communication, not individual stress relief techniques.* You can have a workplace with weekly yoga sessions and still have employees terrified to speak up about a project problem or admit they are overwhelmed. Conversely, you might have a high-strung, hard-charging environment with no frills, yet if people know they can ask for help or acknowledge mistakes without backlash, that environment has psychological safety.

This myth likely stems from the well-intentioned push in recent years toward greater attention to mental health at work. The concept of "safe space" in a mental/emotional context sometimes gets mixed up with "psychologically safe workplace." The distinction is subtle but crucial. Mindfulness and wellness programs typically aim to help individuals cope with stress themselves, whereas psychological safety is rewarded vulnerability with their team. They can be complementary: A psychologically safe environment may encourage people to use wellness resources without stigma. A workforce that is mentally healthy is likely to engage better in a safe climate. But one does not automatically create the other. High safety might reduce workplace stress, but it doesn't eliminate the need for wellness support. *Similarly, wellness perks without a foundation of psychological safety are disingenuous.*

A recent study noted that many frontline workers confuse psychological safety with mental health resources. Some equated it to having an Employee Assistance Program or similar support.[194] That confusion can lead organizations to overly focus on symptoms (burnout, disengagement) with wellness programs, while ignoring the cause (lack of voice, fear of speaking up). To combat this myth, leaders should integrate, not replace. Go ahead and offer well-being programs *and* foster psychological safety.

A White-Collar Luxury

Myth: On a factory floor or emergency room, we just need strict rules and physical safety. Psychological safety is a touchy-feely concept for desk jobs.

Reality: Psychological safety is a necessity, especially in high-hazard industries.

In workplaces where lives are on the line, psychological safety is even more important. Why? Because the cost of not speaking up about a potential hazard or mistake is extraordinarily high. Lives hang in the balance. The applied discipline of physical safety is built on a rubric that identifies four standard hazard categories:

- Physical
- Biological
- Chemical
- Ergonomic

The process is simple. Identify hazards in the work environment in each of these categories and remove them. It's simple, but it's not easy. As a plant manager in manufacturing, I learned firsthand that *improving physical safety is behavioral and cultural before it is physical.* Speaking up to identify a potential hazard, risk, or danger goes against our instincts.[195] But there's nothing more essential than an employee's willingness to call something out.

If a junior technician in a chemical plant notices a pressure gauge anomaly but is afraid to question the senior engineer, the result could be an explosion. If a nurse in an operating room hesitates to warn a surgeon of a possible error due to hierarchy fears, patient safety is compromised. Decades of research in industries like aviation and health care show that encouraging speaking up is essential to prevent accidents. *Psychological safety provides the foundation for speaking up in the context of an asymmetrical power relationship.*

Let me go a little deeper. In the world of physical safety, the DuPont Bradley Curve describes how organizations evolve in their approach to safety, progressing through cultural stages: (1) reactive, (2) dependent, (3) independent, and (4) interdependent.[196] At the lower stages, safety is compliance-driven, enforced by rules and supervision. As organizations mature, safety becomes more self-directed, and at the highest stage, employees actively look out for one another and take shared responsibility for preventing harm. They practice the "duty of care." The curve illustrates that the highest levels of physical safety performance come from strong psychological safety—specifically the norms of intervening and speaking up.

Psychological safety is the engine that makes the DuPont Bradley Curve work. Every upward shift on the curve requires employees to do things that are socially risky, such as report hazards, raise concerns, stop unsafe work, question assumptions, and challenge peers or leaders. These behaviors demand vulnerability, and people will not engage in them if they fear ridicule, retaliation, or relational damage. Thus, psychological safety becomes the enabling condition that transforms physical safety from a compliance activity into a shared norm of voluntarily speaking up.[197]

Fear-based cultures can achieve basic compliance, but they cannot reach the interdependent stage at the top of the DuPont Bradley Curve. That level of safety requires mutual trust, open communication, and peer-to-peer accountability, conditions that emerge only when people feel safe to speak up and challenge the status quo. We already know that many, if not most, major industrial accidents are traceable to suppressed dissent or silence. *In this sense, zero physical harm depends on zero fear of speaking up.* Psychological safety drives advanced safety cultures and is the foundation for sustainable, high-performance safety outcomes.

Despite this, a persistent misconception is that tough, hazardous work settings require an authoritarian, no-nonsense approach where feelings don't matter as much. Some managers in construction, manufacturing, mining, and similar fields may dismiss psychological safety as academic jargon, focusing solely on compliance and procedures. Of course, procedures and training are vital for physical safety, but they often aren't enough if people on the ground hesitate to report that a procedure isn't working or a rule isn't being followed.

A 2025 panel of safety experts highlighted that many frontline employees knew of issues leading to near-misses but didn't voice them until after the fact, because the culture discouraged "rocking the boat."[198]

Building psychological safety in these contexts means creating *an environment where speaking up about hazards becomes normalized.*[199] Consider the practices of companies with excellent safety records. In aviation, crew resource management training explicitly teaches captains to foster an atmosphere where any crew member can question decisions for safety's sake. In organizations like Toyota, the famous andon cord system empowers any worker to stop the production line if they see a defect. This single development revolutionized quality control. These are manifestations of psychological safety in action, incorporated into workflow. They recognize that regardless of industry, humans are prone to errors, and the best defense is an environment where anyone can catch and correct those errors regardless of rank. A systematic review in health care found that units with higher psychological safety had better patient outcomes and fewer errors, precisely because staff felt empowered to speak up about concerns and near-misses.[200]

The mistaken belief that "tough jobs don't need this" is pure denial. Whether it's a software team or a SWAT team, a lack of psychological safety can lead to poor outcomes, bugs left unmentioned, or warnings left unspoken. The context may differ, but the human factors are the same. When it comes to physical safety, psychological safety is the ultimate distant early warning system.

A One-Time Corporate Initiative

Myth: "Our CEO/HR department is responsible for creating psychological safety. I'm just waiting for them to fix the culture." Or, "We did psychological safety training last year, so we should be good now."

Reality: Psychological safety is perishable, and it's everyone's job.

This misconception has two parts: (1) the idea that only those at the top can create or maintain psychological safety, and (2) the notion that it's a project you complete. Both are false. In truth, psychological safety is an ongoing, collective effort. Every team leader and team member contributes to it (or erodes it) through their daily actions. And it's a dynamic, perishable state. It can improve or deteriorate over time, requiring constant care like any other aspect of culture.

Let's tackle the first part: Whose job is it? Certainly, leaders have disproportionate influence. A CEO or executive team that models openness and forbids retaliation sets a powerful tone. Middle managers often dictate the microculture of teams. If they are fearsome or dismissive, no amount of corporate lip service will make subordinates feel safe. So leadership matters greatly. But psychological safety isn't something that can be handed down like a memo. It lives in local interactions. A company could have a great CEO who encourages speaking up, but that won't carry the day. If the team doesn't reward vulnerability, you won't feel safe.

Conversely, even in an otherwise toxic organization, a pocket of psychological safety can exist within a team that consciously supports one another. Ideally, we want it at all levels, but it's instructive to know that everyone has agency. If you're an individual contributor, psychological safety is your job too. You can foster it by responding respectfully to a peer's crazy idea or backing up a coworker when they voice dissent in a meeting. Small acts like that build a layer of psychological safety around you. While organizational climate plays a role, team-level psychological safety plays the most profound role because it is most proximal in shaping the immediate social context. *The reality is that we experience work life at the level of the microculture, on the ground with our team.*

The second part—the myth of arrival ("we've achieved psychological safety!")—likely comes from our desire to treat psychological safety as a program or event. Implement some workshops, announce new values, and then check that item off the list. But psychological safety is more like physical fitness: You don't work out for a month and declare yourself fit for life. It requires maintenance. People come and go, circumstances change (a reorganization, a crisis, new leadership). One serious trust breach can set a team back considerably. That's why vigilance must be constant. Organizations that successfully cultivate psychological safety typically embed it into routines: regular check-ins, continual feedback loops, inclusion as a criterion in performance reviews, periodic surveys to gauge safety levels. They recognize that it's never completely done. That glorious end state never arrives.[201]

Busting this myth requires distributing responsibility for psychological safety. Senior leaders should indeed champion it. But then, every manager must take ownership for their team climate. And within each team, every member should understand they have a role. One particularly important moment is when psychological safety is breached. No team is perfect; maybe one day a leader loses their temper and shuts someone down harshly. If you ignore that event, people will withdraw and assume psychological safety was lip service. But if the leader addresses it, apologizes publicly, and reiterates that such behavior was not acceptable even from themselves, it can actually strengthen the climate: "Wow, they owned up to it. We know they're learning from mistakes." Repairing breaches is part of the maintenance.

Conclusion

Psychological safety is a disciplined interpersonal standard that demands both respect and permission and is sustained through daily behaviors. It is often misunderstood, but its power lies in what it actually does. This is why it's important for leaders to understand what it's not. When they do, they can finally harness what it *is*: the operating condition that allows a team to meet its performance potential and an individual to meet their workplace human needs.

Chapter Summary

- **Definition:** Misunderstanding psychological safety leads to misapplication. To ensure that psychological safety can be used correctly, this chapter clarifies that it is *not*:
    - **A shield from accountability:** Psychological safety strengthens—not weakens—ownership, candor, and responsibility. High psychological safety and high accountability rise together.
    - **Niceness:** Psychological safety is not politeness or conflict avoidance. It requires respectful candor, real debate, and the courage to surface concerns.
    - **Coddling:** Psychological safety is support *with* standards and expectations, not protection from discomfort. It enables tough feedback, resilience, and growth, not indulgence.
    - **Consensus:** Being heard is not being heeded. Psychological safety ensures everyone can speak, but decision rights remain clear and intact.

- **Unearned autonomy:** Safety empowers voice, not entitlement. Autonomy still must be earned through performance and results.
- **Political correctness:** It encourages open, honest conversations, not sanitized language or hypersensitivity. Civility is required; fragility is not.
- **Rhetorical reassurance:** Words without behavior destroy psychological safety. You can't decree it into existence. It must be built through consistent modeling, not slogans or lip service.
- **Wellness programs:** Yoga and meditation help individuals cope but do not replace the interpersonal climate required for productive human interaction.
- **A white-collar luxury:** Psychological safety is essential in high-risk environments, especially high-hazard industries, where silence leads to accidents, injuries, or worse.
- **Someone else's job, nor a one-time fix:** It is a shared, ongoing responsibility. Psychological safety is built through daily behavior and must be continually maintained.

CHAPTER 6

The Catastrophic Consequences of a Nice Culture

Have you ever attended a meeting that wasn't the meeting? Everyone was pleasant and agreeable in the room, but then filed off to engage in back-channel conversations and hold kangaroo courts. This kind of charade is one of the many symptoms of a "nice" culture. But what's touted as niceness is often nothing more than the veneer of civility, a cute nod to psychological safety, a hologram that falsely signals inclusion, collaboration, and high performance. In many of these cultures, leaders have simply *spread a thin layer of politeness over a thick layer of fear*. There is the appearance of harmony and alignment, but in reality there's often dysfunction simmering beneath the surface that results in a lack of honest communication, intellectual bravery, innovation, and accountability.[202] Short of fear, the social expectation to be amiable remains, which leads to an echo chamber and groupthink. As the psychologist Irving Janis explains in his book *Groupthink*, "The more amiability and esprit de corps among the members of a policy-making in-group, the greater is the danger that independent critical thinking will be replaced by groupthink, which is likely to result in irrational and dehumanizing actions directed against out-groups."[203]

Why Organizations Pursue Niceness

The intention behind cultivating a nice culture is often genuine. In my experience, for example, it's common for organizations with a noble institutional mission—such as educational institutions, health-care organizations, government bodies, nonprofits, and voluntary associations—to cultivate an environment of collegiality that emanates from their mission. *A benevolent purpose tends to foster a benevolent culture, and a benevolent culture tends to spawn niceness.* For example, I worked with a biotechnology firm that had a deeply instilled mission to preserve patient safety. Ironically, that sense of compassion for patients mutated into a nice culture that drove truth-telling underground.

There are many reasons why leaders pursue niceness. The top four, based on my experience working with hundreds of organizations and thousands of leaders over the past twenty years, are discussed next.

To Avoid Conflict and Gain Approval

As a reflection of their own desire to be liked, leaders often avoid conflict and stigmatize dissent. They would rather be nice than offend, misbelieving that those are the only two choices.

To Replace Genuine Inclusion

Some organizations see niceness as a proxy for inclusion. They believe that to be nice is to be humane. When you see diverse employee populations self-segregate based on natural affinity groups, it could indicate an unspoken "separate but nice" philosophy.

To Show Exaggerated Deference to the Chain of Command

In rigidly hierarchical fear-based organizations, niceness keeps you safe. The logic is that as long as you don't provoke the ire of those in power, you have a measure of job security. Gradually, authority bias, the tendency to overvalue opinions from the top of the hierarchy and undervalue opinions from the bottom, becomes the norm. Employees tend to give the most credibility to ideas, suggestions, or points of view based on source rather than substance. In fact, source becomes a proxy for substance because we reasonably expect more competency as we move up the hierarchy. But this creates natural disincentives for those at the bottom to raise their voices. The greater the power distance, the higher the perceived risk of speaking up. Thus, the grander the perch, the rarer the feedback.

To Motivate People Instead of Holding Them Accountable

Yes, interpersonal warmth creates a conduit of influence, but you still need accountability. I once worked with a highly affable CEO, who, to his eternal consternation, created a toxic nice culture in which people would hug each other and then not follow through on commitments.

Consider the paradox of nice. In many organizations, being nice is upheld as an unquestioned virtue. While civility and collegiality are essential for cooperation, there is a dangerous threshold at which "nice" turns into false harmony and pseudointimacy, insulating a team from reality. When niceness is enforced to the point that disagreement feels taboo, teams begin to trade candor and truth for comfort and the appearance of harmony. Leaders and employees alike may "smile and nod" in meetings even when they silently disagree.

At the heart of a nice culture's dysfunction is fear—an often unspoken fear of conflict, of displeasing others, or of personal repercussions for speaking one's mind.[204] Employees frequently remain silent out of fear of negative personal or professional consequences. In theory, any member of an organization could speak up with a dissenting view or critical piece of information. In practice, however, fear can become so pervasive that silence feels like the only safe option. People worry that if they voice concerns or challenge consensus, they might damage their reputation, offend a colleague or superior, or even jeopardize their career progression. This climate of fear is the invisible toxin that often underlies an overly nice, conflict-averse culture.

The Catastrophic Downsides

The adverse consequences of this superficial collegiality are not simply inconvenient, they can be catastrophic. Let's consider five downsides.

Choked Innovation

By its very nature, innovation disrupts the status quo. And yet it's the lifeblood of growth. Innovation is also a social process that requires divergent thinking and courageous conversations. Pervasive niceness suppresses this process, turning teams of exceptionally talented people into dysfunctional groups.[205] I frequently work with institutions that desperately need to boost innovation, but their nice cultures slow the speed of discovery.

When niceness becomes the dominant norm, people start avoiding the friction that innovation demands. Ideas are filtered for likability rather than merit, and disagreement feels taboo. In this environment, creativity suffocates—not because people lack ideas, but because they lack permission to challenge or disrupt. The organization drifts into safe, predictable thinking and loses its capacity to explore the unknown. In the end, excessive niceness doesn't just slow innovation, it sterilizes it.

Crisis Activation

At times, inertia becomes so strong in a nice culture that the organization loses its ability to act preemptively. People wait until a problem becomes too big to ignore. How is it possible, for example, that it took the University of Southern California more than twenty-five years to acknowledge and act on the sexual abuse claims against Dr. George Tyndall, a campus gynecologist, eventually culminating in a staggering $1.1 billion settlement? I've personally worked with more than thirty universities over the past twenty years, and I've observed that they are notorious for putting low performers and bad actors in corners rather than directly addressing their performance. Nice cultures tend to nurture the false dichotomy that you can either be nice or hold people accountable, but not both.

This can evolve into a form of organizational complacency, creating an emotional comfort zone where people mistake congeniality for health and consensus for progress. In such environments, warning signals are muffled by optimism and polite silence. Teams reassure themselves that everything is fine because no one wants to be the one to disrupt the mood. As a result, small problems grow roots. Leaders become reactive instead of proactive, addressing issues only when they erupt into full-blown crises. By the time action is finally taken, the cost in reputation, morale, or money is exponentially higher. *A culture of niceness can therefore anesthetize an organization, dulling its sensitivity to risk and blinding it to early signs of trouble.* The organization forgets that its greatest danger is not confrontation but comfort.

Bleeding Talent

Talented people want to make a meaningful contribution. A-players want a healthy culture in which they can be rewarded for challenging the status quo. As one A-player who worked in a large pharmaceutical company said to me, "I'd rather work in an authoritarian toxic culture than a nice toxic culture because in the authoritarian toxic culture, they would at least tell me that I'm wrong when I challenge the status quo. I can provoke the system, force a reaction, and maybe that will lead to something. In a nice toxic culture, they humor you and then nothing ever happens."

High performers don't stay where they can't make an impact. They have options and they exercise them. When initiative is met with avoidance or empty approval, they read the signal: Contribution isn't truly wanted here. Over time, they stop offering their best ideas and start planning their exit. A nice culture confuses retention with loyalty. *Talented people aren't loyal to comfort, they're loyal to purpose and progress.* If they can't find that inside the organization, they'll find it somewhere else.

Low-Velocity Decision-Making

In a nice culture, there's pressure to go along to get along. A low tolerance for candor makes the necessary discussion and analysis for decision-making shallow and slow. Either you get an echo chamber in which the homogenization of thought gives you a flawed decision, or you conduct what seem to be endless rounds of discussion in pursuit of consensus. Eventually, this can lead to chronic indecisiveness. For example, I worked with a health-care organization that became so nice they decided to adopt a consensus-decision-making model. It was an unmitigated disaster. The CEO pulled the plug on this experiment after three painful months of swimming in ambiguity.

Niceness creates a bottleneck where progress gets trapped in politeness. Decisions stall because no one wants to challenge assumptions or take ownership of hard calls. The desire to include every voice morphs into an obligation to please every voice. *As a result, clarity gives way to compromise, and speed gives way to stagnation.* In time, the organization confuses deliberation with diligence, mistaking motionless discussion for thoughtful strategy. The outcome is predictable: Opportunities pass, momentum fades, and the best people stop believing that decisions will ever be made.

Learned Helplessness

An invisible norm of niceness can also induce conformity, passivity, and learned helplessness that lowers the bar of performance. For instance, I've listened to administrators, faculty, and staff at top-tier universities complain bitterly about academe's stultifying brand of politeness and how it destroys morale and extinguishes initiative. One university administrator told me that niceness has become a straitjacket that puts institutional reform at serious risk.

Instead of challenging the environment in hopes of improving the situation, people are throwing their hands up and keeping quiet.

Learned helplessness takes hold when people realize that speaking up changes nothing. In a nice culture, feedback is softened, conflict is avoided, and real problems remain unaddressed. Over time, individuals internalize the futility of effort. They stop pushing, questioning, or proposing new ideas because the system teaches them that initiative leads nowhere. *What begins as a desire to maintain harmony ends as a pattern of resignation.* The collective energy of the organization drains away, replaced by polite disengagement disguised as cooperation.

Combating Niceness

How can organizations create a true idea meritocracy in which they debate issues on their merits? How do they neutralize the liabilities of hierarchy? How can they achieve the *cultural flatness* that I mentioned earlier—the condition in which power distance or structure doesn't restrict collaboration or the flow of information, and a benevolent mission doesn't sedate people into complacency? There are several strategies you can employ to avoid the consequences just discussed, creating a kind and candid culture instead of a "nice" one.

Clarify Expectations, Performance Standards, and Meeting Types

Ambiguity feeds toxic niceness, so clarify how you expect people to treat one another and hold one another accountable. Be explicit that you expect intellectual honesty, candid feedback, and tough questions. This change won't be easy, so it's imperative that you clearly explain the organization's current state, future state, and how the transition between the two will work. As soon as you communicate the new expectations, hold people accountable for violations. Finally, when you have meetings, set an agenda and be explicit in explaining the type of meeting you intend to have. If you're there to discuss and decide issues, say so. If it's an exploratory meeting to ideate and innovate, let everyone know up front. If it's about communication and coordination, don't keep it a secret.

Grant Irrevocable Participation Rights

First, understand the distinction between participation rights and decision rights. *Participation rights* refer to a person's opportunity to participate in discussion, analysis, and advocacy concerning ideas, issues, and questions. *Decision rights*, on the other hand, refer to the authority of a group or individual to make a decision about an idea, issue, or question. Make it clear to both new and existing team members that participation rights are embedded in every role.

Acknowledge that in the past, participation rights were often granted based on criteria such as seniority, time-in-grade, title, experience, and formal status. Explain that your team doesn't subscribe to this norm and that all employees are granted irrevocable participation rights—provided they demonstrate respect, basic contextual understanding, and good faith. Then, present opportunities for team members to exercise their participation rights based on relevant issues, questions, or potential courses of action, and then explicitly invite all team members to weigh in.

This, of course, is easier said than done. Many organizations are dripping with implicit bias, which curtails the participation rights of new and/or underrepresented and marginalized employees. This means that employees in these groups may require reassurance and additional efforts to create psychological safety in the process. They may be slow to respond, but when they see that equal access to participate in the process is fair and consistent, they will gradually opt in.

Finally, cultivate the expectation that innovation is embedded in every job description. Reinforce that innovation is primarily a social process that relies on collaboration.

Practice Exploratory Inquiry

The status quo becomes ingrained over time as our thoughts about it harden into dogma and we become attached to it. Because it carries a high degree of personal risk, most employees conduct careful threat detection before engaging in exploratory inquiry and potentially deviating from the status quo. Also, keep in mind that, for most people, evaluating performance based on data feels more secure than exploring possibilities based on assumptions and predictions. So how do you get over the discomfort associated with exploration?

Practice the *disruptive question sequence*. These three questions are a quick and effective way to get the ball rolling and accelerate bottom-up innovation:

1. **Why?** Why do we do it this way?
2. **What if?** What if we tried this instead?
3. **How?** How might we do it differently?

Ensure that the process is nonjudgmental. Generate and ideate without editing, critiquing, limiting, or censoring.

Finally, once you teach the disruptive question sequence, don't expect the process to run itself. Your team needs to practice. The best way to develop this skill is to run a series of disruptive question sequence sessions with your team with assigned topics. For example, I recently worked with a marketing team that held a session to address its lead-generating process. The leader was careful to model the three-step process and remove every incentive that might motivate her team members to be silent or superficially nice. The dialogue was hard-hitting, yet honest and respectful.

Formally Assign Dissent at the Beginning

It's not enough to model the correct behavior and informally reinforce the norms; you must formally and officially assign dissent. Team members must be given explicit permission, and even the obligation, to disagree. The thinking that causes employees to stay away from innovation goes something like this: *Innovation requires exploration, exploration leads to failure, failure leads to punishment. I'll keep quiet.* Remember, silence is expensive for organizations. It drives out excellence and ushers in mediocrity.

Some industries have mastered this practice out of necessity because they operate in environments of high risk. For example, in the 1960s, NASA started deploying what they called *tiger teams,* which consisted of "undomesticated and uninhibited technical specialists, selected for their experience, energy, and imagination, and assigned to track down relentlessly every possible source of failure in a spacecraft subsystem."[206] It was their job to look for potential problems, flaws, and risks. IT departments do the same thing when they commission so-called white hat hackers to look for vulnerabilities and potential sources of a data security breach.

Finally, I've worked with many technology companies in Silicon Valley who use "red teams" for a similar purpose. You can call it loyal opposition, playing the devil's advocate, or doing a premortem. How you brand it doesn't matter. What matters is that you're formally commissioning and officially dedicating resources to vet ideas and tell you why something might not work, where it's weak, or why it's flawed. Doing this provides the needed cover for candor that helps the team push through the layers of status quo bias and loss aversion that normally guard the current state. It also culturally elevates the role of dissent and makes it socially and politically acceptable. Just make sure that if you reject an individual's suggestion, you show sensitivity by explaining why. Your considerate response will embolden the individual to keep and use their voice.[207]

Assigning dissent to a project, priority, or initiative from the beginning removes the natural fear normally associated with challenging the status quo. You are not only giving people a license to challenge but also setting the expectation. In my experience, assigning dissent is the single most effective mechanism available to a leader to shift a culture toward agility. Nothing can reset cultural norms faster and more powerfully.

Celebrate Dissent and Invite More

After you assign dissent, celebrate it and invite more the moment it happens. *The most significant moments of truth in culture formation happen when a team member takes an interpersonal risk "on stage."* In one team I observed, a team member voiced the unpopular opinion that a proposed decision was a bad idea. Creating a wave of cultural flatness, the team leader responded, "That's fantastic. I'm excited to learn why you feel that way." Then he listened carefully and solicited more dissenting views.

Publicly Criticize Your Own Ideas and Decisions

Think out loud with your team and publicly poke holes in your own thinking and behavior. Invite others to join you. For example, one leader said to her team, "As you know, my fingerprints are all over this decision. I own that, but here we are six months later and it looks like I made the wrong decision. I need your help to think this through."

Inject Empathy

Never a purely intellectual process, dissent is frequently charged with emotion. At its root, dissent is most often an intellectual clash. On the other end of an opinion is a human being coming to the table with some mixture of confidence and fear. People draw different conclusions from the same data sets all the time, and that's why it's hard. You can tell people to hold their opinions lightly, but it rarely works until they come to understand alternative viewpoints with empathy. Empathy is compassionate curiosity about another person's journey from data to conclusions. What data do they have?

What assumptions did they make? What do they care about and why? Finally, how did they reach their conclusions? Injecting empathy into the discussion can turn confrontation into fruitful collaboration. You've probably seen this pattern: Success breeds arrogance, and arrogance breeds a lack of empathy.[208] Don't step in that quicksand.

Publicly Challenge the Status Quo You Helped Create

Don't expect others to muscle through the fear and usher in a new era of truth-telling if you haven't modeled the behavior first. You must be the first mover, demonstrating vulnerability and fallibility, and showing people that candor is rewarded. When others see you cast aside your ego defense mechanisms and pride of authorship for what you built in the past, it will give them courage.

Confront Performance Problems Immediately

When you don't address a performance problem, you condone it. And if you hesitate to take action, you create confusion. Hold people accountable privately and respectfully. People who don't respect these new boundaries have a choice to either adopt the new norm or find a new opportunity. The one thing they won't do is retire on the job, because it's no longer an option.

Conclusion

A culture of extreme niceness may seem benign, even admirable, on the surface. It's a workplace where voices are never raised, disagreement never crosses the threshold of open conflict, and everyone appears considerate at all times. Yet as we have seen, such a culture often rests on a foundation of unspoken fears and unaddressed truths. It breeds silence in the face of crucial issues, encourages conformity over curiosity, and leads teams into the dangerous territory of groupthink and echo chambers. Under the glossy calm of false harmony, a nice culture can rot an organization's health from within. Creativity is stifled, errors accumulate, and decisions go unchallenged until they produce catastrophic consequences. The very problems that niceness seeks to avoid eventually surface with a vengeance.

Martin Luther King Jr. said in his famous "Letter from Birmingham Jail" that "there is a type of constructive, nonviolent tension which is necessary for growth."[209] Don't cover that up in your efforts to be nice. Channel and manage the tension. That's real kindness.

Chapter Summary

- **Definition:** A "nice" culture replaces candor with comfort, creating a veneer of civility that masks fear, silence, and dysfunction.
- **False harmony:** Niceness often signals safety but conceals avoidance, back-channeling, and pseudointimacy that suppress real dialogue.
- **Fear under the surface:** Niceness is frequently driven by fear of conflict, fear of disapproval, or fear of repercussions.
- **Why leaders pursue niceness:**
    - To avoid conflict and gain approval
    - To substitute niceness for genuine inclusion
    - To defer excessively to hierarchy
    - To use warmth as a substitute for accountability
- **Catastrophic consequences of niceness:**
    - **Choked innovation:** Niceness suppresses dissent and divergent thinking, suffocating the friction innovation requires.
    - **Crisis activation:** Nice cultures ignore problems until crisis forces action. Comfort anesthetizes vigilance and delays intervention.
    - **Bleeding talent:** High performers leave when they cannot challenge, influence, or meaningfully contribute within a polite-but-paralyzed culture.
    - **Low-velocity decisions:** Fear of disagreement slows decision-making, creates consensus-seeking paralysis, and traps progress in politeness.
    - **Learned helplessness:** When candor goes nowhere, people stop trying. Silence becomes the rational strategy.
- **Ways to combat niceness:**
    - **Clarify expectations:** Set explicit norms for candor, accountability, and meeting types.
    - **Grant irrevocable participation rights:** Reduce hierarchy's grip on voice.

- **Practice exploratory inquiry:** Apply disciplined questions ("Why? What if? How?").
- **Formally assign dissent and then invite more:** Make disagreement routine and valued. Invite critique.
- **Celebrate dissent and invite more:** Reward unpopular opinions.
- **Criticize your own ideas and decisions in public:** Think out loud and poke holes in your own thinking and behavior.
- **Inject empathy:** Show compassionate curiosity.
- **Publicly challenge the status quo you helped create:** Be the first one to question past decisions and practices.
- **Confront performance problems immediately:** Address issues directly and respectfully so niceness never shields poor performance.

CHAPTER 7

How the Leader Warms or Chills the Air

There's a power dynamic in every room. If you're the leader and you're in the room, you control that dynamic. Positional power is consolidated in your hands, and what you say and do can draw people out or make them recoil with anxiety and fear. You have a trailing force field, an invisible current of authority, hierarchy, and expectation. That force field can inspire openness or instill fear, invite candor or suppress dissent. The more senior the leader, the more powerful the gravitational pull of silence and conformity. What unfolds in that room—whether ideas are unleashed or muted—depends not only on the agenda or intellect in the room, but on how you use or sabotage your own positional power.

In my work with thousands of leaders over the past thirty years, I've observed some who intellectually and emotionally muzzle the room, creating an echo chamber, and others who unleash the room, creating an idea meritocracy. There's no arena where "the treacherous curtain of deference"—a phrase coined by American diplomat George Kennan—creates a more dangerous reality distortion field than when the leader gathers with other members of the organization.

A leader's job is to encourage useful ideas, and yet your very presence can work against that objective. At all costs, avoid the desire to indulge in the dark side of charisma to seek admiration. Ironically, you must overcome the interpersonal liability of your role in order to perform it. This is the paradox of power: The more you have, the more you must neutralize it to get to the truth. By default, you have a profound influence on the room by regulating the quality of inputs, conversion, and outputs.

Consider the fact that for your people, their personal reputation, career opportunity, and job security are on the line. For you, the viability and success of the organization are on the line. You understand that silence is expensive, but your people understand that silence is safe. You understand that unvarnished feedback leads to good decision-making, but your people understand that varnished feedback is a form of self-preservation. You know that fear breaks the feedback loop, but your people know that fear surrounds the feedback loop. In one study, 85 percent of employees said they withheld feedback because they feared negative consequences. That fear is amplified in hierarchical organizations, especially when leaders fail to recognize the chilling effect of status, authority bias, and the so-called HiPPO effect—where the highest-paid person's opinion dominates discourse.[210]

How, then, can you create high levels of psychological safety to promote the unencumbered exchange of ideas and unedited circulation of feedback? How do you warm and not chill the air? The following sections describe some practical ways to make that happen.[211]

Assign Someone Else to Conduct the Meeting

Because you occupy the apex of power on your team, you can change the power dynamic with small adjustments to the way you orchestrate a meeting. For example, when you assign someone else to conduct the meeting instead of taking the reins yourself, you're visibly redistributing power by leveling yourself down to be more of a player-coach. This has the added benefit of giving you a better vantage point to dual-monitor content and interaction.

To neutralize the authority gradient in a room is to share or relinquish control of the meeting itself. Delegate the role of meeting facilitator to another team member (or rotate it among attendees). This move immediately redistributes power: It sends the message that you're not there to dominate the agenda or micromanage the conversation. Research on hierarchy suggests that when the highest-ranking person steps back, it encourages others to step up. This is an effective way to create cultural flatness—an atmosphere where people become almost agnostic to title, position, and authority. They focus on the substance of an idea rather than the source.

By letting someone else run the meeting, you demonstrate confidence in the team's capability and create space for more voices to be heard. Importantly, as a participant you have a better vantage point to read the room and hear more honest information. You will be the leader at the "side of the table" rather than the head. Social science research supports this concept: Groups are more likely to share unique or unpopular information when the leader is not directing every exchange. Delegating meeting facilitation is thus a conscious flattening of the hierarchy, mitigating the instinct people have to defer to the highest authority. Academic studies on leader inclusiveness echo this approach: When leaders invite others to guide discussions and decisions, it elevates junior members' sense of ownership and psychological safety.[212] As a practical tip, be explicit about this hand-off. For instance, I might open the meeting by saying, "Today, Dana will guide us through the agenda—I'm here to listen and learn along with the rest of you."

Don't Sit at the Head of the Table

In many physical spaces, seating reflects the hierarchy.[213] When you uphold rituals that reflect the power structure, it fosters guarded behavior and laundered language. Disrupt those rituals by not sitting at the head of the table. Mix it up. Don't allow people to get comfortable in designated spots. Show others that you don't care about the accoutrements of power by continually reconfiguring the physical space, including your personal proximity to the same people.

Physical symbols of power exert psychological influence. The classic boardroom image of a CEO presiding from the head of a long table carries centuries of hierarchical baggage. People associate the "head" seat with authority, command, and power. To create a more egalitarian atmosphere, don't plant yourself on that symbolic throne. Instead, choose a seat that downplays rank: perhaps in the middle of a side, or wherever others might normally sit. Better yet, if the setting allows, I opt for a circular or dispersed seating arrangement that visually reinforces that we're all in this together. This may seem like a trivial detail, but small signals have outsized effects on group dynamics. Studies in environmental psychology have found that leaders who remove traditional status markers (such as special chairs or separate offices) help reduce employees' perceptions of distance and fear. By contrast, the head seat can unwittingly turn the CEO into an oracle—everyone waits for pronouncements and approval from that end of the table, which discourages organic debate. This physical decentering complements strategy #1 (delegating meeting conduct) to further erode the psychological barriers that often come with hierarchy.

Create Warmth and Informality

It would be nice if you could personally greet and connect with every person in every meeting, but you can't. What you can do is create an atmosphere of psychological safety by using your emotional intelligence to convey warmth and encourage collaboration. Pay attention to the slightest signals you send, including your gestures, facial expressions, and vocal characteristics (intensity, tone, volume, rate, and pitch).

Your emotional tone is contagious. A leader who exudes coldness or formality—however unintentionally—can send an implicit message: Be on your guard. Conversely, leaders who convey warmth, approachability, and a bit of informality signal to everyone in the room that "it's safe here; we're all human and on the same team." Academic research shows that when we meet someone, the first questions we subconsciously ask are *Can I trust this person?* and *Can I respect this person?*—in other words, we gauge their warmth and their competence. It is crucial that warmth comes first. Warmth is often the single most important factor in forming a positive impression of a leader, even before competence is assessed.[214]

Warmth in practice can be communicated in many small ways—a genuine smile, a friendly greeting by first name, an open posture, light humor, or a personal anecdote. Even the choice to remove a bit of formality can reduce the psychological distance that inhibits people from speaking candidly. Cultivating informality goes hand in hand with warmth. One powerful aspect of warmth is conveying empathy and care. If I regularly acknowledge people's feelings and well-being ("I know this project has been stressful—how is everyone holding up?"), it signals that candor about challenges or concerns will be met with understanding.

Model Acts of Vulnerability

You have a first-mover obligation to model acts of vulnerability to give others permission to do the same. This is disarming, especially when the people in the room are doing risk/reward calculations about what to say or not say. The quality of the clash of ideas will hinge on the permission and respect others sense through your behavior. If you show no personal vulnerability, silence will substitute for productive tension. So, try the following:

- Openly challenge yourself.
- Ask for help.
- Admit what you don't know.
- Point out a past mistake.
- Express your uncertainty.

Nothing crushes psychological safety more effectively than perfectionism at the top. If you project an image of infallibility—never admitting to uncertainty, ignorance, or error—employees will quickly conclude that they too must appear infallible. The result is a culture of blame avoidance and hiding mistakes, where learning and honest dialogue die on the vine. To counter this, be the first to model vulnerability: Demonstrate the courage to be imperfect. This means openly acknowledging your own fallibility and limitations. For example, admit when you don't know something, own up to a mistake, or express that you're still learning. Such acts of humility have a powerful effect: They normalize taking risks and being candid about problems.[215]

When I say, "I might be missing something here—what do you all think?" or "I was wrong about that approach, and here's what I learned," it undercuts the culture of fear. It tells people that no one is expected to be perfect, and that it's not only acceptable but desirable to discuss mistakes and uncertainties openly. To model vulnerability effectively, I go first. I share a story of a mistake I made and what it taught me. I say "I need help" in front of the team when appropriate. Even something as small as saying, "I'm nervous about this presentation" or "I'm not an expert in this area—please correct me if I'm off track," can have a profound influence. It dismantles the myth that leaders are omnipotent superheroes and instead sets a norm that being human is not only okay, it's encouraged. One CEO I know begins project postmortems by detailing his own missteps on the project. The effect is electric: Once the top dog has shown vulnerability, everyone else readily chimes in with lessons learned from their mistakes, rather than hiding or spinning them.

Stimulate Inquiry Before Advocacy

You need lateral, divergent, and nonlinear thinking in the room. If you move from asking questions to advocating your position too soon, it softly censors your team and signals the end of the discussion. Understand that there are two forms of inquiry: explanatory and exploratory. *Explanatory inquiry* uses data to understand current performance based on cause-and-effect relationships. *Exploratory inquiry* uses data to make assumptions and predictions about what could be possible. Explanatory inquiry helps improve execution, while exploratory inquiry drives innovation. Whether your focus is execution or innovation, ask thoughtful questions surrounded by compassionate curiosity. This acts as an equalizer and dilutes the power differential. Make statements such as:

- Help me think this through . . .
- I'd like to know . . .
- I'm fascinated by . . .
- I wonder why . . .
- I can't wait until we figure out how to . . .
- Let's see if we can tackle this problem together.

Have you been in a meeting where you spoke first—declaring an opinion or solution—and a timid, superficial discussion ensues? *When the leader advocates early, it often freezes the flow of ideas.* Team members may either quietly acquiesce ("the decision's already made") or confine their input to what they think you want to hear. To avoid this groupthink trap, flip the script: Encourage inquiry before advocacy. In practice, this means starting discussions with open-ended questions and exploration, rather than premature decision statements. Invite multiple perspectives and spend adequate time probing issues before anyone argues for a particular course. Deliberately create time and space for nonlinear, divergent thinking before converging on answers. You might say, "We'll get to decisions, but first let's make sure we've fully explored the terrain."

One best practice is the leader-speaks-last rule. You might say, "I have some thoughts, but I want to hear from everyone else first." Not only does this yield a richer set of views, but it also sends a clear signal that healthy debate is welcome.

Reward Challenges to the Status Quo

One CEO I've worked with likes to raise an issue and then ask everyone in the room to challenge her point of view. She'll say, "Tell me why I might be wrong. Help me see my blind spots." Then she pauses and lets everyone sit in the silence until the first person is brave enough to challenge her. She immediately rewards the vulnerability by saying, "Thank you. I may have missed something. Let's explore your perspective." Keenly aware that smothering dissent increases the risk of poor judgment, she has done this so often that challenging the status quo has become normalized behavior.

When someone in the room musters the courage to voice a dissenting opinion or to point out that "the emperor has no clothes," how you respond in that split second will echo throughout the organization. If you shoot the messenger, you will create a legion of silent observers. But if you "hug the messenger," as the saying goes, you send an unmistakable signal that speaking up is valued. To cultivate psychological safety, publicly reward those who challenge the status quo or bring up uncomfortable truths. Use simple praise and gratitude in the moment and then engage with the idea. The key is that when someone takes an interpersonal risk—disagreeing with the boss or questioning a plan—that risk earns them respect rather than retribution. You might do something unconventional, such as creating an award for "Best Idea That Contradicted Consensus" or highlighting in company communications instances where an employee's unorthodox suggestion led to a positive change. Some companies have instituted practices like "red team" reviews, where a team is lauded for finding holes in a project plan. *In summary, make heroes of the truth-tellers.*

Push Back with Humor and Enthusiasm

To increase the productive tension in the room, another leader I've worked with makes smart use of humor and enthusiasm. For example, he'll ask, "May I arm wrestle you on that point?" which always elicits a smile and positive response. It communicates, "I'm not rejecting you or your input; I actually relish the back-and-forth." The person being challenged doesn't feel attacked; if anything, they feel encouraged to engage in a friendly sparring of ideas. Humor and enthusiasm not only are disarming but also inject excitement into the process and communicate a commitment to rigorous debate. This approach also takes the emotional edge off high-stakes discussions. If you can disagree without being autocratic, it leaves the discussion open for others to do the same.

Even in an open culture, disagreements and critiques can be tense moments. As the leader, your challenge to someone else's idea carries extra weight—if delivered harshly, it can shut down dialogue and bruise the very psychological safety you're trying to build. That's why how you push back matters. Do it with humor and enthusiasm rather than with anger, condescension, or defensiveness. In practice, this means disagreeing in a positive, light-hearted, or upbeat manner, keeping the tone collegial and forward-looking ("we're all trying to solve this together") rather than adversarial. The goal is to signal that intellectual friction is welcome and not a personal attack. By infusing humor and enthusiasm into a counterpoint, you can defuse the potential intimidation factor of your dissent.

Enthusiasm plays a similar role. If my posture in a disagreement is enthusiastic curiosity—leaning forward, smiling, saying things like "I love the passion around this topic" or "This is great, we're really digging in!"—it frames the disagreement as a positive endeavor. That's completely different than if you let your body language signal irritation ("claws out and teeth bared"). Enthusiastic, good-natured pushback has the opposite effect: It keeps the energy in the room high and positive. The focus stays on the ideas, not on ego or status. In fact, a bit of laughter can release any interpersonal anxiety that a disagreement creates. *Remember, you're debating the idea, not each other.*

Buffer Strong Personalities

Chances are you have introverts, extroverts, and strong personalities in the room. Keep in mind that introverts may prefer to process quietly and nonverbally, whereas extroverts may relish verbal, public processing. Contain strong personalities, especially those who lack self-awareness. Don't allow assertions of dominance. One leader does this by saying, "As we discuss this issue, don't take more than your fair share of airtime. I want each of you to ensure equal participation." Remember, insecure people tend to elevate themselves by subordinating others. Your job is to create a shame- and embarrassment-free environment. The higher the arena of power, the deeper the potential humiliation if things go south. Finally, draw out the quiet ones. Ask a question up front and give time for reflection.

Do you notice who talks more and who hangs back? You have to play the role of traffic cop in discussions, buffering the strong personalities so they don't crowd others out, and drawing in the quieter contributors. The idea is to prevent a few voices from monopolizing the airtime or bulldozing the conversation, which can erode safety for others. If left unchecked, a forceful debater or a high-status expert can intimidate teammates, who then withdraw rather than engage. One of the central findings of Google's study of psychological safety was that "equality in conversational turn-taking" was a key determinant of the overall level of psychological safety.[216] It's your job to ensure that equity of voice.

Tactically, buffering strong personalities can be done up front and in the moment. I set expectations at the start of a meeting—for example, "I'd like everyone to get a chance to speak today. If you're typically outspoken, be mindful to leave room for others; if you're usually quiet, know that we really want to hear from you." This kind of gentle norm-setting can make a big difference. It explicitly legitimizes you stepping in if needed. Again, I might say at the outset, "As we discuss this issue, please don't take more than your fair share of airtime. I want to ensure equal participation." By framing it positively (an equal-opportunity meeting) rather than as a scold, you enlist everyone in the goal. Many strong talkers will self-regulate once they're aware of the norm.

Take advantage of pre-meeting preparation to help introverts and less assertive folks engage. For example, circulating an agenda or key questions in advance allows reflective thinkers to formulate ideas ahead of time. Then, in the meeting, they're more ready to share. Some teams even use hand-raising or turn-taking protocols in virtual meetings to prevent the loudest voice from constantly grabbing the mic. Finally, be on the lookout for people with high expertise or seniority whose comments might carry extra weight. For instance, a domineering technical expert might habitually dismiss others' ideas.

Intervene in those moments to protect the space for the original speaker. I might say, "Hold on, let's fully consider Maria's point before we evaluate it," thereby preventing a premature critique from silencing her. If a heated exchange between a strong personality and another team member starts to escalate, pause and reframe: "I think we have two passionate viewpoints here. Let's take a step back and make sure we understand both. Lisa, can you elaborate on your thought? Then we'll hear Mark's concerns." In conclusion, buffering strong personalities is about creating a fair and productive conversation space.

It ensures that extroversion or assertiveness alone doesn't set the agenda—merit does. *Make balanced participation the norm.*

Listen and Pause

When you listen and pause, you're communicating respect in an unmistakable way. You're telling the person that they deserve to be seen, heard, and understood. There is perhaps no more powerful way to validate another human being. When you do this in the presence of other members of your organization, you send a clear message that the individual matters. I know a leader who does this exceptionally well. He listens with intensity and will sometimes pause for a long time. People often try to break the awkward silence, but he raises his hand gently to signal a no-interruption rule. In time, the leader acculturated his team to tolerate brief silences as moments to think, rather than to fear silence and rush to fill it. Nonverbally, he was saying, "Don't take that silence away." That trained extroverted team members to let a quiet beat linger so deeper thinking could happen. By literally pausing the room, he gave introverts time to formulate their input and prevented the quick talkers from dominating by sheer momentum. These moments embolden others to think harder and contribute more fully.

In a fast-paced discussion, especially when challenging issues arise, there's a natural temptation for a leader to fill the silence and respond to every comment. Leaders often feel pressure to be decisive and quick-thinking. *Remember, patience can be more powerful than speed.* "Listen and pause" is a reminder to practice active listening and to embrace moments of silence or reflection rather than rushing to reply or decide. When you truly listen—fully present, not interrupting, not multitasking or formulating rebuttals in your head—it makes people feel valued and heard. And when you allow a pause before responding, it demonstrates thoughtfulness and signals that you're weighing ideas carefully rather than dismissing them offhand.

Consider how it feels for an employee to voice a delicate concern. If you immediately fire back a solution or an answer, the employee may wonder if their comment was really understood (or if it triggered annoyance). But if you sit for a moment in silence, processing, and perhaps even ask a follow-up question or simply nod, it shows respect for the comment. That pause can be worth gold; it indicates contemplation rather than knee-jerk judgment. In some cases, the silence invites the speaker to elaborate further, filling the space with additional details or thoughts they might have initially withheld. Psychologically, your comfort with a bit of silence conveys confidence and absence of threat. It's the opposite of an interrogation, where silence feels ominous. Instead, silence is more like space being given for consideration.

Active listening is the other half of this coin. It involves truly hearing the speaker's words, observing their tone and body language, and maybe paraphrasing or asking clarifying questions to ensure understanding. You might say, "Let me make sure I got that—are you saying X, and worried about Y?" Such responses validate that the person's voice made it through. Active listening also means not interrupting and not preemptively answering your own question. It can be as basic as maintaining eye contact and nodding. If the busiest person in the room can listen without distraction, it encourages everyone else to grant that same courtesy to their peers' ideas.

Give Highly Targeted Praise and Recognition

Inject precision into your praise and recognition. Instead of saying, "I appreciate that insight," make it highly targeted by explaining why. The "why" describes how the contribution is valuable, which both reinforces the behavior and coaches the individual to engage in deeper analysis. You might say instead, "I appreciate that insight, because you're helping us identify other areas of risk that we weren't paying attention to." One leader I've worked with avoids any hint of gratuitous or uncritical praise because he believes his job is to constantly stretch the critical-thinking capacity of his people. Don't withhold or be stingy with praise or recognition. Just give it in the moment, and make it precise with an explanation and genuine encouragement.

Positive reinforcement is a powerful shaper of behavior and norms. But not all praise is created equal. Generic, vague compliments ("Good job, everyone!") might provide a brief feel-good boost, but they miss the opportunity to reinforce specific behaviors that drive psychological safety. Targeted praise and recognition clarify which actions and values are appreciated and should be emulated. In essence, targeted praise turns your positive feedback into a teaching moment and a culture-setting mechanism.

Consider the difference: Imagine an employee in a meeting raises a novel idea and also candidly points out a potential flaw in the current plan. I could simply say afterward, "Thanks for your contributions." That's nice, but broad. Alternatively, I could say, "I want to thank you for sharing that idea and especially for highlighting the risk in our plan. Because you did that, we're now able to address a critical issue we might have missed." This specific praise does three important things: (1) it recognizes the individual's exact behavior (speaking up with a new idea and a constructive critical viewpoint), (2) it links that behavior to a positive outcome (preventing a problem), and (3) it implicitly encourages others to do the same (it's now clear that raising concerns is not just tolerated but valued). The praised person feels genuinely seen and appreciated, and their colleagues receive a clear signal about what success looks like in this team's culture.

This approach aligns with insights from organizational culture research, notably Edgar Schein's concept of *embedding mechanisms*.[217] Schein found that one of the primary ways leaders shape culture is through what they reward and recognize publicly. Targeted praise and recognition—where essentially you shine a spotlight on desired behaviors—is an embedding mechanism for creating culture by design. Aim for micro-praises delivered in context: "Alex, the way you asked that question in the meeting was really constructive. It opened up the dialogue and got us unstuck. Well done." Finally, public recognition of behaviors that bolster psychological safety can inspire peer-to-peer reinforcement. When others hear me highlight a colleague's brave question, diligent listening, or collaborative support, they may start acknowledging each other for those things, not just leaving it to the boss. That's when you know it's starting to be embedded in the culture.

Separate Worth from Worthiness

Inclusion is the key that unlocks a team's cognitive diversity, but that inclusion must be built on a basic acceptance of any individual's worth—not their worthiness, which implies a performance test to meet a standard or requirement of some kind. If we're assessing someone's competency in a particular area like customer service, a worthiness/performance test is valid and appropriate. But when it comes to inclusion, there is no performance test. Simply being human qualifies you for inclusion.[218]

If you want your employees to feel confident to speak up, they must first feel a sense of acceptance based on their fixed, intrinsic worth. If their belonging needs are not being met, if their acceptance is subject to a worthiness test, why would they risk the sting of further social rejection by speaking up? Speaking up is nothing less than an expression of one's authentic self. People will retreat from the opportunity to be their authentic selves if doing so is expensive. But if their worth is separate and distinct from the worthiness of their input, opinions, and views, they'll be more willing to use their voice.

In this social exchange, who has the first-mover obligation? Clearly, the organization. It must prove to the individual that their worth is a nonnegotiable constant. How can an organization do that? By treating every employee with equal respect regardless of performance—not as a shield from accountability, but as a guide for fair, equitable, and compassionate accountability. No one has special dispensation from accountability, and yet all are entitled to the same dignity based on intrinsic worth. When people believe they're included for who they are, without fear of reprisal for speaking up, they speak up.

Separate Loyalty from Agreement

I once attended an executive meeting in which the CEO would frequently ask, "Are we aligned?" to which everyone in the room would nod their heads and say yes. In this culture, loyalty meant agreement—a stifling agreement that silenced the team into compliance rather than commitment.

When loyalty becomes contingent on agreement, it produces manipulated conformity, which isn't loyalty at all. True loyalty—which refers to genuine concern for and dedication to the best interests of an institution and its people—must not only allow but also encourage independent thought. Unless the organization divorces loyalty from agreement, the pressure to conform can produce dangerous groupthink.

At some point, nearly every employee privately wonders whether their job comes with a voice. Then they watch, listen, and observe. If disagreement is considered disloyal, they will likely witness fear-induced intimidation. But if they see rigorous debate and constructive dissent without fear of retaliation, they will feel encouraged to participate and permitted to question any default in the organization. Ultimately, when loyalty and disagreement peacefully coexist, a speak-up culture can flourish.

Separate Status from Opinion

In human hierarchies, distance from power often prevents people from speaking up. An asymmetrical power relationship between employees typically puts pressure on the lower-status person to agree with the higher-status person.

Unfortunately, many organizations develop a debilitating norm that stigmatizes—and even punishes—contrary opinion, motivating each person to become their own gated community. As long as that norm is in place, fear exacts a tax on open dialogue. But it doesn't have to be that way. Smart people don't make a smart team unless they can harness their collective intelligence by networking their minds and engaging in multidisciplinary learning. This depends on their ability to invite and process dissent.

I've worked with several CEOs who have successfully decoupled opinion from status. They do it by teaching and modeling the art of disagreement. Then they ask for thoughtful disagreement delivered in good faith. When leaders reward challenging the status quo from the top to the bottom of the hierarchy in this way, they accelerate the formation of a speak-up culture.

Separate Permission from Adoption

Most employees understand that a speak-up culture means they have permission to speak their minds and weigh in with suggestions, opinions, and concerns. Unfortunately, some employees mistakenly believe that to be heard is to be heeded. This, of course, is not possible—you can't say yes to everything. Which brings us to the next step: removing the misconception that permission to speak up translates into an obligation to adopt the suggestion.

Leaders should not only make this separation between permission and adoption clear to employees, but also make it a point to acknowledge and commend those who speak up, even when you won't be adopting their suggestion. *To speak up, an employee needs some evidence of organizational receptivity.* Is someone listening? Does it even matter? Will it make a difference? In the absence of adoption, emphasize recognition. We all need the reassurance that when the answer is no, the very act of speaking up is appreciated and encouraged.

Conclusion

As the leader of the team, you are first among equals, yet your mere presence dictates the power dynamic. Take the opportunity to deliberately design that dynamic. If you induce fear, seek admiration, or allow hierarchy to outrank truth, you chill the air. But if you nurture psychological safety, you warm the air. Remember Dickens's description of Fezziwig's impact on the room: "He has the power to render us happy or unhappy; to make our service light or burdensome; a pleasure or a toil. Say that his power lies in words and looks; in things so slight and insignificant that it is impossible to add and count 'em up."[219]

Chapter Summary

- **Definition:** A leader's presence shapes the climate of every room; positional power can either draw people out or shut them down.
- **Power dynamic:** Authority, hierarchy, and status create a gravitational pull toward silence, conformity, and self-protection unless consciously neutralized.
- **Perception gap:** Leaders want unvarnished truth; employees want self-preservation. Fear surrounds the feedback loop unless psychological safety is deliberately created.
- **HiPPO effect:** The highest-paid person's opinion can dominate by default, softly censoring dissent and distorting decision quality.
- **Warm versus chill:** Leaders either warm the air, inviting candor, creativity, and participation, or chill it, producing fear, deference, and filtered information.
  - **Assign someone else to run the meeting:** Redistribute power, flatten the hierarchy, and encourage broader participation.
  - **Don't sit at the head of the table:** Remove symbolic status cues to reduce guarded behavior and increase openness.
  - **Create warmth and informality:** Use emotional intelligence, including tone, presence, and facial expression, to lower threat and invite human connection.

- **Model vulnerability:** Admit mistakes, uncertainties, and learning limits to signal that risk-taking and honesty are safe.
- **Stimulate inquiry before advocacy:** Ask questions first, speak last. Inquiry dilutes power, expands thinking, and prevents premature conformity.
- **Reward challenges to the status quo:** Publicly praise dissent to make courage contagious and normalize constructive dissent.
- **Push back with humor and enthusiasm:** Disarm tension, keep debate alive, and frame disagreement as collaborative rather than adversarial.
- **Buffer strong personalities:** Regulate airtime, protect quieter voices, and maintain equality in contribution.
- **Listen and pause:** Use silence and deep listening to convey respect, validate contributions, and slow down a fear response.
- **Give highly targeted praise:** Identify and recognize specific behaviors that strengthen psychological safety, reinforcing them as cultural norms.
- **Separate worth from worthiness:** Include people based on intrinsic human worth so they feel safe enough to speak authentically.
- **Separate loyalty from agreement:** Make it clear that disagreement is not disloyalty; healthy critique strengthens the mission.
- **Separate status from opinion:** Ensure that ideas compete on merit, not hierarchy, to unleash collective intelligence.
- **Separate permission from adoption:** Being heard does not guarantee adoption; acknowledge contributions even when you choose another path.

CHAPTER 8

How to Create a Sanctuary of Inclusion

This chapter focuses on the "how" of creating more inclusion safety (stage 1). Before we jump into the practical and applied side of this stage, let's zoom out and talk about the personal and organizational journey of increasing inclusion safety. In all cases, it's a journey *from awareness to action.*

Unfortunately, many people would like to be more inclusive, but they feel paralyzed by fear and don't know how. Similarly, many organizations fail in their attempts to create sanctuaries of inclusion. They want to change their calcified norms, but they face the same obstacle: How? They launch awareness campaigns, adjust policies, and mandate training on the theory that behavioral change will follow. It doesn't. When exclusion compounds, an organization may reach the state that Émile Durkheim called *anomie*, or a state of normlessness, in which social regulation is failing due to a collapse of shared values, rules, and moral frameworks that hold it together.[220] In every case, a lack of inclusion safety is at root. *It's everyone's job to make the world safe for differences.*[221]

Remember, while diversity is a matter of makeup and composition, inclusion is a matter of intent and behavior. Inclusion activates diversity and unleashes its power, but it requires both skill and will, which the trifecta of awareness, policy, and training can never deliver. In the end, it comes down to behavior and what Alexis de Tocqueville called the "art of association."[222]

For example, Millennial Corporation (not its real name) has worked tirelessly over the past three years to become more inclusive. Like many organizations, it launched a massive campaign to increase awareness, understanding, and appreciation of differences; it issued new policies to eliminate systemic bias; it rolled out inclusion training to every employee. Yet the prevailing norm in the organization—rigid self-segregation based on lines of natural affinity—didn't budge. Employees still clung to a pattern of *homophily*, a term coined by sociologists Paul Lazarsfeld and Robert K. Merton to refer to association based on similarity.[223] It's true that humans tend to be attracted to and bond with those who are demographically and culturally like them. We are drawn to similarity and tend to fear differences which easily lead to divisions. Especially when our sense of inclusion is threatened, we often feel provoked, turn hostile, and lash out.[224]

Bonding Versus Bridging

The political scientist Robert Putnam helps us understand that to get to real inclusion safety, we have to go beyond bonding to bridging. We can't always be looking for our tribe.

Bonding is the act of connecting with someone like you or in agreement with you. It's usually not hard to do if you have conditions that include equal status and common goals. If you get to know each other better, you'll find that you like each other. Proximity prevents hostility. So goes the "contact hypothesis" proposed by Gordon Allport.[225] The challenge is that bonding will never take an organization to deep and abiding inclusion. Natural bonding patterns inevitably become exclusive, creating cultural fault lines and pushing some to the margins because they are inward-looking. Yes, these patterns promote solidarity, but they also create insularity.[226]

Organizations must add intentional bridging behavior to the natural bonding behavior that already exists. *Bridging* connects people across diverse groups, fostering broader identities and reciprocity. It is outward-looking and more likely to link individuals from different backgrounds, supporting inclusion, tolerance, and wider social cooperation. Does the contact hypothesis hold true between people who are not alike? Yes, if you work hard enough at it. For example, I agree with Robert Livingston that racism is caused primarily by fear and insecurity, so it's easy to see how a refusal to bridge can ultimately lead to the toxic polarization we see today.[227] The bottom line is that you need both: bonding for support and cohesion, and bridging for openness and innovation. The problem is that bonding is easy and bridging is hard.

First, bridging is an act of vulnerability that comes with increased risk of interpersonal harm or embarrassment. Second, it requires skill. Employees avoid bridging because they don't feel confident or comfortable, or know how to approach a dissimilar person. So even well-intentioned employees either choose not to bridge or make an awkward attempt that is brief and transactional. Both parties come away from the encounter feeling unconnected, and often with their vulnerability punished rather than rewarded.

How can organizations help their employees bridge across lines of natural affinity? In my client experience, organizations that move immediately from a state of awareness to a state of action make progress. Why? Because only through real human exchange, dialogue, and conversation does change occur. Divisions begin to disappear when individuals generate their own confirming evidence that bridging works. To help, you can *accelerate the natural pace of social integration and actually move beyond natural affinity* by deliberately adding more bridging to the bonding. My team and I have field-tested the following four-step process in many organizations with great success.

Step 1: Hold Bridging Discussions

Because people fear differences, they recoil from extending themselves to dissimilar persons. But if you formally assign employees to get to know each other, that assignment can replace personal fear with institutional permission.[228] An effective way to do this is to arrange fifteen-minute bridging discussions. Assign employees from different parts of the organization to meet virtually or face-to-face for fifteen minutes. Randomizing assignments across functions and levels of responsibility provides an egalitarian coaching relationship that stimulates cross-affinity connection. You can institutionalize this practice and do it on a monthly basis.

Because natural bridging behavior is slow, or sometimes even nonexistent, assigned bridging discussions can accelerate the normal pace of social integration and change the structure of informal networks almost instantaneously. More importantly, it can be a vehicle to slice through lines of natural affinity related to age, race, gender, rank, and several other demographics and psychographics. Over time, assigned bridging can redraw the lines of natural affinity and help remove exclusionary bias throughout the organization.

Step 2: Follow a Discussion Guide

Remember, interaction is not connection. Interaction is a mere exchange, while connection is satisfying each other's need to matter. Until there is empathic inquiry, the exchange may stall in a state of obligatory surface acting in which individuals merely tolerate the ritual. But if the conversation moves into genuine mutual discovery, bridging happens. To facilitate that, provide a discussion guide with the following guidelines and questions:

GUIDELINES:

- Hold eye contact.
- Physically or virtually face the person.
- Learn to pronounce the person's name properly.
- Ask questions with genuine intent.
- Listen without interrupting.
- Summarize what you learn about that person.

QUESTIONS (CHOOSE AT LEAST THREE):

1. When did you feel included at work?
2. When did you not feel included at work?
3. What makes you feel most vulnerable at work?
4. What would you like others to know and appreciate about you?
5. Whom do you know that is skilled at modeling inclusion? What do they do?

The goal is to generate real connection between dissimilar persons (*heterophily*). Only when two people feel psychologically safe enough to be their authentic selves does the relationship building begin. *If you can't be you, there is no chance to be understood.*

Step 3: Commit to Practice One Inclusive Behavior

At the end of the discussion, each employee commits to practice one inclusive behavior. The following seven behavioral families, when modeled, create cross-affinity connection and inclusion as a natural by-product:

- Greeting
- Asking
- Listening
- Sharing
- Inviting
- Helping
- Protecting

Have each employee choose a behavior from one of the seven families to practice over the subsequent fourteen days. Each behavior is distinct in purpose, yet similar in impact. As affirming behaviors, they validate others in any situation, provided they are performed with genuine interest.

Step 4: Report on Performance and Learning

To report progress, assign employees to arrange a thirty-minute follow-up discussion with their assigned partners after fourteen days. Have employees discuss and answer these four questions:

1. How effectively did you model your inclusive behavior?
2. What impact did modeling your inclusive behavior have on you?
3. What impact did modeling your inclusive behavior have on others?
4. What did you learn in the process?

In his *Nicomachean Ethics*, Aristotle observed, "People love those who are like themselves."[229]

As organizations try to create sanctuaries of inclusion, however, they reach a point where no amount of bonding behavior within the lines of natural affinity will help. Nor will an awareness campaign, policy changes, or training be enough to move people to action and behavioral change. Ultimately, organizations need their employees to cross lines of affinity through bridging behavior. But employees need help. They tend to cling to the familiar and fear the strange. So, a guided effort in which dissimilar employees meet each other, engage in mutual discovery, and model inclusive behaviors can dramatically extend inclusion and activate the latent power of diversity. *Remember, humans step into vulnerability to feel connected and step out of it to feel protected.*

Applying the L.I.V.E. Model

If modeling and rewarding vulnerability is the central mechanism for building psychological safety, how do you apply that behaviorally? After working with thousands of teams across many organizations, I have distilled the process into four concrete steps that are represented in what we call the L.I.V.E. Model (figure 21; table 9).

You can apply the L.I.V.E. Model, especially in meetings, one-on-ones, and day-to-day team interactions. The goal is to turn each step into a conscious habit that reinforces a culture of rewarded vulnerability:

1. *Look* at the interactions and social dynamics around you. Be a student of the room. Notice who speaks up and who doesn't, whose ideas are heard or ignored, and how people respond to mistakes or questions. For example, in a meeting, pause before moving to the next agenda item and observe who hasn't contributed. Note patterns: Do certain voices dominate? Do people defer to authority or remain quiet in disagreement? Tip: Rotate meeting facilitation occasionally so different people experience what it feels like to manage group dynamics.
2. *Identify* acts of vulnerability in real time. Train yourself to spot behaviors that involve risk—asking for help, admitting an error, challenging a group consensus, or sharing a half-formed idea. For example, an employee says, "I might be wrong, but I think our customer feedback process is broken." A teammate admits, "I missed that deadline—I should have asked for help sooner." Tip: Recognize that these are moments of courage, not weakness. Mentally label them as "vulnerability moments" to help you respond intentionally instead of reflexively.

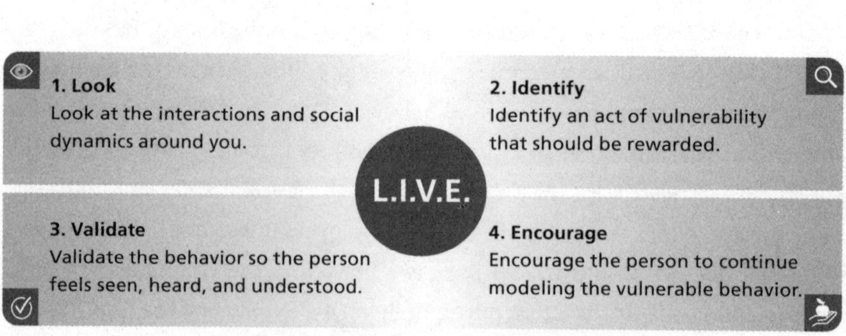

Figure 21. The L.I.V.E. Model for Teams

3. *Validate* the behavior so the person feels understood. Respond in a way that shows appreciation for the person's honesty, rather than focusing immediately on the content of what they said. For example, you might say, "Thanks for being up front about that—that's exactly the kind of transparency we need." Or, "That's a really helpful observation. I appreciate you raising it." Tip: Use your tone, body language, and timing. A short, sincere acknowledgment in the moment can have more impact than a long speech later. If at all possible, get one-on-one with the person you are validating. Calculus teacher Craig Smith will go to a student's desk and kneel next to them to help them with a problem and validate their efforts. It's a powerful gesture of servant leadership that reduces the status gap.
4. *Encourage* the person to continue modeling vulnerability. Reinforce the behavior by linking it to the team's values or goals. Encourage follow-up action that keeps the momentum. For example, you might say, "Would you be willing to walk us through what you learned so others can benefit too?" Or, "Let's build on your point—what ideas do others have?" Or, "That was a tough call to make. Thanks for setting the example." Tip: Recognition can be public or private, but the key is consistency. When vulnerability is consistently rewarded, it becomes normalized and contagious.

Table 9. Applying the L.I.V.E. Model in team meetings

Situation	Application	Outcome
Team member raises a concern about workload.	1. Identify it as vulnerability. 2. Validate it ("Thanks for saying that—it's not easy to bring up"). 3. Encourage discussion on solutions.	Builds openness about capacity and stress
Someone admits they made a mistake.	1. Acknowledge courage. 2. Focus on learning instead of blame.	Reduces fear of failure
A junior member hesitates to share an idea.	1. Look for nonverbal cues. 2. Invite input ("You looked like you had a thought—want to share?").	Increases participation and inclusion
Conflict arises between two colleagues.	1. Recognize both sides' vulnerability in speaking up. 2. Validate both. 3. Encourage constructive dialogue.	Strengthens trust and resolution skills

Chapter Summary

- **The inclusion journey:** Creating inclusion safety is a journey from *awareness to action*. It's the "art of association," not the by-product of awareness campaigns or policy shifts.
- **The failure pattern:** Organizations often stall because they try to fix exclusion with messaging, rules, and training. They drift toward what Durkheim called *anomie*—normlessness and the collapse of shared values.
- **Bonding versus bridging:** Bonding between similar people fosters solidarity, but reinforces insularity. Bridging connects across differences; it expands identity, reciprocity, and cooperation. Bonding is easy. Bridging is hard.
- **Why bridging is essential:** Diversity's power is unlocked only when employees cross lines of natural affinity. Fear, insecurity, and homophily create silos.
- **Four-step bridging process:**
  1. **Hold bridging discussions:** Assign fifteen-minute cross-affinity conversations to accelerate integration and redraw informal networks.
  2. **Follow a discussion guide:** Move from interaction to genuine connection through empathic inquiry and mutual discovery.
  3. **Practice one inclusive behavior:** Employees choose one behavior (greeting, asking, listening, sharing, inviting, helping, protecting) to model for fourteen days.
  4. **Report on learning:** Partners reconvene to reflect on behavior modeled, its impact, and personal insights gained.
- **Why bridging works:** Structured vulnerability normalizes connection across differences and dissolves fault lines bonding alone cannot fix.
- **Connecting and protecting:** Employees step into vulnerability to connect and step out of it to protect.
- **Applying the L.I.V.E. Model:** Inclusion grows through the daily mechanics of rewarded vulnerability:
  - **Look** at the interactions and social dynamics around you.
  - **Identify** an act of vulnerability that should be rewarded.
  - **Validate** the behavior so the person feels seen, heard, and understood.
  - **Encourage** the person to continue modeling the vulnerable behavior.

CHAPTER 9

How to Challenge the Status Quo

Arguments are extremely vulgar, for everybody in good society holds exactly the same opinions.

—Oscar Wilde

Innovation requires deviation. In fact, every aspect of innovation, radical or slight, begins with at least a small dose of constructive dissent, some kernel of an idea to shake up the system.[230] But shaking up the system is the easy part. It's not the system that fossilizes, gets territorial, and pushes back—it's humans who stand in the way of subsequent progress. *In fact, the deeper the attachment to the status quo, the greater the willful blindness to its growing irrelevance.* Therein lies the danger.

So how should you go about sharing an idea or feedback that goes against the status quo? It's more about dislodging a deeply entrenched paradigm than it is presenting clear logic and unimpeachable data. Even if what you have to say doesn't feel earth-shattering, what you're calling for is the destruction of dogma, the abolition of a mindset, the transfer of an allegiance—much of which becomes more emotional and political than rational.

It's no wonder, then, that challenging the status quo can feel risky, leading you to self-censor and shy away from speaking up. *Threatening the edifice threatens those who built the edifice.* You could bruise egos, reveal poor performance, redistribute power, or upend hierarchy. You probably will. At a minimum, the business of challenging the status quo calls into play context, personalities, and self-interest.

Ironically, challenging the status quo is how we keep each other safe, yet we often feel terrified to do it. For example, how do you convince marketing that they're wasting ad spend on poor messaging? How do you challenge finance to relax the hurdle rate for smaller capital budget requests? How do you inform your division that the current onboarding process for new hires is tedious and ineffective? How do you let HR know that you see systemic gender bias in the promotion of production managers? How do you raise a concern about the potential unintended consequences of a new product launch?

Just shine the light of logic and data, right? And as if an entrenched status quo isn't enough, what if you have no positional power? What if you're new to the organization? What if you want to challenge something not in your area of expertise? What if you're a member of an underrepresented and marginalized group, which makes challenging the status quo especially risky and potentially costly to your reputation and chances for advancement?

In working with organizations around the world, I've learned that challenging the status quo requires not only courage but also skill. The following ten tips will help you build that skill, mitigate the risk, and increase the chances of success.

Anticipate the Opportunity

Very few organizations have open-mic forums for challenging the status quo, so expect to do so in the context of your natural workflow. It won't be like standing in front of venture capitalists with a pitch deck, but you should prepare as if it were. *The lower your seat in the hierarchy, the tighter the case you must bring.*

Odds are that it will be an informal opportunity or chance encounter that allows you to introduce your idea. You never know when you might have the ear of the right stakeholder.

Anticipating means being ready when the chance comes. Research shows that people at lower levels of the hierarchy often have plenty of ideas for improvement but rarely get a chance to voice them under normal conditions.[231] Formal invitations to challenge the status quo are rare. Studies of "issue selling" (how employees sell new ideas upward) show that successful change agents are "ready to act . . . when the time is right."[232] Many of those who fail wish later that they had seized a better moment. Being prepared with a tight case allows you to indirectly control the process by waiting patiently and then striking when conditions are favorable.

Ask for Permission

When it comes to challenging the status quo, employees are often unsure of their participation rights. So ask explicitly for permission to challenge—for example, "May I have your permission to push back on this? Do you mind if I offer a different perspective? May I suggest an alternative way to look at this?" The moment someone with positional power gives you the okay, you trade your personal risk for institutional permission, and those in charge feel the assurance of retaining control. *This allows you to position your interaction as a contribution rather than a confrontation.*

In practice, this simple step can significantly lower the perceived audacity of your dissent. Many employees stay silent out of fear or uncertainty about whether it's their place to speak up. *By explicitly asking to offer a different perspective, you frame your challenge as deference to the leader's authority rather than defiance.* Notably, people tend to take cues from authority figures: When leaders openly invite input, team members are far more likely to speak up. Your request for permission effectively prompts that invitation. It also transforms the power dynamic: Once the boss says "Go ahead," your challenge becomes sanctioned. Psychologically, you've shifted the exchange from *you* versus *them* to a joint examination of an idea under the leader's purview. The person in power retains a sense of control over the discussion.[233] By securing institutional permission up front, you create a safe container for dissent.

Lead with Inquiry, Not Advocacy

Challenging the status quo often evokes defensiveness. To neutralize this response, begin your challenge with inquiry, not advocacy. Make it a conversation. Rather than advocating a position that might divide, exclude, or marginalize, disarm with questions that recruit others into dialogue.

Good inquiry engages the intellect and reduces the chance of emotional escalation. For example, to start the inquiry process, you might ask the "do-nothing" question: "If we don't change anything, what will happen?" This question transfers critical thinking to others and invites them to think through potential consequences out loud.

Leading with inquiry helps avoid triggering a fight-or-flight reaction. If you launch straight into arguing your point, colleagues or bosses may dig into defensive positions. In fact, too much forceful advocacy can backfire. People will answer a push with a push. On the other hand, asking thoughtful questions puts everyone in problem-solving mode. Posing a question like "What outcomes do we expect if we continue on the current path?" prompts others to analyze the status quo themselves. They become partners in identifying issues, rather than targets of your critique. Scholars of organizational learning have long advocated balancing advocacy with inquiry for this reason.[234] Inquiry signals humility and an openness to dialogue.

In team interactions, I call direct and unsympathetic forms of disagreement "head-on collisions."[235] Even when team members try to be objective and avoid personal criticism, head-on collisions almost always arouse strong emotions and may provoke defensiveness. *The harder the intellectual collision, the more likely the parties will react with strong emotions, potentially intentionally or unintentionally sabotaging the effort.* Instead of clashing directly with another person's point of view, engage in "soft angle" dissent by leading with inquiry. Use questions like:

- Why do you feel that way?
- Have you ever considered such and such? Would you consider another way to look at this?
- May I share my experience, which may be a little different?
- If I walk you through a different approach, would you tell me what you think?

Model Emotional Intelligence

Paradoxically, the challenger must often create psychological safety for the challenged, giving them space to acknowledge and come to terms with needed change. To foster that safety, let your emotional intelligence be your guide. This includes demonstrating self-awareness to inform your own behavior while paying close attention to the nonverbal cues of others.

Interact with poise, humility, and sincerity. Remember that respect defuses defensiveness and humor de-escalates tension. If a topic is sensitive, raise it privately. Show your stakeholders that you're acting in good faith and that you appreciate their concerns and objections. Use empathy to ensure that they feel seen, heard, and understood.

Emotionally intelligent challengers manage both their own emotions and the emotions of those they are challenging. This means maintaining composure (no matter how passionate you feel about your idea) and showing empathy toward the defenders of the status quo. You can sense when someone is growing defensive. Perhaps their tone sharpens or body language closes off. Adjust your approach. Small behaviors signal respect: A calm, friendly tone of voice, receptive listening, and nodding can all convey that you're not there to attack the person. When people feel respected, their defensiveness tends to dissipate.

Another facet of emotional intelligence is knowing when and where to challenge. If an issue is particularly sensitive or might embarrass someone, don't bring it up in a crowded meeting. *Emotional intelligence means protecting others from humiliation*. If you need to intervene, pull the person aside in private to discuss a delicate matter. By showing that courtesy, you protect their dignity and signal that your intent is *not* to publicly shame but to genuinely solve a problem.

Demonstrate a Grasp of the Past

In his book *The Thing*, G. K. Chesterton describes a situation in which a fence has been erected across a road. An eager reformer comes along to challenge the status quo—"I don't see the use of this; let us clear it away"—to which someone representing the status quo responds, "If you don't see the use of it, I certainly won't let you clear it away. Go away and think. Then, when you can come back and tell me that you do see the use of it, I may allow you to destroy it."[236]

The lesson is simple, but often overlooked: If you want to challenge the status quo, grasp the past. Demonstrate contextual understanding by acquiring a thorough knowledge of previous decisions and how the status quo came to be. Sure, you can spitball ideas anytime, but when you're ready to push back on the status quo, demonstrate mastery of the current state first.

This is about showing respect for the institutional memory and the efforts of those who came before you. In short: "Don't remove a fence until you know why it was put up in the first place." If you haven't bothered to learn the original rationale, people will (rightly) question the credibility of your proposal to tear it down. By contrast, when you can articulate both the merits and the flaws of the status quo, you gain trust. This approach honors the past before arguing for change, making your challenge feel less like an attack on your predecessors' competence or values.

Be Transparent About Potential Unintended Consequences

If you're proposing a different course of action, you bear the burden of proof to explain how your proposal will make things better. This means being candid about the risks. Think through first-, second-, and third-order consequences, both intended and unintended.

When you take aim at the status quo, there's often a susceptibility to confirmation bias. *It's easy to dismiss disconfirming evidence and focus solely on first-order intended consequences as if they were already facts in evidence.* Don't do that. If you're transparent and impartial in your analysis, that candid disclosure of risk will create trust with stakeholders.

Every proposal for change has downsides or uncertainties. Wise challengers acknowledge these up front. By openly discussing the potential negatives of your idea, you actually strengthen your persuasiveness. Why? Because you preempt the audience's skeptical inner voice. Instead of them thinking, *This person is naive or hiding something*, they hear you say it for them. In fact, persuasion research has long documented that two-sided arguments (those that mention both pros and cons) tend to be seen as more credible and trustworthy. If you say, "Here's my recommendation, but here are the risks," you come across as a fair, objective analyst rather than a biased promoter of your own idea. Stakeholders are more inclined to greenlight an experiment or pilot of a new approach if they believe you've realistically assessed the risks and have safeguards in place.

Bring Credibility

As a matter of principle, every employee should have participation rights and be encouraged to challenge the status quo. That's nice in theory, but what percentage of organizations have truly embedded the obligation of dissent into their DNA?

Every day you don't challenge the status quo should be a day spent preparing. And how do you prepare? By growing your credibility through a track record of performance. In *The Structure of Scientific Revolutions*, Thomas Kuhn explains that advances in science are inherently subversive—not only to current theory, but, perhaps more importantly, to existing commitments as well.[237] So even if you're right in your analysis and recommendations, your challenge is a threat that naturally stirs up opposition, especially among those who benefit from the current incentive structure. Your personal credibility will be table stakes. If you're not credible, people may listen, but choose to not hear you.

Organizational life isn't a pure meritocracy of ideas; *who* delivers a message often matters as much as *what* the message is. This step is about building the capital you need so that when you challenge the status quo, your voice carries weight. One way to think of credibility is as *currency* or "credits" you earn over time. Social psychologists have a term for this: *idiosyncrasy credits*.[238] You accumulate these credits by contributing to the group and meeting expectations. Later, you can "spend" them by deviating from the norm (such as suggesting a change that others might initially resist). Keep some in the bank before you destabilize the status quo.

Consider Kuhn's point about scientific revolutions. He noted that "normal science" actively *suppresses* disruptive novelties because they threaten the established commitments of the field. In a company, normal operations often suppress disruptive ideas for the same reason. They challenge existing commitments, budgets, power structures, or comfort zones. People invested in those commitments will, consciously or not, resist. Kuhn's observation implies that even an *objectively correct* new idea might fail unless it comes from someone the community deems legitimate. If you aren't that person yet, consider bolstering your idea by partnering with someone who has the needed clout. For example, get a well-regarded manager or technical expert to co-sponsor your proposal. *Credibility must carry the weight of your dissent.*

Know Your Boss

Understand your boss's personality, biases, preferences, and goals. I know one executive who simply can't tolerate being challenged in a public setting. One of his direct reports was convinced that several metrics in the KPI dashboard were no longer useful and could be eliminated. He surprised his boss with this blunt advice in an executive meeting. He was right in his challenge and wrong in his approach.

If you know your boss, don't collide with them. To determine the best approach, ask: When does your boss get defensive and territorial? Do they invite challenge and dissent? How willing are they to be wrong? How do they handle bad news? How emotional or unflappable are they? How entrenched in the status quo are they?

No two leaders are exactly alike. Challenging an idea championed by your boss requires tailoring your approach to that boss's temperament and values. Some bosses pride themselves on being open-minded and even *expect* vigorous debate; others have fragile egos and will perceive any disagreement as disloyalty, especially if it's in front of others. And regardless of your boss's style and temperament, it's almost never a good idea to make a frontal challenge, especially in front of others, which provokes an ego audience effect. With rare exception, that will create defensiveness. By knowing your boss, you can at least avoid *unforced errors* in the way you present your ideas.

Frame Dissent as Exploration

Even if you think you have the perfect solution to fix or enhance the status quo, be careful in the way you frame your dissent. Think, for instance, about the natural response to curiosity compared to contradiction. When you're contradicted, it can trigger a fear response, spike emotion, and thrust you into fight-or-flight mode.

Try using statements such as, "I'd really like to learn more about this," "I wonder what else the data is telling us," and "Please poke holes in this." Then show your own cognitive flexibility. Think and challenge yourself out loud. When others see you as curious rather than dogmatic, they'll be more willing to join the expedition.

Your stance when challenging should be that of a discoverer, not a crusader; an innovator, not an agitator. By framing your challenge as an invitation to explore an issue together, you reduce the psychological threat. The idea is to make the whole endeavor feel like a joint problem-solving quest, rather than you versus them. Practically, this means adopting the language and tone of curiosity. Phrases like "I'm curious what everyone thinks about . . ." or "This is a tough nut—I've been trying to figure it out; maybe we can all put our heads together" encourage others to participate rather than take sides.

This approach taps into people's natural intellectual curiosity. It also frames the status quo not as "stupid" or "wrong," but as an opportunity for learning and improvement. In a Stanford course on civil disagreement, instructors emphasized seeing disagreements as "opportunities to expand your own perspective and build empathy."[239] In practice, that means approaching debates with a mindset of trying to understand, rather than trying to win. Doing so helps ensure that even conversations on divisive topics can remain constructive and collegial.

Framing dissent as exploration also means showing intellectual humility. You might explicitly say, "This is just a hypothesis. If there's data that contradicts it, I want to know." The conversation becomes a mutual learning process rather than a zero-sum debate.

Use Data

Data has the power to de-personalize and de-risk challenging the status quo. If you have compelling quantitative data to make your case, use it. If you don't, move down the data hierarchy. Do you have meaningful qualitative data? If not, move down again to less-reliable anecdotal data. If you don't have that, you're down to impressionistic data, or what we call a hunch.

All categories of data are admissible, but may not be compelling enough to get the attention of your stakeholders. Use the best data you can get your hands on. If you're low on evidence and high on gut, ask for an opportunity to test your hypothesis, such as an experiment, trial, or pilot. This lowers the perceived threat of the challenge as well as the anticipated risks and costs of trying something new.

Whenever possible, ground your challenge in facts and evidence. A data-driven approach shifts the focus from *opinions* and personalities to something more objective. It's harder to argue with numbers (assuming they're good numbers) than with personal assertions. In challenging the status quo, using data can make the discussion feel less like *your idea versus my idea* and more like *what the evidence indicates*. This reduces the likelihood that people feel personally attacked or that egos dominate the debate.

Studies have found that statistical evidence is generally more persuasive than anecdotal stories in changing minds.[240] Numbers bring objectivity and rigor. Be honest about the strength of your evidence. If you only have a hunch, it's not a death knell—you can still challenge the status quo by proposing to *get* data. Say something like "I can't prove this yet, but I have a hypothesis that doing X instead of Y might improve outcomes. Can we run a small pilot to gather data on this?" This approach is smart organizationally. It translates an instinct or idea into a low-risk experiment, which is often more palatable to decision-makers than a wholesale change based on a guess. Pilots and experiments are the allies of challengers because they say, "We don't have to bet the farm; let's test this and see."

Using data also helps you check your own confirmation bias. We all can fall in love with our ideas. Data keeps us honest. It might even reveal that the status quo is better than you thought, or that your proposed change has unintended downsides, which you can then factor in. Ultimately, evidence is your friend. Even if the final decision is subjective or political, you want to be the person in the room who did their homework.

Conclusion

Challenging the status quo is the mechanism that leads to innovation and improvement. It's also a behavior that causes fear and trembling. Yet summoning the courage to challenge the status quo is almost never enough. Yes, you need courage, but you also need skills.

Chapter Summary

- **Definition:** Challenging the status quo is the engine of innovation. It disrupts entrenched paradigms, confronts dogma, and overcomes human resistance to change.
- **Emotional reality:** Challenging the status quo feels risky because it threatens egos, power structures, habits, and identities.
- **Courage + skill:** Speaking up requires both bravery and technique. Without skill, courage alone often fails.
- **Risk factors:** Lower power, newness, lack of expertise, and being part of a marginalized group increase the interpersonal risk of dissent.

- **Practical ways:**
  - **Anticipate the opportunity:** Prepare ahead of time. Informal windows to challenge are rare and often unanticipated. Be ready with a tight, ready-to-go case.
  - **Ask for permission:** Get explicit authorization to offer a dissenting view. Sanctioned challenge lowers defensiveness and legitimizes your voice.
  - **Lead with inquiry, not advocacy:** Begin with questions, not assertions, to defuse defensiveness and recruit others into problem-solving.
  - **Use emotional intelligence:** Regulate your own emotions, read others' cues, and frame dissent with empathy, humility, and respect.
  - **Understand the past:** Demonstrate contextual awareness of why the status quo exists—"Chesterton's fence"—to earn credibility for change.
  - **Acknowledge unintended consequences:** Build trust by presenting both risks and rewards. Two-sided arguments increase credibility.
  - **Bring credibility:** Credibility is currency. Build a track record or partner with someone who has clout to carry the weight of dissent.
  - **Know your boss:** Tailor your approach to temperament, ego, triggers, and preferences. Avoid surprise, public challenges unless appropriate.
  - **Frame dissent as exploration:** Position your challenge as curiosity-driven, not combative; an expedition, not a rebellion.
  - **Use the best available data:** Lead with evidence, quantitative if possible, qualitative if necessary. Use pilots and experiments if evidence is thin.
- **Innovation requires deviation:** Challenging the status quo is uncomfortable but essential. Responsible dissent is the precursor to discovery and improvement.

CHAPTER 10

The Behavioral Guide

This guide is designed to help you move quickly from the theory of psychological safety to actual practice. Many of the behaviors summarize or reinforce my suggestions from the previous chapters, and I've added several others. Here's a suggested approach to using the Behavioral Guide:

1. Choose one behavior at a time to maintain focus and a manageable scope.
2. Choose a behavior that is relevant to your role and visible to your team.
3. Make a list of places and interactions where you can model the behavior you've chosen. Be specific. Then think about your team. How can you not only model the behavior but also reward the vulnerability of others when they do?
4. If you feel that you accomplished your behavioral goal after seven days of practice, choose a new behavior and start again. If not, go another week. What could you do differently this time around?

Please note that each behavior is coded with the letters T, I, M, or some combination. A "T" behavior is relevant for teams. An "I" behavior is relevant for individuals, and an "M" behavior is relevant for managers.

Behaviors to Increase Inclusion Safety (Stage 1)

1. **Teach inclusion as a human need and right.** (T, I, M) Inclusion isn't something we earn; it's something we're owed. Teach your team members

to approach each other with the understanding that everyone is entitled to the human need to be included.

2. **Introduce yourself at the first opportunity.** (I) Be proactive to introduce yourself to those who are new or you don't know. Once you break the ice and display warmth and acceptance, people will believe they belong.
3. **Learn people's names and how to pronounce them.** (T, I, M) Nothing is more personal than a name. When a new person joins the team, learn their name immediately. If you don't know how to pronounce it, ask.
4. **Physically face people.** (I) Your job, whether you're speaking or listening, is to be actively engaged in that conversation. Face people directly and look them in the eyes. Without knowing it, you're communicating deep validation, value, and belonging.
5. **Listen and pause.** (T, I, M) Have you ever been talking to someone and you can tell that they're simply waiting for you to finish your sentence so they can jump in? Listen with intent to comprehend rather than the intent to respond. Do this by listening, pausing to reflect, and then responding thoughtfully.
6. **Ask twice as much as you tell.** (M) When you ask someone a question, it's an invitation to engage and a form of validation. Telling can be fine too, but if you tell too much, it's self-serving and it signals selfishness, arrogance, and dominance, all of which are off-putting.
7. **Conduct hop on, hop off tours.** (M) Have you ever done a tour on one of those hop on/hop off buses? Do the same thing when someone joins your organization. Have a personal guide give social tours to accelerate relationship-building. Make sure those interactions are meaningful enough to move the relationship beyond the acquaintance stage.
8. **Meet a person in their physical space.** (M) Don't make them come to you. This sends a clear message that you value them, their time, and their input because you are extending yourself on their behalf. People feel more comfortable to engage in their own space, which will lead to higher-quality interactions.
9. **Move to mutual discovery quickly.** (T) Ask your colleagues questions to discover their personal interests and find common ground. Don't probe into personal or sensitive topics—just ask natural questions about their

background and interests. Once conversation doesn't feel like an obligation, everyone will feel more included.

10. **Create deep bonding opportunities.** (T) When a new team member arrives, that individual needs warmth and civility to feel comfortable. Then you need to move from creating comfort to creating a real sense of belonging. Find projects that allow individuals to spend significant time together to develop inclusion.
11. **Avoid comparisons and competitions.** (T, I, M) We lose the ability to connect when we compare and compete with each other. Identify and recognize each person's talents and abilities and point them out. Celebrate others' strengths, especially when they are strengths you may not possess.
12. **Define and communicate the purpose and values of your team.** (M) To feel a part of the team, each member must understand why the team exists, how it works, and what it stands for. The team must first define its values, purpose, and goals and continuously communicate those things to team members.
13. **Identify negative bias.** (M) A bias is a preference for or against a human characteristic, individual, or group of people. As humans, we all have them. Sometimes they're hidden, and sometimes they're obvious. Periodically ask team members if they can identify any patterns of negative bias in the team, then act to remove them.
14. **Check alignment.** (M) Both the sense of belonging that each person feels and the sense of alignment the entire team feels are delicate and dynamic, not permanent. Pull members of the team aside informally and ask them how well they understand the vision, purpose, and goals of the team, and how committed they are to achieving them.
15. **Conduct frequent, brief touchpoints.** (M) Humans are hypersocial creatures, born to connect. Short, frequent interactions are far more effective than long but infrequent ones. It's the frequency that builds and strengthens the connection.
16. **Share your story, learn their story.** (T) Build rapport by sharing appropriate background and experiences about your life. Be the first to expose yourself emotionally. Then invite the other person: "Tell me your story."

17. **Don't flaunt perks or status symbols.** (M) You might have certain perks that come with your job title, like office size, parking privileges, or compensation structure. People are sensitive to differences and might assume they indicate who they can and can't interact with. There will always be differences. Just don't call undue attention to them.

18. **Forbid personal attacks.** (M) People make mistakes, fail, and often get things wrong, but that's never a justification for a personal attack. Your team members are still entitled to respect and the permission to participate. Call out any comment or behavior that could make a person feel marginalized or disrespected.

19. **Create opportunities to socialize outside of work.** (T) When we remove the work agenda from our conversations, we come to know and appreciate each other much better, which allows us to collaborate more effectively when we come back to work.

20. **Never hide behind title, position, or authority.** (M) Titles are just artifacts an organization gives you to get work done. Don't confuse them with your own identity. If you hide behind these things out of insecurity, it creates a barrier to inclusion.

21. **Avoid exclusive patterns of social interaction.** (I, M) Reach out to team members that you don't normally talk to. Do you interact with the same few people socially? What's keeping you from branching out? Be democratic with your time and attention. Make an effort to include people that aren't in your immediate circle.

22. **Respond to messages promptly.** (I) In part, the timeliness of your response communicates your respect for that person. Although there are times that justify a delayed response, try to respond promptly to those who message you. When you are consistent in your response pattern, you communicate inclusion.

23. **Avoid self-serving references to status.** (M) In any hierarchy, there are differences in roles and responsibilities. Sometimes we assume that those differences also determine our value and importance based on status. Make an effort to minimize those differences and create a feeling of equality between you and other team members.

24. **Control nonverbal cues.** (M) Your team members will read your body language as much as they listen to what you say. Be careful that you don't

send nonverbal cues that communicate exclusion. Examples include rolling eyes, fidgeting or drumming your fingers, looking bored, or allowing yourself to be distracted in the middle of a conversation.

25. **Follow through on small commitments.** (I) If you make a commitment, follow through, especially if it's a small one. Sweating the small stuff is an expression that you respect and value others.

26. **Use appropriate humor as a relief valve.** (I, M) When the pressure mounts and people are feeling the stress, look for ways to relieve that stress with humor. Using humor to point out silly or ironic things, or your own mistakes and inadequacies, can relieve pressure in a healthy way while still affirming the value of people.

27. **Ask about needs and challenges.** (M) Your team members probably won't say anything when they're experiencing a problem or challenge. Sometimes those needs are job-related. Other times, they are more personal. People often simply need to be asked before they open up and give you the opportunity to offer your support.

28. **Ask for feedback and help.** (I) When you run into a problem or challenge, don't be afraid to ask others for help. This does two things: First, it acknowledges the fact that you're human and you need help. Second, it gives others a legitimate opportunity to help you in a meaningful way.

29. **Express gratitude and appreciation.** (T, I, M) Your team members aren't included and excluded as members of your team on the basis of success and failure. When team members perform well, express genuine gratitude and appreciation. When they try hard but fail to meet their goals, recognize their efforts with empathy.

30. **Avoid digital addiction and overdose.** (I) We're flooded with ways to connect. Some bring a sense of real inclusion, while others leave us feeling alone. Ask yourself and the members of your team: Which connections leave you feeling depleted? Which connections leave you feeling energized with a real sense of inclusion?

31. **Reinforce inclusion daily.** (T) The sense of inclusion that people feel on a team is fragile. Even when it's not broken, it will fade away with time if it's not strengthened. The perishable nature of inclusion requires constant reinforcement. Talk about inclusion often, and make sure people know the concept is important to you.

Behaviors to Increase Learner Safety (Stage 2)

1. **Unite your team with learning.** (M) Learning is a highly individual process, but it can also be richly collaborative. It shouldn't be a divisive competition. Don't allow learning to divide people, pitting them against each other in unhealthy ways. Encourage everyone to participate in the learning process by demonstrating compassionate curiosity with each other.

2. **Adopt a student mindset.** (I, M) Use the word *student* with your team. Students approach learning with humility and consistency and avoid complacency and arrogance. Help them understand that although we may develop expertise, we're always learning and will never arrive at a place of permanent competency.

3. **Assess the learning style and temperament of each person.** (M) Each member of your team has a different learning approach and disposition, and your task is to understand what those are. Do this by observing each individual and asking them about their learning preferences.

4. **Help people one-on-one in their space.** (M) Some team members may be reluctant to "learn publicly" in a group setting. Work with them one-on-one in their space or in a neutral space that is comfortable to them. Your goal is to take away the inhibition and anxiety that they associate with learning.

5. **Share what you're learning.** (I) One of the most powerful ways to encourage others to learn is to share what you're learning. Share the topic, the insights, and, most importantly, the joy and satisfaction you have gained in the learning process. Your optimism and enthusiasm for learning is contagious.

6. **Invite your team to learn.** (M) Some members of your team will be aggressive in their learning habits, and others will be tentative. Sometimes all a person needs is an invitation to be a part of the learning process. Identify questions, problems, or challenges that you can give to your more tentative team members as learning assignments.

7. **Invite others to share their roles.** (M) Because people take pride in what they do, it's almost always true that they like to talk about their individual roles. Invite team members to explain their roles or share something they've

recently done in their role and how it influences other team members. Let your team learn from each other.

8. **Share past mistakes.** (I) It's hard to learn from mistakes if a team has a culture that hides its mistakes. Take the opportunity to mention some of your mistakes, laugh at them, and share what you learned from them. This will encourage others to be more comfortable sharing their mistakes, learning from them, and moving forward.
9. **Ask for help from those in different roles, especially of lower status.** (M) Model humility in learning by asking for help from those who work outside, or under, your role. This gives the other person the chance to teach and be helpful, which leads to increased confidence and engagement.
10. **Frame problems before you solve problems.** (T, I, M) Teach your team to frame problems before they solve problems. Otherwise, we often end up solving the wrong problem. Find a problem and say, "I'd like you to help me frame this problem, not solve it. I want to make sure I'm defining the problem correctly first."
11. **Reinforce learning potential.** (M) The learning potential of your team is unknown and unknowable. Consistently remind your team that to earn their living is to learn their living. Ask members of the team what new thing they learned during the week that they are now implementing in their work.
12. **Formulate questions.** (T, I) Asking thoughtful questions requires thought and preparation. In fact, it's part of the learning process itself. The next time you tackle a problem with your team, have them take ten minutes to formulate a set of questions to ask about the issue before you begin discussing the issue itself.
13. **Ask questions to activate learning.** (M) Asking a question is the activator that starts the learning process. When we ask a question, we catalyze the learning process for ourselves and those we're asking. Encourage team members to ask meaningful questions to push their thinking, skills, and experience.
14. **Implement rotating mentoring.** (M) Rotating mentoring is a system in which members of the team have a monthly forty-five-minute mentoring session with a different individual outside of the team. This provides a

concentrated learning opportunity for each member to learn from someone with a different perspective, skills, and experience.

15. **Share your personal learning goals.** (M) Set the example by setting and sharing your own learning goals with your team. Think about technical and nontechnical learning goals. Your example will often motivate other team members to set and pursue their own goals.
16. **Help team members set learning goals.** (M) Individuals learn more effectively and consistently when they have set clear goals about what they want to learn. Encourage your team members to set concrete and time-bound learning goals. Help them find goals that might be appropriate given their roles, responsibility, and aspirations.
17. **Explain formal versus informal learning.** (M) Most of the learning we do in life is informal. Once we finish any formal schooling, we spend very little time in structured learning environments. Help your team members understand that in the long run their personal informal learning habits will make all the difference.
18. **Identify and share what you unlearn.** (M) In a dynamic environment, our knowledge, skills, and experience can become obsolete. Identify the times when you see this happening to you. Point it out to others. Acknowledge that you are in a cycle of unlearning and relearning.
19. **Remove learning obstacles.** (M) Analyze your team's learning environment and identify any obstacles to the learning process. Maybe a team member needs the right colleagues or better resources. Determine how to enhance the learning conditions for each person on your team.
20. **Embrace quality feedback.** (I) Demonstrate a pattern of embracing quality, actionable feedback from any direction. Focus on the substance of the feedback, not the source. If it's worthwhile, let others see you embrace it. Even if it isn't, be gracious and appreciative to the person who gave it.
21. **Model an example of taking notes.** (I, M) Taking notes is perhaps the most obvious outward sign that a person is actively learning. Whether on paper or an electronic device, take notes. Capture facts, insights, and observations that you want to remember and ponder later. This habit will influence others to do the same.

22. **Ask for feedback at the moment of need.** (M) It's normal to encounter questions, problems, or challenges in the course of normal workflow. Unless there's an obvious solution, teach your team to engage in collaborative learning and formulate a learning response (not an answer) to the problem, and then ask a colleague to give feedback (not an answer).
23. **Provide unwavering support through the low points.** (M) As your team members progress through learning cycles, they will often encounter points of discouragement. When this happens, provide extra support to keep their efforts moving forward. Find evidence of progress that you can point out to them, however small they may be.
24. **Assign action learning projects.** (M) Assign a small group or subteam a real and meaningful problem to solve. Provide clear objectives, timelines, resources, and ground rules for solving the problem. Have the team present their recommendations in a formal setting. Adopt the suggestions if they make sense, and recognize those who participated.
25. **Celebrate failures.** (T, M) Failure is evidence that an individual is learning through trial and effort. As long as team members fail within defined limits, you should encourage this behavior. When a team member fails and learns from it, celebrate it. Destigmatize failure and create a culture where failure is seen not as an accident but as the way forward.
26. **Dedicate time and resources to learning.** (T, I, M) If you talk about the importance of learning but don't dedicate any time or resources to it, it's really not a priority. Formally allocate budget and dedicate time to learning. There's no perfect approach. Just make sure that you offer everyone consistent resources and time.
27. **Acknowledge that learning is "error-driven."** (M) If you aren't making mistakes, you aren't learning. Be intentional in how you talk about others' development and education, as well as your own. They aren't going to get it right the first time; that's how you know that learning is happening.
28. **Admit your ignorance and say, "I don't know."** (M) When we step out of our areas of competency, we often feel insecure. It's refreshing to your team if you can confidently acknowledge your ignorance in areas that go beyond your know-how. When you gracefully acknowledge your own limitations, others will learn without fear.

29. **Demonstrate patience and empathy.** (M) People often stop learning when they meet a harsh, critical, indifferent, or sarcastic response in the learning process. Avoid demeaning, belittling, or disrespectful response patterns that increase personal vulnerability and shut off the motivation to learn. Show empathy instead.
30. **Challenge your teams with hard problems.** (M) Customize the learning process based on the needs of each individual. For team members who are confident, capable, and aggressive learners, challenge them with hard problems they may have no idea how to solve. Check in regularly to provide appropriate coaching and guidance.
31. **Establish a book/video/podcast club.** (T) To create incentives for additional learning, create a book/video/podcast club and provide monetary and nonmonetary incentives for team members to consume content on topics that are relevant to the team's work. Have team members share their insights and lessons as they learn.
32. **Incorporate a daily learning segment.** (T, M) Learning doesn't have to take long. In fact, micro-learning segments can take as little as five minutes. Make it a habit to do short learning segments in your regular meetings. Rotate the assignment to teach among all team members.
33. **Communicate a vision of potential.** (M) People often can't see their potential. Help them see what they can become if they maintain a disposition for continuous learning. If they keep learning, their vision of themselves will catch up with the potential that you already see.
34. **Encourage the emotional side of learning to build confidence.** (M) The learning process is both intellectual and emotional. You can't pull them apart. A person's emotional state influences their desire and ability to learn. As a leader, encourage both the head and the heart to want to learn.
35. **Be a self-sufficient learner.** (I) It's crucial that you learn how to learn in informal settings. Never become dependent on an organization or other people to tell you what to learn, why, or how. Set an example of aggressive, self-directed learning by sharing your personal learning goals and plans.
36. **Teach the concept of learning agility.** (M) Learning agility is the ability to learn at or above the speed of change. If you emphasize and model this concept, you reduce the sense of risk your team members feel when they

engage in the learning process. They need to be convinced that not taking learning risks is a greater risk than taking them.

37. **Journal your learning observations.** (I) As you lead your team, you naturally observe their work patterns, but do you observe their learning patterns? Write down your observations. They'll serve as a benchmark and help you be more deliberate and purposeful in your efforts to enhance the learning patterns of your team.

Behaviors to Increase Contributor Safety (Stage 3)

1. **Rotate who conducts meetings.** (M) Traditionally, the leader conducts the meeting, but if you rotate that assignment, your team members will gain greater confidence to contribute. Giving them an assignment acknowledges their ability to do the job. Remember, you may need to coach them through the process.
2. **Clarify roles.** (T, M) More complexity requires greater teamwork, and more role ambiguity causes people to make assumptions about how to contribute. Clarify roles at the beginning to reduce both anxiety and ambiguity. You will need to do this periodically to ensure role clarity.
3. **Recognize accomplishment.** (I, M) Certainly, accomplishment is its own reward, but receiving genuine recognition from your peers makes it all the sweeter. As a leader, recognize the successes of your team quickly. Never delay or resent the opportunity to show genuine excitement for their accomplishments.
4. **Don't correct with anger, blame, or shame.** (M) Things won't always go right. Sometimes mistakes are due to complacency and carelessness. Even in that situation, don't correct with anger, blame, or shame. Even candid, corrective feedback can be given respectfully.
5. **Identify stall points.** (M) There are times when your team members don't know what to do or how to proceed, and they may be embarrassed to ask what to do. Notice when this happens. Rather than making them feel bad about it, engage with them and ask them what they think the next steps should be. Make it safe for them to be in this stalled situation.
6. **Celebrate small wins.** (T, I, M) Small wins increase confidence and build momentum. When your team members see a series of small wins, it creates

a sense of forward motion. Ultimate success may be a way off, but it's the small wins that fuel the team members' efforts to continue contributing at a high level.

7. **Shift from tell to ask.** (M) A leader's coaching continuum ranges from telling at one end to asking at the other. A good leader uses the entire continuum. Too much telling breeds dependency and learned helplessness. Shift as much as you can to the ask end. Lead through questions more than answers.
8. **Share your values.** (T, I) Your values define you and what's important to you. They always define the way you want to work. Share your values with your team and have them share theirs with you. This is the first important step in defining the ground rules and terms of engagement for a team.
9. **Share your workstyle and communication preferences.** (T, I) Beyond your values, share your workstyle and communication preferences with your team. Have your team members share theirs as well. The better you understand the preferences of your team members, the more effectively you'll be able to work together.
10. **Align work with passion.** (M) Passion is an intense desire or enthusiasm for something. Where do you find passion in what you do? Have your team members share the sources of their passion. To increase and sustain contribution, try to make work assignments that align with the individual passions of your team members.
11. **Create conditions for peak engagement.** (M) We've all had peak engagement experiences in professional life—times when we're in the groove and doing our best work. Have your team reflect on and share their peak engagement experiences, then work to create peak engagement conditions for each other.
12. **Set ground rules.** (M) After sharing your values, set practical terms of engagement with your team tied to your values. Once team members know the ground rules, they'll be more likely to engage because they know what's expected.
13. **Shape the experience.** (M) There are, of course, limits and constraints, but help shape the team experience for each member as much as you can. Customize, personalize, and tailor the experiences based on the individual's

preferences. There are often neglected opportunities to shape work and boost contribution.

14. **Give stretch assignments.** (I, M) Move your people out of their comfort zones. We build our capacity to contribute when we're stretched and out of our comfort zones. Don't stretch so much that it becomes destructive. Give your team members stretch assignments, but do it in a way that the exhilaration outweighs the discomfort.
15. **Avoid boredom and burnout.** (M) Boredom and burnout are the two ends of the engagement spectrum. Both are destructive and unsustainable. As a leader, it's your job to monitor the contribution of your team and help them avoid both. Encourage team members to work hard, reap the rewards, and find renewal in the process.
16. **Distinguish ability versus motivation problems.** (M) When contribution begins to lag, your first task is to understand why. Ask: Is this an ability problem or a motivation problem? Ability problems need increased skills, knowledge, and experience. Motivation problems need understanding, confidence, self-efficacy, and accountability.
17. **Paint the vision.** (M) A vision is a portrait of the future, a seedling of reality, a destination that hasn't yet been achieved. A compelling vision provides excitement, enthusiasm, and line-of-sight understanding that connects our personal contribution with a desired end state.
18. **Help others see their strengths.** (M) Many team members deliver mediocre performance because they don't realize their strengths. Identify your team members' hidden or undervalued strengths and bring them to each person's attention. This will ignite the desire to contribute more.
19. **Own your own contribution.** (T) Team members are responsible for their own contribution and have three options: (1) Accept what they've been given, (2) change and improve what they've been given, or (3) leave what they've been given. Emphasize that they'll have the direction, resources, and support they need, but your role is secondary.
20. **Give people the why.** (T, I) The strongest driver of engagement and performance is when we find meaning and purpose in the work we do. Team members often have a hard time connecting the work they're doing with a larger and more significant purpose. Help them understand that they're contributing to something worthwhile.

21. **Remove a sense of entitlement.** (I) The most entitled team members are generally not contributing all they could. Their sense of entitlement gets in the way and leads them to believe that others should be doing more for them. We owe each other psychological safety and are entitled to little else.
22. **Keep focused with trade-offs.** (T) Teams that lack a clear focus become confused, lose steam, and dilute their efforts. Keep your team focused by saying no to other options and priorities. Your success is based on the allocation of scarce resources, so protect your team's focus using strategic trade-offs.
23. **Make the team customer-centric.** (M) Every team has a customer. When a team loses sight of its customer, it often becomes careless, jaded, and cynical, and loses pride in its work and contribution. Keep the customer in front of the team. Communicate and collaborate with the customer's goals and satisfaction in mind.
24. **Let them do it their way.** (M) Human beings want to make a difference in their own unique way. Delegate with clear expectations and then get out of the way. Allow your team members the creativity and independence to approach things as they see fit. If you micromanage them, you will extinguish their motivation to contribute.
25. **Measure performance.** (M) When our contributions aren't measured, we get discouraged or lose interest in what we're doing. Make sure you have meaningful metrics for the areas of contribution that really matter. Keep in mind that you can discourage your team if you're measuring too many things, which causes you to lose a sense of priority.
26. **Approach failure with curiosity rather than criticism.** (M) When performance falters, it means our inputs are not producing the outputs we expected. When this happens, approach your team members with curiosity rather than criticism. Defuse the stress and emotional tension that often surrounds poor performance.
27. **Clarify the decision-making process.** (I, M) There are three basic ways to make a decision with a team: (1) unilateral, (2) collaborative, and (3) consensus. Ensure that your team members understand their roles in the decision-making process so they know how to contribute appropriately and confidently.
28. **Compliment participation from quiet team members.** (T) Some team members aren't comfortable participating in a formal group setting. And yet

the team needs their real-time input to solve problems and create solutions. Compliment and encourage that behavior without bringing too much attention to them.

29. **Avoid shutdown statements.** (M) Some team leaders use statements such as "bad idea," "nice try," or "I told you so." Those statements stem from ego and insecurity and quickly trigger team members' self-censoring instinct. Avoid statements that shut down rather than draw out your team members' discretionary effort.

30. **Report your own mistakes and errors.** (T, M) Leaders who share their mistakes are acknowledging what we all know—that humans make mistakes—and, by doing so, they earn deep trust with their teams and discourage them from hiding errors. Teams that follow this behavior can correct mistakes and increase contribution more quickly.

31. **Ask people what they think.** (M) Ask a team member, "What do you think?" Those four simple words invite contribution and increase confidence in the process. Don't say those words when you don't really mean it. At the same time, don't move to a decision or action without asking, even if you think you know the right answer.

32. **Check skills and resources.** (M) For your team members to contribute effectively, they'll need the skills and resources to do the job. It's your job to ensure that they can do their job. Sometimes, team members don't have the skills or resources to do the job even when there's a ready solution to solve the problem.

33. **Accept bad news.** (M) Bad news is part of every team's experience. Show your team that you want to hear bad news, because it's a measure of performance—and performance can't improve until the team knows and accepts where they are today. You may be disappointed, but express appreciation to those who bring bad news.

34. **Reward those who accept additional responsibility.** (M) Taking on additional responsibility means greater performance expectations and more stress. It also means the opportunity to make a greater contribution. Praise and reward your team members who take on more responsibility willingly. Help them recognize when they're taking on too much.

35. **Create outcome accountability.** (M) Accountability happens at three levels: (1) task, (2) process, and (3) outcome. Create a cultural expectation

that you want team members to move to outcome accountability and have maximum autonomy and ownership for what they do, how they do it, and the results they get.

36. **Teach the compounding principle.** (M) Often your team members may not think their contributions are amounting to anything. Help them understand that big contributions are incremental, and often you can't recognize their effects early on. Praise their consistent efforts, especially when there are no visible signs of success.

Behaviors to Increase Challenger Safety (Stage 4)

1. **Take your finger off the fear button.** (T, I, M) Fear triggers a self-censoring instinct that causes people to retreat into silence. When a leader uses fear, it's normally a punitive response borne of frustration and insecurity. More importantly, it's an abdication of leadership.
2. **Respond constructively to disruptive ideas and bad news.** (M) Your positive emotional response to disruptive ideas and bad news is a clear signal that you have a high tolerance for candor and will protect your people in their right to dissent.
3. **When you reject feedback, explain why.** (M) When you reject a team member's input or suggestion, explain why you didn't adopt it. Your considerate response will embolden the individual to continue giving feedback.
4. **Weigh in last.** (T, I, M) Speaking first when you hold positional power softly censors your team. Listen carefully, acknowledge the contributions of others, and then register your point of view.
5. **Encourage others to think beyond their roles.** (M) Inviting your people to venture out of their tactical and functional silos creates more opportunity for divergent thinking and allows them to connect things that aren't normally connected. Manage the process carefully and discern when constructive dissent is giving way to destructive derailment.
6. **Reward vulnerability.** (T, I, M) Remember, challenger safety must protect the individual and the team at the highest point of personal and interpersonal vulnerability. It's about generating and harnessing diverse perspectives (and even disagreement) without emotional escalation and destructive social friction.

7. **Challenge your own decisions.** (M) Leaders make decisions that are right today and then wrong tomorrow. Openly discuss some of the decisions that you've made to demonstrate that even correct decisions aren't correct forever. Help your team know that you are willing to revisit old decisions, courses of action, and points of view.
8. **Look for R.O.T.** (T, I) Everything we do eventually becomes obsolete. Every source of competitive advantage we have is temporary. Engage your team to look at the way you do things. Identify anything that is redundant, obsolete, or trivial (R.O.T.). These sources represent the low-hanging fruit of the status quo that needs to be dismantled.
9. **Teach deliberate versus emergent strategy.** (M) Deliberate strategy is the formal, long-term strategy that we are all familiar with. But when that deliberate strategy meets reality, it's riddled with flaws. Emergent strategy, on the other hand, is the process of adapting your strategy in real time in the context of a dynamic environment.
10. **Model the art of disagreement.** (T, I, M) Having challenger safety means that the members of your team can debate issues on their merits and find the best one without creating fear and interpersonal conflict. It's your job to teach them how to have marvelous disagreement to create this idea meritocracy.
11. **Share challenge experiences.** (T, I) You can't remove all of the risk associated with challenging the status quo, but you can eliminate much of it simply by sharing your own successful challenge experiences. Identify the best examples from your professional life and share them with your team at opportune times.
12. **Identify tangible and intangible sources of value.** (T, I) When we challenge the status quo, it means we have an idea about how to create more value, either tangible or intangible. Tangible value might come in the form of design, comfort, durability, or ease of use. Intangible value might come in the form of prestige, security, or reputation.
13. **Model vulnerability.** (I) Remember that vulnerability is exposing yourself to the possibility of harm or loss. If you model and reinforce a pattern of vulnerability, others will do the same.
14. **Reward shots on the goal.** (M) Reward your team members with recognition and enthusiasm when they attempt to challenge the status quo. Not

all ideas and suggestions will have merit, but if you encourage the attempts, those shots will increase.

15. **Mandate a no-interruption rule.** (M) As the leader, model and mandate a respectful and collaborative temperament and set of rules to make them everyday behaviors. Mandate a non-interruption rule in group discussions. That rule will empower team members with the respect and permission they need to challenge the status quo.
16. **Break before breakdowns.** (M) When interpersonal dynamics start breaking down, immediately take a break. Don't let social friction shut down intellectual friction. When the team gets tired, it's easy for social friction to increase. Take a break when you see this happen. Refresh the team before you come back together.
17. **Create diverse teams.** (M) Assign diverse people with diverse perspectives to work together on meaningful projects. Diverse teams possess cognitive diversity and naturally produce divergent thinking.
18. **Define what is in and out of scope.** (M) Define what can and should be challenged based on the team's defined scope of activity. This will avoid needless frustration that results when team members challenge out-of-scope or irrelevant issues.
19. **Identify and avoid defensive routines.** (M) Defensive routines are the things we do and say to avoid potential threats and embarrassment. Gain the team's permission to identify defensive routines at the earliest opportunity. This will help activate new behaviors that promote a higher tolerance for candor.
20. **Ask for bad news.** (M) This may seem counterintuitive, but asking for bad news is a way of speeding up the process of identifying areas for experimentation and innovation. When there's bad news, it allows us to challenge the status quo more easily because something is already broken or not working right.
21. **Tee up challenge-the-status-quo questions.** (M) Ask your team one challenge-the-status-quo question at the end of the day and have them ponder that question with the expectation of discussing it the next day. Hold a short meeting the next day and have each person share their thoughts.

22. **Praise quantity over quality in brainstorming.** (M) Research clearly shows that the best approach to brainstorming is to generate ideas rather than focusing on the quality of those ideas. Unconstrained thinking is the vehicle to the best solutions, so don't limit or constrain the process.

23. **Put a hypothesis on the table.** (T) Invite the members of your team to propose hypotheses—explanations about why things are the way they are. This is a healthy, apolitical way of putting an idea or challenge on the table.

24. **Protect your team from groupthink.** (M) When team members start to think alike, we call that groupthink. Team members worry more about fitting in with the group's conventional thinking instead of performing the hard labor of critical thinking. Say, "I don't want an echo chamber. What's another way to think about this?"

25. **Scan the environment for adaptive challenges.** (M) Teams and organizations have to respond to three kinds of adaptive challenges: (1) opportunities, (2) threats, and (3) crises. Opportunities offer potential benefit. Threats offer potential harm. Crises offer certain harm. Scan for each and determine how to respond.

26. **Identify inflection points.** (T) An inflection point is a turning point. Teams have the responsibility to identify, interpret, and respond to inflection points that might have an impact on what they do. Lead your team in a discussion to ask: What's beginning to change? What does it mean to us? What should we do about it?

27. **Engage in recombination.** (T) Challenges to the status quo often come as the natural result of connecting things that we don't normally connect. Hold a recombination session. Take one thing and combine it with a host of other things that you wouldn't normally think of connecting. Try some outlandish combinations just to see what happens.

28. **Hold a "do-nothing scenario" session.** (T) To put the status quo to the test, bring your team together and propose a do-nothing scenario: Think through the consequences of preserving the status quo instead of changing it. Mention both planned intended and proposed unintended consequences and show that keeping the status quo often presents a higher risk than changing it.

29. **Recognize patterns.** (T) Before we can challenge the status quo with a credible idea or suggestion, we need to identify a pattern of cause and

effect that we think we can improve. Teach the members of your team that they are in the pattern recognition business.

30. **Identify your status quo bias.** (M) A status quo bias favors what we believe is the right thing and the best way. When our status quo bias is strong, we stop looking for ways to improve things. Ask your team, "What would you do if there were no status quo and we could start fresh? How would you do it?"

31. **Come with half-baked questions and raggedy solutions.** (I) You've heard leaders say, "Don't come to me with questions. Come to me with solutions." That's nonsense. Encourage your team to come to you with unrefined thinking. If you expect polished and tested questions and solutions, be prepared to wait a long time.

32. **Respect local knowledge.** (M) When you talk to one of your team members, view them as the expert. They have access to local knowledge, context, experience, and relationships that you don't. Respect that local knowledge and be willing to solicit and circulate it throughout the team.

33. **Bring in outsiders.** (M) Even when you have diversity of thought in your team, it's typically within a narrow range. Bringing in outsiders can recharge your team with energy and fresh thinking. It can explode your assumptions and elevate your vision. It can push out the limits of what you believe is possible.

34. **Follow the disruption question sequence.** (M) An effective way to challenge the status quo is to use the disruption question sequence: Begin with a "why?" question. Move to a "what if?" question. End with a "how?" question. Model and teach the members of your team to implement this three-question process.

Conclusion

The Gutters of Paternalism and Exploitation

Just remember that your real job is that if you are free, you need to free somebody else. If you have some power, then your job is to empower somebody else.

—Toni Morrison

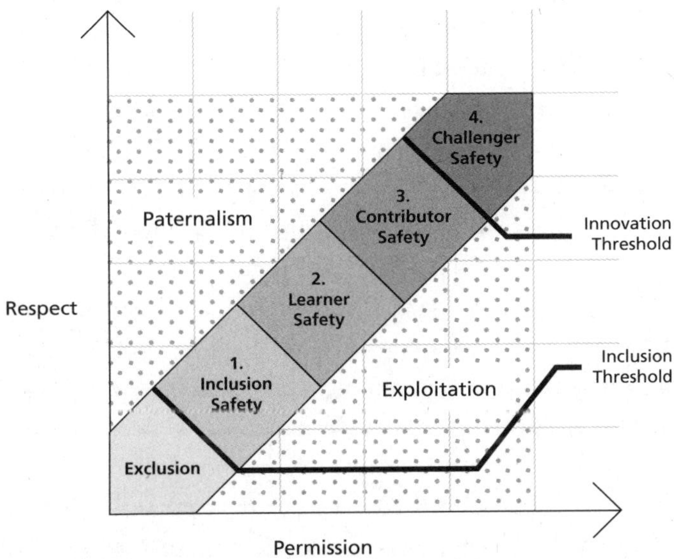

Figure 22. Paternalism and exploitation

In 1788, British Parliament passed the Chimney Sweepers Act to stop the practice of conscripting boys as young as four years old to be apprenticed to master chimney sweeps. As an early child-labor reform law, it gave expression to a moral position that employers had a responsibility to keep their employees safe, a concept that had been evolving from the time William Blake described England's "dark, satanic mills" and Charles Dickens called them "soot-vomiting."[241]

In time, the legal doctrine of *duty of care* emerged—the idea that people should take reasonable steps to avoid dangers, risks, and hazards. During the convulsions of the Industrial Revolution, however, *safety meant little more than not dying*. Today, as I've tried to make the case, it means helping others flourish by satisfying the Workplace Hierarchy of Needs: To be included and belong, learn and grow, choose and contribute, and challenge and improve the status quo.

While the primary hazard of past centuries was dying, the primary hazards of our day are paternalism and exploitation (figure 22). As we have discussed, psychological safety requires both respect and permission to participate. One without the other creates a dangerous imbalance that hurts people in different ways. A serious deficiency in permission pushes the team into the gutter of paternalism, whereas a serious deficiency in respect moves us into the gutter of exploitation. In either case, the organization lacks the motivation, confidence, and unit cohesion to perform at its best because the gutters of paternalism and exploitation flood the organization with fear. For example, paternalism's lack of permission creates paralysis and isolation. When you're constantly told what to do, you get used to it, becoming passive and unsure of yourself to the point that being self-reliant becomes a frightening prospect. *You seek comfort more than freedom, security more than independence.*

How can the social pressure to conform be stronger than the desire to express your opinions and make your own decisions?[242] Paternalism and exploitation hold the answer. Either you've been taught to be servile and compliant or you've been forced to be. I spent some time in Poland a few years after Eastern Europe had been liberated. As I met with men and women and toured several manufacturing plants, the lingering Soviet influence and long night of despotism revealed itself in stubborn patterns of paternalism and exploitation that wouldn't go away. Some people yielded to communist paternalism and were content to face a hopeless future. Others remained unbowed, shook off the chains of oppression, and were busy starting businesses and making things better.

In a similar way, exploitation's lack of respect creates the fear of harm in addition to the fear of isolation. Once when I was in Shanghai on business, the gentleman I was meeting with told me that he would hold confidential meetings on the street rather than in his office because he feared his office was bugged and that he was being monitored under the watchful eye of the government.

In both cases, paternalism and exploitation lack the balanced quantities of respect and permission that create psychological safety, leading individuals and organizations to perform below their potential. I interviewed a woman who had lived and worked under a repressive and autocratic regime in South America. "We were never allowed to be creative," she said. The patterns of paternalism and exploitation are universal, inhabiting every society and penetrating every culture. Let's take a closer look at each pattern.

The Gutter of Paternalism

Paternalism is telling you what to do, supposedly in your own best interest. A higher authority will supply your needs or regulate your behavior because it doesn't believe you can do it yourself.[243] Laws are the most common form of paternalism. You must be eighteen to vote. You must wear a seatbelt. You must not swim in a riptide. These are sensible measures, but let me give you some less enlightened examples of actual laws on the books: You can't pump your own gas, can't harass Bigfoot, can't eat fried chicken except with your bare hands, and can't walk backward after sunset.

We're often told that we need a benevolent parent, teacher, coach, or boss to protect us, manage our freedom, and direct our actions so we don't hurt ourselves or others, especially with fried chicken. There are certainly times when this sort of benign despotism is warranted. Remember my son who was practicing his driving to get his driver's license? He got it, and when we went to the Division of Motor Vehicles to pick it up, the woman who issued his license made it very clear to him that his parents had the right to revoke his license at any time. The power of paternalism is often good and necessary. It protects us until we are wise enough to protect ourselves and others.

Misguided paternalism means we're granting some respect to the individual but withholding the power to choose. There's a time and place for appropriate paternalism, but when it continues after the individual has demonstrated the ability to learn, contribute, or innovate without a lot of direction and guidance, it's time to back off. Not only that, it's time to listen, encourage, and empower the individual. When you're controlled by extrinsic motivation, you look outside yourself for punishments or rewards. You're stripped of autonomy and, in the process, an internal impetus to action. *Unnecessary paternalism runs the risk of breeding dependency and learned helplessness on the one hand and frustration and rebellion on the other.*

Higher education and health care are sectors marked by professionalism, competence, and a deep sense of collegiality. But these sectors are also more risk-averse than the private sector and typically have no established norm or process for pitching or testing new ideas. They tend to hang a Do Not Disturb sign, coalesce into a "make nice" culture, and lead from the gutter of paternalism.

I've worked with many universities, health-care organizations, and government agencies and consistently encounter this pattern. Health-care organizations are animated by a mission to extend life and do no harm, and yet most hospitals are dominated by broken authoritarian cultures no different from the one in my steel mill. Similarly, institutions of higher learning are dedicated to the mission of education and research and are inclined to be driven by consensus. The deeply ingrained sense of respect these institutions have for humanity is beyond reproach. Where they struggle, however, is in the way they grant permission to their members to learn, participate, and, most of all, innovate. Each sector is deeply entrenched in a tradition of glacial incremental change and paternalistic leadership. If you don't think paternalism is a liability in tumultuous times, consider that 138 institutions of higher learning in the United States have closed their doors or been consolidated since 2016.[244]

Rather than discourage people from challenging the status quo out of fear, these sectors tend to do it through neglect. They listen to ideas, tolerate debate, express appreciation for proposed disruptive courses of action, take it under advisement, and smile. And then not much happens. As a result, people don't self-censor out of fear; they simply leave out of frustration.

I helped lead an organizational transformation with a leading research hospital that lasted a year. On both the clinical and administrative sides of the house, we spent months putting together transition plans that would take the organization from its current state to a better one. We had long-term strategic plans, shorter-term tactical plans, and even shorter-term operational plans that included assignments, due dates, and other details. After all this preparation, the executive team came back and said, "We just don't think the organization is quite ready for the transition. We're going to think about doing it next year."

What this hospital learned was the lesson that most paternalistic leaders eventually learn: Paternalism is safe in the short term but grows dangerous in the long term. In your benevolence, you cut off the circulation of local knowledge that is flowing to you from the bottom of the organization, suffer the consequences of isolation, and find yourself in crisis later.

Health care, higher education, and government are good examples of paternalism, but it exists in every industry and sector. In most paternalistic societies, there's strong deference to authority and a desire to honor the past. People try to say yes to every request because they don't want to appear disloyal. Saying no is an unpopular answer, and no one wants to face social disapproval. Over time, paternalism leads to a low tolerance for candor and a lack of bravery. If the pattern becomes widely and deeply institutionalized, it compounds risk and often explodes in crisis.

Except for natural disasters, nearly every human crisis announces itself in advance. In paternalistic organizations, the warnings often go unheeded. Scandals and business failures don't come out of nowhere. But why would an organization repeatedly choose not to respond to early warning signs? Agile, alert organizations do respond. Lumbering, paternalistic ones don't.

The Gutter of Exploitation

Exploitation combines high permission with low respect. It tends to be motivated by the universal temptation toward despotism—the urge to control others for gain and gratification. *Whether personal or organizational, exploitation requires some type of repressive apparatus by which to extract value from humans, either by manipulation or coercion.*

Exploitation comes in degrees, but it is always based on the exploiter's allegiance to selfish ambition. James Madison reminded us in "Federalist Paper No. 10" that "enlightened statesmen will not always be at the helm."[245] Think of

Jack Ma, the founder of China's internet giant, Alibaba, and his promotion of what he calls the 996 work schedule: You work from 9 a.m. to 9 p.m., six days a week, with no overtime pay. Isn't it interesting that he frames it as a "philosophy" to give it more legitimacy? Similarly, my nephew recently finished a stint at a major investment bank and was required to work from 6 a.m. to 9 p.m. every day. Is there any concern for the needs of human beings in this case? No, it's the pure extraction of utility. The asymmetry in the way value is created and captured is the dead giveaway. When acquisition becomes an addiction, corporate chieftains tune their organizations based on a pure shareholder-return theory of the corporation.[246] That's the beginning and the end of their stewardship, which often leads to predatory tendencies toward employees.

Another example is the gender wage gap and the implicit bias that continues to sustain it. Aside from such prominent public or systemic examples, there are numerous everyday examples, and they can be very small and seemingly insignificant. For example, I worked with a team leader who was anxious for a promotion and would steal credit for the contributions of his colleagues.

What concerns me most is that people can become conditioned to accept exploitation, which leads to the normalization of abuse. Reflect on these words from the great Russian novelist Aleksandr Solzhenitsyn, "Peasants are a silent people, without a literary voice, nor do they write complaints or memoirs."[247] He may have been talking about another time and place, but the pattern is the same: When exploitation is permitted, people learn to accept it without complaint. Even those who are exploited can become defenders of the very exploitation they suffer. What makes it confusing, and therefore sustains it, is when leaders alternate acts of kindness and generosity with acts of violence, humiliation, harassment, bullying, and abuse. *Exploitation is the process of extracting value from another human being while disregarding that person's inherent value.*

In civil society, most forms of coercive exploitation are illegal and therefore less visible. Ironically, we have officially purged civil society of slavery, and yet human trafficking is at an all-time high, with an estimated forty million persons working in forced labor and servitude. But the most common forms of exploitation are not illegal, just immoral. They take the form of rudeness, unkindness, incivility, and abuse, and they exact a terrifying toll. Christine Porath and Christine Pearson, for example, show in their research that

98 percent of workers have experienced uncivil behavior at work. Half report being treated rudely at work at least once a week.[248]

Beware the Land of False Fellowship

I said in the preface that human beings long to belong. But that longing can be taken too far. When others prey on your need to belong, there comes a point when you must say adios, when it's far better to live without approval because that approval is feigned and destructive. As the philosopher C. Terry Warner has rightly observed, "Approval is held out as relief from this insecurity."[249]

At some point, we simply need to stop caring about what others think. If not, we become vulnerable to further exploitation, giving others the power to control or manipulate us, and turning us into victims. Social approval, belonging, and connectedness are needs. But no one really needs constant validation. If your most consuming fear is to be alone, you're easy prey to a shaming culture, and you would do well to pry yourself away from the social mirror. Do you always need an audience? Do you always need to be noticed? In the digital world, to be happy in your own company is a survival skill. When necessary, healthy rejection of popular opinion is a beautiful thing. *We crave attention, sometimes even if it's the wrong kind. Attention alone never satisfies, but it can deeply hurt.*

My son came home from middle school one day and was talking about how many followers his friends had on Instagram. He then proceeded to tell me that several of them use their parents' credit cards to purchase followers. As if that weren't alarming enough, he added that some of the parents encourage it. The like button has become an altar of worship.

If you want to be happy, you will sometimes need to politely disconnect to protect yourself. Anyone who thinks that their inherent worth will diminish if they don't have constant validation from others doesn't understand the meaning of *inherent*.[250]

Many people stand ready to shame you if you don't join their ranks, do what they do, think what they think, or wear what they wear. If your happiness depends on popular opinion, prepare to be unhappy.

A shaming culture demands compliance and hurls contempt on those who dare leave its company. In such a place, relationships are based on the reciprocation of flattery and false praise. In this self-imposed reality distortion field, we breathe fiction to our neighbors, and they to us. We feed on appearance and image, and drink the strong wine of self-deceit. If you live or work in such a congress of cowards, please remember that humans have always created social units where anyone is welcome and admission is free, but the truth is forbidden. You can be anyone you want to be except your true and authentic self.

In the land of false fellowship, members gain their sense of identity from the common sense of superiority they feel for themselves and the common sense of disdain they feel for others. Relationships are superficial and loyalty conditional. People enter those relationships to deflect the truth about themselves. *In the land of false fellowship, unnatural competition replaces natural affection.*

But what if you're already in the land of false fellowship? What if you're in a relationship you need to escape, enduring abusive treatment, tolerating destructive behavior? What do you do? First, understand that the other party will often try to convince you that you need them or that you must accept their treatment. Prepare for skillful manipulation or coercion. The control response is as predictable as the sunrise. As the Eagles song goes, "You can check out anytime you like. But you can never leave."[251] The truth is, you *can* leave.

If you're being exploited, abused, or harassed, you're being denied the respect and permission you're entitled to as a human being. If that's not going to change, give yourself inclusion safety. Sometimes that means standing alone, absorbing an economic loss, being misunderstood, or taking a hit to your reputation. In my own professional life, I've witnessed psychological terrorism at its worst and watched it demolish self-worth and drown initiative and creativity. I've worked with business associates who have been driven by greed and unbridled ambition and think it no crime to leave a wake of economic and emotional destruction behind them. There have been times when I was too trusting and didn't acknowledge the warning signs of ulterior motive and ill intent. We've all been scraped by an insecure leader, a cruel pretender, a small-time exploiter on the take. Sooner or later, we find ourselves swimming in a red zone, on the receiving end of hurt and humiliation.

As fellow travelers, we bump into each other. But when the hurt comes deliberately and continually, that's abuse. It's time to create boundaries and change the terms of engagement. I can't possibly address the vast ocean of human suffering, and I fully understand the threat of real danger. In my volunteer work, I've helped abuse victims in tragic circumstances and seen the wreckage that surrounds them. In the end, we can and must help ourselves.

Nobody is a nobody. Whether or not you're accepted, you're acceptable. If you're human, you're enough. But you must act to protect yourself. Here are some suggestions:

- Love yourself first. Give yourself inclusion safety—the respect and permission you inherently deserve. If others won't give you psychological safety, you must at least give it to yourself as you work to change your circumstances.
- Be alert to the motives of those around you. If you observe others acting maliciously toward you, even if it's mild, act early to confront the behavior or remove yourself from the situation.
- Don't believe that you must accept abusive treatment. That's a lie. Do everything in your power to protect yourself.
- Learn resilience in your resistance. As you work to liberate yourself from unhealthy treatment, fight back in healthy ways. Because of the hurt, anger, guilt, self-hatred, and anguish people suffer as a result of social and emotional persecution, they often resort to equally unhealthy response patterns. That just makes things worse. Avoid drugs and all forms of self-harm and self-indulgence. Don't heap more hurt on yourself.
- If you feel dominated, controlled, or trapped, with no apparent means of escape, search for a way out or leave immediately. In the meantime, refuse to entertain damaging thoughts about yourself. You can eventually heal and overcome everything.
- Find and connect with trustworthy, happy people who genuinely want your success and are willing to help. Consult with them as you make decisions and consider options.

Why Psychological Safety Terrifies Some Leaders

Some leaders bristle at the mention of psychological safety.[252] Why? Think about the definition: Psychological safety ensures that your acts of vulnerability will be rewarded, not punished. When leaders nurture it, teams flourish. When leaders neglect it, teams falter. Despite the transformative benefits of psychological safety, it puts insecure, mediocre, or poor leaders—and certainly imposters—to the test. As a leveling device, it redistributes influence. For leaders who feed on title and status, it threatens their positional power. For those lacking competence, it threatens their exposure. Let's consider how psychological safety causes alarm for leaders in these two camps.

Leaders Who Feed On Title and Status

Title, position, and authority are artifacts of power the organization grants to its leaders. We need hierarchy, a division of labor, and defined roles and responsibilities to function effectively and hold each other accountable to our commitments. Psychological safety, however, neutralizes authority bias, a central liability of hierarchy. We become more willing to debate issues on their merits, creating a genuine idea and skill meritocracy based on capability, not title.

That's wonderful—unless you're a leader who feeds on status, indulges in grandiosity, enjoys disproportionate privilege, or is addicted to the narcotic of power. The cultural anthropologist Ralph Linton's distinction between "achieved" and "ascribed" status helps us understand why some leaders shun equity and jealously guard their toxic cultures lacking in psychological safety.[253]

If your sense of identity as a leader is based on what you've accomplished through performance and effort, you have what Linton termed *achieved status*. You've worked hard to develop the competence necessary to get where you are. You welcome psychological safety because your sense of identity is tied more to your efforts and accomplishments than your status and position.

But if your sense of self is bound up in title, position, and authority—artifacts that give you what Linton called *ascribed status*—then anything that might reduce your stature and reputation based on those factors signals a threat. Leaders with ascribed status are resistant to sharing "their" stage of aggrandizement. They will try to protect privilege and consolidate power.

Leaders Who Try to Hide Their Incompetence

Some leaders shudder at psychological safety because it threatens to expose their incompetence. When psychological safety abounds, the mediocre leader no longer has the weight of position to hide their lack of skill or judgment.

Psychological safety shifts the focus from a power hierarchy to a competence hierarchy. It may not redistribute decision rights, but it does broaden and redistribute participation rights. In organizations with psychologically safe cultures, everyone has an opportunity to influence decisions and courses of action related to their areas of responsibility.

When it comes to finding the right solution, decision, or answer to a problem, psychological safety makes the power hierarchy more of an arbitrary distinction. The best ideas win when they don't yield to power, but power yields to them. Psychological safety offers those with diverse perspectives the opportunity to share their opinions without fear of retribution.

The less competent a leader is, the more likely they will be to exercise control through fear, intimidation, shame, or manipulation. Conversely, the more effective the leader, the more that leader will genuinely listen, collaborate effortlessly, and lavish credit on others rather than hoard it themselves.

Sixty Billion Interactions Every Day

The world's population is fast approaching eight billion. Every day those nearly eight billion people have sixty billion interactions with each other. Each one of those interactions either nourishes or neglects human potential. We either affirm each other or we don't. In each interaction we extend a measure of respect and permission, which determines a certain level of psychological safety.

The more we create psychological safety, the more we allow each other to satisfy the Workplace Hierarchy of Needs. The less we create it, the more we suffer the bitterness and sting of splendid isolation.

As we scan the history of our species, on balance, we see a species technologically advanced and sociologically primitive. We seem to be stuck in an existential fog in which the complex social matrix in which we live our lives is our biggest challenge. We alone are responsible for the antagonisms we create among ourselves, yet we continue to shed emotional blood—not just occasionally, but constantly. Are we medieval? Have we not ripened in wisdom?

Psychological safety is built on a moral foundation of looking upon our fellow creatures with respect and giving them permission to satisfy their basic human needs. At the same time, we must judge each other's skill and performance. We're all accountable. But when it comes to worth, people are owed respect because they're people. The moment we begin to devalue, objectify, or dehumanize each other, we forsake humanity.

Don't tell me you have a company to run or results to deliver. Don't tell me you're important. Don't tell me this is high stakes, or you're under pressure, or you have your triggers, or you're prone to grown-up meltdowns. If you make any excuse for not extending psychological safety, you're choosing to value something else more than human beings. Consider, for example, the thirty-five employees at France Télécom who took their own lives as a result of relentless and systematic harassment.[254] Rather than creating a supportive, humanistic workplace, the leaders dehumanized their lower-ranking colleagues with institutionalized oppression, leading to tragic consequences.

We can give ourselves warm baths of self-satisfaction and blame our poor behavior on personality, work style, pressure, stress, anxiety, deadlines, or a disadvantaged past. Welcome to the human race. We don't get a pass for those things. Remember, we can't claim special status. But isn't that what we're doing when we refuse to extend psychological safety to another person? So is hiding behind the guise of tolerance or political correctness only to excoriate those who don't share our values or agenda.

Harvard's seventy-five-year study of human happiness, which is now in its fourth generation, has identified what we already know intuitively: As the grant study's director, Robert Waldinger, summarizes, "The clearest message that we get from this 75-year study is this: Good relationships keep us happier and healthier."[255] In the end, it's connection that brings us sustained happiness. With its restorative and healing powers, cultivating relationships is the one nonpharmaceutical therapy, the one redemptive act, that continues to bring us the most joy.

A Swelling Demand for Leaders Who Create Psychological Safety

When I say the words *human potential*, what comes to mind? How do those words make you feel? Think about the potential of those around you—your family, friends, neighbors, classmates, coworkers. Ironically, whether or not you care about their potential, you have an impact on it, and others have a profound impact on yours. The people you spend the most time with are the ones you influence the most. But even those you rarely see, even those with whom you may have had only a chance encounter, may be profoundly affected by your influence. Even a few words can change a life. Through our interactions, we cultivate or crush potential. Which always brings us back to the concept of psychological safety.

In the days ahead, you will see a swelling demand for leaders who create a high level of psychological safety on their teams and in their organizations. This demand is the natural consequence of competing in a highly dynamic environment that relies on constant innovation. It's also the natural consequence of highly intelligent people who've had one too many bosses dripping with ego and control issues. *At an individual level, we need personal fulfillment and happiness. At an organizational level, we need innovation and a sustained competitive advantage.*

In fact, we're starting to see the beginning of a sea change in how many of the best organizations in the world choose their leaders. It's counterintuitive to the conventional thinking that a leader must be a charismatic, hard-driving repository of vision and answers. In fact, the traditional archetype of a leader, forged on the imperial model of leadership, abundant with hubris and advocacy skills, is fast becoming an occupational hazard. The primary characteristic of this new variety is an individual who possesses superb emotional intelligence with a highly controlled ego.

A growing body of research confirms that emotional intelligence creates psychological safety in the organization, which, as a mediating variable, accelerates innovation. In hypercompetitive markets, innovation is the lifeblood of survival and the mainspring of growth. Thus, the leader of the twenty-first century must be able to thrive in this context as an example of collaboration, creative abrasion, and humility.

The industrial concepts of command and control on the one hand and benevolent paternalism on the other are dying an ignominious death because they activate the self-censoring instinct and shut down the ability to innovate. If we don't cultivate a higher tolerance for candor, we can't convince people to release their discretionary efforts. They're already hypervigilant to any threat. So the single most important question in the selection of a leader is fast becoming this: Does the individual create or destroy psychological safety and therefore stimulate or stifle innovation?

Pluralism is our reality. In our hierarchy of loyalties, let's think above personal and tribal differences and enshrine our central tie, the allegiance and affinity that matters most: the bond of belonging to the human family. Let me return to the call to action I issued at the beginning of the book. I invited you to conduct a searching personal inventory about the way you behave toward others, especially those who are strangers or against whom you have a lingering bias or prejudice.

1. **Inclusion safety:** Are you prepared to cross the threshold of inclusion, bridge differences, and invite others into your society?
2. **Learner safety:** Are you prepared to encourage others to learn and grow?
3. **Contributor safety:** Are you prepared to give others choice and the opportunity to contribute?
4. **Challenger safety:** And finally, are you prepared to cross the threshold of innovation and provide air cover for others to challenge the status quo and innovate?

To conclude, let me share an ancient case study in psychological safety. Regardless of your religious or metaphysical persuasion, the story is awesomely powerful. In the New Testament, in the book of Acts, Peter, a Jew, is taken to Cornelius, a Roman centurion. Peter had grown up with the understanding that non-Jews were common or unclean. He had lived his entire life in a segregated society based on this paradigm and prejudice. Yet when Peter encounters Cornelius, he says, "Ye know how that it is an unlawful thing for a man that is a Jew to keep company, or come unto one of another nation; but God hath shewed me that I should not call any man common or unclean."[256]

Alexander the Great allegedly remarked that there were "no more worlds to conquer." There is at least one—the inclination to conquer itself.

The greatest source of fulfillment in life comes from including others, helping them learn and grow, unleashing their potential, and finding deep communion together. "Wherever the barriers to the free exercise of human ingenuity were removed," the economist Friedrich von Hayek argues, "man became rapidly able to satisfy ever widening ranges of desire."[257] That's the lesson. Now look around and see others with fresh amazement.

Conclusion Summary

- **Modern hazards:** Today's cultural risks are the gutters of paternalism (low permission) and exploitation (low respect).
- **Fear imbalance:** Both patterns create fear that suppresses identity, motivation, confidence, and performance.
- **Paternalism:** This gutter grants respect but withholds autonomy, producing dependency, passivity, and learned helplessness.
- **Exploitation:** This gutter grants autonomy but withholds dignity, extracting value while disregarding human worth.
- **False fellowship:** Weaponizes belonging through conformity, flattery, image, and shame. Unnatural competition replaces natural affection.
- **Leader insecurity:** Psychological safety threatens status-dependent or incompetent leaders by exposing weakness.
- **Redistributed influence:** Psychological safety shifts emphasis from hierarchy to merit, capability, and contribution.
- **Moral foundation:** Respect is owed because people are people, and every interaction either cultivates or crushes potential.
- **Leadership shift:** Modern environments demand emotionally intelligent leaders who elevate candor, inclusion, and innovation.
- **Core test:** The defining question is whether a leader creates or destroys psychological safety.

Acknowledgments

I pay special tribute to my wife, Tracey, who models and rewards vulnerability and practices unfeigned love toward all human beings. She is a living example of one who has mastered the art of creating and maintaining psychological safety. I'm grateful to Neal Maillet, the editorial director at Berrett-Koehler. He is both candid and kind. He brings creative abrasion and genuine personal concern that motivate me to give my very best efforts. I also thank the entire Berrett-Koehler team and appreciate the distinctive culture of collaboration they have created for me as an author. I'm thankful for the craftsmanship of Rachel Monaghan, Maureen Forys at Happenstance Type-O-Rama, and Ashely Ingram (cover design), and to Dr. Sajid Ali for his assistance with quantitative analysis. To my team at Leaderfactor, I express profound appreciation for the quality of their execution and innovation as we support organizations around the world in their cultural transformation journeys. Finally, I thank my children for relentlessly challenging the status quo and helping us love and serve each other better!

APPENDIX

Empirical Validation of the 4 Stages Model

This appendix provides a comprehensive quantitative validation of the proposed 4 Stages model. Building upon the qualitative and theoretical foundations of the framework, the analysis empirically examines whether individuals follow a predictable behavioral sequence when entering new organizational settings. Specifically, the study investigates whether participants naturally prioritize inclusion first, learning second, contribution third, and challenging and improving the status quo fourth. We sought to answer the following two research questions:

- **Research question 1:** Do individuals follow the hypothesized sequential order (Inclusion → Learner → Contributor → Challenger) when engaging in new team settings in the workplace?
- **Research question 2:** Does the randomized display order of the four stages influence participants' selection bias?

In our PSindex® survey, we gathered responses from 3,366 employees in more than twenty organizations around the world and asked this question:[258]

If you were assigned to work with a new team at work, in what order would you engage in the following activities:

1. *Meet and get to know the members of the team.*
2. *Learn my role.*
3. *Contribute and add value.*
4. *Challenge the way things are done.*

Note that this question measures the self-reported perceived order of importance of these behaviors rather than actual observed behaviors. To ensure methodological rigor, the order of stage presentation was randomized across respondents to eliminate potential response bias. The analyses, therefore, serve two purposes: (1) to determine whether participants' selections follow the hypothesized sequential order, and (2) to assess whether the randomized display order influenced their responses. Descriptive statistics, Friedman and Wilcoxon nonparametric tests, and Spearman rank correlations were applied to address the study's research questions. These analyses examined the sequential validity of the 4 Stages of Psychological Safety model and tested whether the randomized display order influenced participants' stage selections.

Descriptive Analysis of Participants' Stage Selection Patterns

Descriptive statistics were used to examine how participants ordered the 4 Stages of Psychological Safety. Frequencies and percentages were calculated for each stage across the four selection positions. The results reveal a clear sequential pattern, with the majority of participants assigning inclusion as the first stage, followed by learner, contributor, and challenger in subsequent positions. This consistent ordering across participants reflects a systematic behavioral progression from social belonging to learning, contribution, and, ultimately, confident challenge.

The frequency distribution provides a clear empirical pattern in how participants prioritize stages of psychological safety when entering a new work setting (see table 10). Results from stage 1, which captures participants' *first behavioral preference*, reveal that a substantial majority (65.1 percent) indicated inclusion as their initial stage of engagement. This was followed by learner at 30.6 percent, contributor at 3.2 percent, and challenger at only 1.1 percent. This ordering demonstrates that most individuals seek belonging and connection before attempting to learn, contribute, or challenge existing norms within a new team environment. Please note that percentages are row percentages and may not sum to 100 due to rounding.

Table 10. Cross-tabulation of stages of psychological safety by selection order (*N* = 3,366)

Actual stage	**1st selection *n***	**1st selection %**	**2nd selection *n***	**2nd selection %**	**3rd selection *n***	**3rd selection %**	**4th selection *n***	**4th selection %**	**Dominant stage position**
Inclusion	2190	**65%**	977	29%	136	4%	63	2%	1st (65%)
Learner	1031	31%	2116	**63%**	138	4%	81	2%	2nd (63%)
Contributor	107	3%	231	7%	2713	**81%**	315	9%	3rd (81%)
Challenger	38	1%	42	1%	379	11%	2907	**86%**	4th (86%)

Results from stage 2, which represents the activity participants identified as their second behavioral step in a new team setting, indicate that the majority of respondents (62.9 percent) selected learner safety—that is, the desire to understand one's role and develop competence as the second stage of engagement. This was followed by inclusion (29.0 percent), contributor (6.9 percent), and challenger (1.2 percent). The dominance of learner safety at this stage shows that, after achieving a sense of belonging, participants naturally prioritize learning and skill acquisition before seeking to contribute or challenge existing norms.

Findings from stage 3 show that the vast majority of respondents (80.6 percent) selected contributor safety, the willingness to add value and contribute, as their third step when integrating into a new team environment. Far fewer participants identified challenger safety (11.3 percent), inclusion safety (4.0 percent), or learner safety (4.1 percent) as their third stage. This clear dominance of contributor safety indicates that, after experiencing inclusion and engaging in learning, most individuals naturally progress to a phase where they feel safe to demonstrate competence and autonomy by contributing to the group's goals.

Results from stage 4 indicate that the overwhelming majority of respondents (86.4 percent) selected challenger safety, a willingness to advocate for constructive change, as the fourth and final stage in their behavioral sequence. In contrast, only 9.4 percent identified contributor safety, 2.4 percent selected learner safety, and 1.9 percent chose inclusion safety at this stage. This clear concentration at the challenger level suggests that participants generally perceive challenging the status quo as the final need category they wish to satisfy, and requiring the other three need categories to be satisfied, at least to some threshold degree.

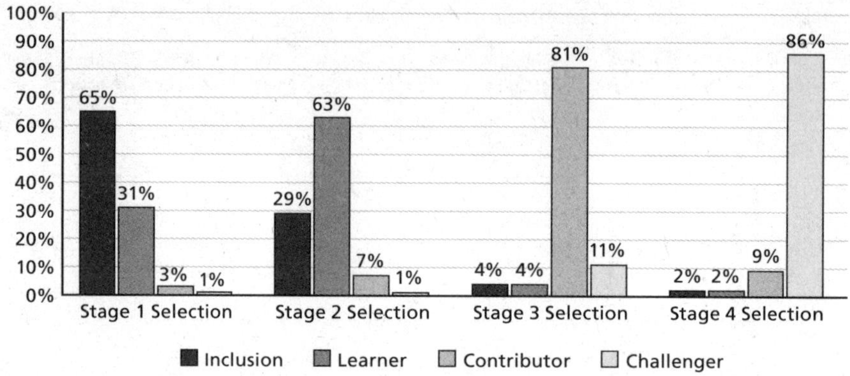

Figure 23. Sequential distribution of participants across the 4 Stages

Figure 23 illustrates the percentage of participants who selected each stage of psychological safety—inclusion, learner, contributor, and challenger—at each step in their behavioral sequence. The pattern reveals a distinct and orderly progression consistent with the proposed theoretical model. Specifically, 65 percent of respondents selected inclusion as their first step, followed by 63 percent selecting learner as the second, 81 percent selecting contributor as the third, and 86 percent selecting challenger as the final stage. The figure illustrates a pronounced progression consistent with the theoretical model.

Inferential Validation of the Sequential Model

The Friedman test was used to determine overall differences in ranking among the stages, followed by Wilcoxon signed-rank tests to assess pairwise differences between consecutive stages. These inferential analyses evaluate the sequential validity of the proposed model by testing whether participants' mean ranks systematically increase from the first to the final stage.

A Friedman test was conducted to examine whether participants' rankings of the 4 Stages of Psychological Safety differed significantly in their mean rank order (table 11). The test yielded a highly significant result, $\chi^2(3, N = 3366) = 7357.81$, $p < .001$, indicating that participants did not assign equal importance or sequence to the four stages. The observed mean ranks followed a clear ascending pattern: inclusion ($M = 1.43$), learner ($M = 1.78$), contributor ($M = 2.96$), and challenger ($M = 3.83$). This pattern strongly supports the hypothesized sequence in which individuals first seek inclusion and learning

Table 11. Mean ranks and Friedman test of differences among stage rankings

Stages	Mean rank	Chi-square	df	Asymp. sig.	Kendall's *W* (effect size)
Inclusion	1.43	7357.809	3	<.001	0.73
Learner	1.78				
Contributor	2.96				
Challenger	3.83				

Note. Lower mean rank indicates earlier behavioral prioritization.

opportunities before progressing toward contribution and ultimately challenging the status quo. Kendall's $W = .73$ indicates a strong degree of agreement among participants in the relative ordering of the stages.

Taken together, these results provide strong descriptive support for the hypothesized four-stage progression model (inclusion → learner → contributor → challenger). The data suggest that individuals naturally begin by seeking inclusion and social acceptance before advancing to learning and contribution, and only later, once safety and confidence are established, do they move toward challenging the status quo.

The Wilcoxon signed-rank test was used to assess whether there's a meaningful difference between how people ranked two consecutive stages (table 12). Results revealed significant pairwise differences between all adjacent stages:

- Learner versus inclusion: $Z = -18.22$, $p < .001$
- Contributor versus learner: $Z = -43.70$, $p < .001$
- Challenger versus contributor: $Z = -44.24$, $p < .001$

In each case, the median rank of the latter stage was higher, confirming a statistically reliable progression through the four stages.

Table 12. Wilcoxon signed-rank pairwise comparisons between consecutive stages

Comparison (paired stages)	*Z*-value	Asymp. sig. (2-tailed)	Direction of difference
Learner – inclusion	–18.22	**< .001**	Learner > inclusion
Contributor – learner	–43.70	**< .001**	Contributor > learner
Challenger – contributor	–44.24	**< .001**	Challenger > contributor

The results show that participants clearly moved through the stages in a step-by-step manner. Each stage was ranked significantly higher than the one before it, meaning people naturally began by seeking inclusion, then focused on learning, followed by contributing, and finally felt confident to challenge. This confirms that individuals seek to meet their workplace needs in a predictable order.

Validation of Randomization: Testing for Display-Order Bias in Stage Selection

To determine whether the randomized display order of the four stages influenced participants' selection sequence, a series of Spearman rank correlation analyses were conducted. This analysis compared the rank position in which each stage was displayed with the rank position in which it was subsequently selected by participants. The purpose was to verify whether the randomization procedure successfully mitigated potential order bias in participant responses.

Results revealed statistically significant *p*-values for all four stages (table 13). Associations between display order and selection order were statistically significant but trivially small, indicating no practically meaningful display-order effects. However, the corresponding correlation coefficients were extremely small, ranging from $r = .043$ to $r = .072$. Specifically, inclusion ($\rho = .055, p = .001$), learner ($\rho = .052, p = .003$), contributor ($\rho = .072, p < .001$), and challenger ($\rho = .043, p = .014$) all exhibited negligible effect sizes. Although these associations reached statistical significance, this outcome is attributable primarily to the large sample size ($N = 3{,}366$) rather than to a meaningful relationship between variables.

Table 13. Spearman rank correlations between display order and selection order for each stage

Stage of psychological safety	Mean selection rank	Mean display rank	Spearman's ρ	*p*-value	Interpretation
Inclusion safety	1.43	2.48	0.055	0.001	No meaningful relationship
Learner safety	1.78	2.51	0.052	0.003	No meaningful relationship
Contributor safety	2.96	2.52	0.072	< .001	No meaningful relationship
Challenger safety	3.83	2.48	0.043	0.014	No meaningful relationship

In substantive terms, the results indicate that there is no noticeable relationship between the display order of stages and the order in which participants selected them. This finding demonstrates that the randomization strategy effectively eliminated any display-order bias, confirming that participants' stage selections reflected genuine psychological sequencing rather than experimental artifact. Hence, participants consistently followed the hypothesized progression (inclusion → learner → contributor → challenger) even when the stages were presented in varying orders. This provides further evidence that the observed pattern represents an authentic and cognitively grounded behavioral sequence rather than a response bias induced by item presentation.

Summary of Findings

The quantitative analyses collectively provide strong empirical support for the proposed 4 Stages of Psychological Safety framework. Descriptive results revealed that participants predominantly followed the hypothesized sequence—beginning with inclusion, followed by learner, contributor, and finally challenger safety. Nonparametric analyses (Friedman and Wilcoxon tests) confirmed statistically significant differences among stage rankings, demonstrating that participants consistently perceived each stage as a distinct and progressive step in developing psychological safety. Additionally, the Spearman correlation analyses showed no meaningful relationship between the randomized display order and participants' selection order, confirming that the randomization procedure effectively prevented order bias. Taken together, these findings validate the sequential structure of the model and affirm that the observed order of responses reflects authentic behavioral tendencies rather than artifacts of survey design.

Limitations

These findings should be interpreted in light of several limitations. First, responses are based on self-reported, hypothetical sequences rather than observed behavior over time in actual teams. Second, the survey used single ranked items to represent each stage, which limits assessment of reliability. Third, the sample, while large, may not be fully representative of all industries and cultures. Future research using longitudinal and multimethod designs could test how closely these perceived sequences match real behavioral trajectories.

Notes

1 Albert Bandura, *Social Learning Theory* (Prentice-Hall, 1977), 22.

2 Kurt Lewin, Ronald Lippitt, and Ralph K. White, "Patterns of Aggressive Behavior in Experimentally Created Social Climates," *Journal of Social Psychology* 10, no. 2 (1939): 271–299.

3 Margaret Mead, *Coming of Age in Samoa: A Psychological Study of Primitive Youth for Western Civilisation* (William Morrow, 1928), 17.

4 Clifford Geertz, *The Interpretation of Cultures* (Basic Books, 1973), 49.

5 Edmondson has argued that psychological safety is a "shared belief that the team is safe for interpersonal risk taking." Our PSindex® survey shows wide variation in individual perceptions of psychological safety at a team level, and no evidence that the concept is necessarily a shared belief. See Amy C. Edmondson, "Psychological Safety and Learning Behavior in Work Teams," *Administrative Science Quarterly* 44, no. 2 (1999): 354.

6 As a newcomer, my experience was overflowing with change, contrast, and surprises of all kinds. See Meryl Reis Louis, "Surprise and Sense-Making: What Newcomers Experience in Entering Unfamiliar Organizational Settings," *Administrative Science Quarterly* 25, no. 2 (1980): 227–251.

7 C. Wright Mills, *The Power Elite*, new edition (Oxford University Press, 1956, 2000), 9.

8 Robert Conquest, *History, Humanity, and Truth: The Jefferson Lecture in the Humanities* (Hoover Institution Press, 1993), 7.

9 Immanuel Kant made the precursor argument that civil freedom enables intellectual freedom. See Hans Reiss, ed., *Kant: Political Writings* (Cambridge University Press, 2010), 59.

10 "If any human emotion is as old as our species it must, surely, be fear, and the end of its hold on us is not in sight." David Scruton, ed., *Sociophobics: The Anthropology of Fear* (Westview Press, 1986).

11 American Psychological Association, *2024 Work in America Survey: Psychological Safety in the Changing Workplace* (APA, 2024).

12 Steven W. Cole, "The Conserved Transcriptional Response to Adversity," *Current Opinion in Behavioral Sciences* 28 (2019): 31–37, cited in Sheldon Cohen, *Psychosocial Pathways Linking Affective States and Physical Health* (Oxford University Press, 2020), 268.

13 See Naomi I. Eisenberger et al., "An Experimental Study of Shared Sensitivity to Physical Pain and Social Rejection," *Pain* 126, nos. 1–3 (2006): 132–138; Naomi I. Eisenberger and Matthew D. Lieberman, "Why Rejection Hurts: A Common Neural Alarm System for Physical and Social Pain," *Trends in Cognitive Sciences* 8, no. 7 (2004): 294–300; Naomi I. Eisenberger,

Matthew D. Lieberman, and Kipling D. Williams, "Does Rejection Hurt? An fMRI Study of Social Exclusion," *Science* 302, no. 5643 (2003): 290–292.

14 See Albert O. Hirschman, *Exit, Voice, and Loyalty: Responses to Decline in Firms, Organizations, and States* (Harvard University Press, 1970).

15 W. Edwards Deming, *Out of the Crisis* (Massachusetts Institute of Technology, Center for Advanced Engineering Study, 1982), 125.

16 Maya Angelou, *Wouldn't Take Nothing for My Journey Now* (Random House, 1993), 81.

17 Jake Herway, "How to Create a Culture of Psychological Safety," *Workplace*, December 7, 2017.

18 Langston Hughes, *Selected Poems of Langston Hughes* (Vintage Classics, 1959), 20.

19 Hannah Arendt, *Men in Dark Times* (New York: Harcourt, Brace & World, 1968), 4.

20 Thomas Hobbes, *Leviathan*, in *The Harvard Classics: French and English Philosophers: Descartes, Rousseau, Voltaire, Hobbes*, ed. Charles W. Eliot (F. F. Collier & Son, 1910), 385.

21 Rowan Williams, address to Wheaton College Theology Conference, April 6, 2018, video, 49:13.

22 Robert Livingston, *The Conversation: How Seeking and Speaking the Truth about Racism Can Radically Transform Individuals and Organizations* (Currency, 2021), 91.

23 Matthew Stewart, "The 9,9 Percent Is the New American Aristocracy," *The Atlantic*, June 2018.

24 W. B. Yeats, "The Circus Animals' Desertion," in *The Collected Poems of W. B. Yeats* (Macmillan, 1956), 389.

25 See Jacob Cohen, *Statistical Power Analysis for the Behavioral Sciences*, 2nd ed. (Lawrence Erlbaum Associates, 1988), 79–81; Frank L. Schmidt and John E. Hunter, *Methods of Meta-Analysis: Correcting Error and Bias in Research Findings*, 3rd ed. (Sage Publications, 2015), 35–38; Robert Rosenthal and Ralph L. Rosnow, *Essentials of Behavioral Research: Methods and Data Analysis*, 3rd ed. (McGraw-Hill, 2008), 521–522. I include four different coefficients, r, β, r, and ρ, which are complementary but not interchangeable measures of association. In all cases, a coefficient of .30 or greater indicates a moderate effect, and .50 or higher indicates a strong relationship.

26 ($r = .54$). Michael J. Kerrissey et al., "How Psychological Safety and Feeling Heard Relate to Burnout and Adaptation During Uncertainty," *Health Care Management Review* 47, no. 4 (2022): 308–316.

27 ($r = .68$). Emil Viduranga Mogård, Ole Bendik Rørstad, and Henning Bang, "The Relationship between Psychological Safety and Management Team Effectiveness: The Mediating Role of Behavioral Integration," *International Journal of Environmental Research and Public Health* 20, no. 1 (2023): 406.

28 ($r = .31$). D. Cai, "Improving the Agility of Employees through Enterprise Social Media: The Mediating Role of Psychological Conditions," *Information & Management* 55, no. 8 (2018): 103–114.

29 ($r = .87$). Kathryn C. Adair et al., "The Psychological Safety Scale of the Safety, Communication, Operational, Reliability, and Engagement (SCORE) Survey: A Brief, Diagnostic,

and Actionable Metric for the Ability to Speak Up in Healthcare Settings," *Journal of Patient Safety* 18, no. 6 (2022): 513–520.

30 (β = .59). Natsu Sasaki et al., "The Survey Measure of Psychological Safety and Its Association with Mental Health and Job Performance: A Validation Study and Cross-Sectional Analysis," *International Journal of Environmental Research and Public Health* 19, no. 16 (2022): 9879.

31 (ρ = .46). Mary L. Frazier et al., "Psychological Safety: A Meta-Analytic Review and Extension," *Personnel Psychology* 70, no. 1 (2017): 113–165.

32 (β = .37). Holly Bahadurzada, Amy C. Edmondson, and Michael J. Kerrissey, "Psychological Safety as an Enduring Resource amid Constraints: A Multi-Year Study of Healthcare Workers," *International Journal of Public Health* 69 (2024): 1607332.

33 (β = .50). Xingyu Wang, Priyanko Guchait, and Ayşın Paşamehmetoğlu, "Tolerating Errors in Hospitality Organizations: Relationships with Learning Behavior, Error Reporting and Service Recovery Performance," *International Journal of Contemporary Hospitality Management* 32, no. 8 (2020).

34 (β = .41). Reuven Hiraket al., "Linking Leader Inclusiveness to Work Unit Performance: The Importance of Psychological Safety and Learning from Failures," *The Leadership Quarterly* 23, no. 1 (2012): 107–117.

35 (ρ = .44). Jiaqi Zhu, L. Zhang, and H. Zhang, "The Effect of Psychological Safety on Innovation Behavior: A Meta-Analysis," *Advances in Economics, Business and Management Research* 658 (2022): 142–149.

36 Abraham H. Maslow, "A Theory of Human Motivation," *Psychological Review* 50, no. 4 (1943): 376–377.

37 Abraham H. Maslow, *Toward a Psychology of Being* (Van Nostrand, 1962), 26–27.

38 PSindex® is a twelve-item psychometrically validated scale that we use to measure the level of psychological safety in each of the four stages at the team level. We house the largest normative database for psychological safety in the world.

39 The Workplace Hierarchy of Needs has remarkable conceptual alignment with Edward Deci and Richard Ryan's Self-Determination Theory (SDT). They argue that human motivation and well-being are driven by three innate psychological needs: relatedness, competence, and autonomy. These designations map closely to inclusion and belonging, learning and growth, and choice and contribution. However, these scholars reject the idea of a hierarchy or sequence. I agree that the need categories are simultaneous and not developmental, but in the social context of the workplace, it is clear that most individuals engage their needs in the same sequence. Further, SDT theory does not account for a fourth need category: to challenge and improve, which represents the ultimate application and culmination of competence and contribution. SDT stops short of describing what those capacities are ultimately for. Human beings don't pursue autonomy and competence in isolation; they pursue them in the service of something meaningful beyond themselves. Thus, competence and autonomy are instrumental need categories, and ultimately a means to an end. That end may contribute

to supporting the status quo, but it may also be an improvement or innovation that disrupts the status quo. See Edward L. Deci and Richard M. Ryan, *Self-Determination Theory: Basic Psychological Needs in Motivation, Development, and Wellness* (Guilford Press, 2017), 10; Richard M. Ryan and Edward L. Deci, "Self-Determination Theory and the Facilitation of Intrinsic Motivation, Social Development, and Well-Being," *American Psychologist* 55, no. 1 (2000): 68–78; Marylène Gagné and Edward L. Deci, "Self-Determination Theory and Work Motivation," *Journal of Organizational Behavior* 26 (2005): 331–362; Edward L. Deci and Richard M. Ryan, *Handbook of Self-Determination Research* (University of Rochester Press, 2002), 22; Maarten Vansteenkiste, Richard M. Ryan, and Bart Soenens, "Basic Psychological Need Theory: Advancements, Critical Themes, and Future Directions," *Motivation and Emotion* 44 (2020): 1–31.

40 For a useful review of the psychological safety literature, see Alexander Newman, Ross Donohue, and Nathan Evans, "Psychological Safety: A Systematic Review of the Literature," *Human Resource Management Review* 27, no. 3 (2017): 521–535; Amy C. Edmondson and Zhike Lei, "Psychological Safety: The History, Renaissance, and Future of an Interpersonal Construct," *Annual Review of Organizational Psychology and Organizational Behavior* 1 (2014): 23–43. Also see findings from Aspen Institute National Commission on Social, Emotional, and Academic Development, *From a Nation at Risk to a Nation at Hope* (Aspen Institute, 2019), https://www.aspeninstitute.org/wp-content/uploads/2025/05/Nation-at-Hope.pdf.

41 Søren Kierkegaard, *The Concept of Anxiety: A Simple Psychologically Orienting Deliberation on the Dogmatic Issue of Hereditary Sin*, in *Kierkegaard's Writings*, vol. 8, ed. Vigilius Haufniensis, trans. Reidar Thomte (Princeton University Press, 1980; originally published 1844).

42 Joseph Schumpeter, *Capitalism, Socialism and Democracy* (Routledge, 1994; originally published 1942), 82–83.

43 "When a man's physiological needs are satisfied and he is no longer fearful about his physical welfare, his social needs become important motivators of his behavior. These are such needs as those for belonging, for association, for acceptance by one's fellows, for giving and receiving love." Abraham H. Maslow, "A Theory of Human Motivation," *Psychological Review* 50 (1943): 380.

44 Herbert A. Simon, *Administrative Behavior* (Free Press, 1997; originally published 1947), 214.

45 Carl R. Rogers, "The Necessary and Sufficient Conditions of Therapeutic Personality Change," *Journal of Consulting Psychology* 21 (1957): 95–103. See also Carl R. Rogers, *On Becoming a Person* (Little Brown, 1967; originally published in 1961); Carl R. Rogers, "Toward a Theory of Creativity," *Etc.: A Review of General Semantics* 11, no. 4 (1954): 249–260.

46 Douglas McGregor, *The Human Side of Enterprise* (McGraw-Hill, 1960), 37; Edgar H. Schein and Warren G. Bennis, *Personal and Organizational Change through Group Methods: The Laboratory Approach* (John Wiley & Sons, 1965), 44.

47 Schein and Bennis, *Personal and Organizational Change*, 44.

48 William A. Kahn, "Psychological Conditions of Personal Engagement and Disengagement at Work," *The Academy of Management Journal* 33, no. 4 (1990): 692–724.

49 Edmondson, "Psychological Safety and Learning Behavior in Work Teams," 350–383.

50 See Charles Duhigg, "What Google Learned from Its Quest to Build the Perfect Team," *New York Times*, February 25, 2016.

51 Arlie Russell Hochschild, *The Managed Heart: Commercialization of Human Feeling* (University of California Press, 1983), 56.

52 Megan S. Jones et al., "Facilitating Psychological Safety in Science and Research Teams," *Humanities and Social Sciences Communications* 11, no. 1 (2024): Article 220.

53 Yasutaka Ojio et al., "Understanding the Relationship between Sport-Related Psychological Safety and Mental Toughness in Male Elite Athletes," *BMC Sports Science, Medicine and Rehabilitation* 16, no. 1 (2024): 38.

54 Erich Fromm, *Escape from Freedom* (Farrar & Rinehart, 1941), 72.

55 American College Health Association, *American College Health Association–National College Health Assessment II: Reference Group Executive Summary Fall 2017* (American College Health Association, 2018).

56 See Marshall Sahlins, "The Original Affluent Society" (abridged) in *The Politics of Egalitarianism: Theory and Practice*, ed. Jacqueline Solway (Berghahn Books, 2006), 78–98.

57 William James, *The Principles of Psychology*, vol. 1 (Henry Holt and Company, 1890), 293.

58 Holly Hedegaard, Sally C. Curtin, and Margaret Warner, *Suicide Mortality in the United States, 1999–2017*, NCHS data brief no. 330 (National Center for Health Statistics, Centers for Disease Control, November 2018).

59 Albert Camus, *Letters to a German Friend and Other Writings*, trans. Philip Thody (Hamish Hamilton, 1961), 173.

60 Paul Petrone, "The Skills Companies Need Most in 2019," *LinkedIn Learning*, https://learning.linkedin.com/blog/top-skills/the-skills-companies-need-most-in-2019-and-how-to-learn-them.

61 Henry David Thoreau, *A Week on the Concord and Merrimack Rivers* (Ticknor and Fields, 1862), 59.

62 Garry Kasparov, *How Life Imitates Chess: Making the Right Moves, from the Board to the Boardroom* (Bloomsbury, 2007), 174.

63 Scott D. Anthony et al., *2018 Corporate Longevity Forecast: Creative Destruction Is Accelerating* (Innosight, 2018), 2, https://www.innosight.com/wp-content/uploads/2017/11/Innosight-Corporate-Longevity-2018.pdf.

64 For a bio-cultural argument, see Sebastian Junger, *Tribe: On Homecoming and Belonging* (Twelve, 2016).

65 See Robert M. Sapolsky, *Behave: The Biology of Humans at Our Best and Worst* (Penguin Press, 2017), 484–487; Henri Tajfel et al., "Social Categorization and Intergroup Behaviour," *European Journal of Social Psychology* 1, no. 2 (1971): 149–178; Robert Trivers, *The Folly of Fools: The Logic of Deceit and Self-Deception in Human Life* (Basic Books, 2011), 19.

66 Robin I. M. Dunbar, *Friends: Understanding the Power of Our Most Important Relationships* (Little, Brown, 2021), 7.

67 Stephen Porges calls it *neuroception* in *The Pocket Guide to the Polyvagal Theory: The Transformative Power of Feeling Safe* (W. W. Norton & Company, 2017), 81, 193.

68 Sheldon Cohen, *Psychosocial Pathways Linking Affective States and Physical Health* (Oxford University Press, 2020), 296.

69 Christopher F. Karpowitz and Tali Mendelberg, *The Silent Sex: Gender, Deliberation and Institutions* (Princeton University Press, 2014), 52. See also Yuxin Ma, "Silence as a Survival Strategy: Will the Silent Be Worse Off? A Study of Chinese Migrant Workers in Guangdong," *Asian Journal of Social Psychology* 24, no. 2 (2021): 103–115.

70 Kristin Bain et al., "Research: Incivility at Work Silences Everyone, but Especially Women," *Harvard Business Review*, January 21, 2025.

71 Alison S. Schormans et al., "Which Ideas for Change Are Endorsed? How Agentic and Communal Voice Affects Endorsement Differently for Men and for Women," *Journal of Applied Psychology* 108, no. 3 (2023): 448–467.

72 Laurie A. Rudman and Peter Glick, "Feminized Management and Backlash toward Agentic Women: The Hidden Costs to Women of a Kinder, Gentler Image of Middle Managers," *Journal of Personality and Social Psychology* 77, no. 5 (1999): 1004–1010.

73 Christine Porath, *Mastering Civility: A Manifesto for the Workplace* (Grand Central Publishing, 2016), 23; Thomas A. Foulk et al., "Catching Rudeness Is Like Catching a Cold: The Contagion Effects of Low-Intensity Negative Behaviors," *Journal of Applied Psychology* 101, no. 1 (2016): 50–67; Christine L. Porath et al., "How Incivility Hijacks Performance: It Robs Cognitive Resources, Increases Dysfunctional Behavior, and Infects Team Dynamics and Functioning," *Organizational Dynamics* 44, no. 4 (2015): 258–65.

74 Ta-Nehisi Coates, *Between the World and Me* (Spiegel & Grau, 2015), 17–20.

75 *The Impact of Equality and Values Driven Business*, Salesforce Research, 12, https://www.salesforce.com/contents/impact-of-equality/.

76 Martin Luther King Jr., "I Have a Dream" (speech, Washington, DC, August 28, 1963), American Rhetoric, http://www.americanrhetoric.com/speeches/mlkihaveadream.htm.

77 Reinhold Niebuhr, *The Irony of American History* (Charles Scribner's Sons, 1952), 63. See also William Law, *A Serious Call to a Devout and Holy Life* (ReadaClassic, 2010), 244. Law underscores the point that "there is no dependence upon the merits of men."

78 Abraham Lincoln, *Abraham Lincoln papers: Series 1. General Correspondence. 1833–1916: Abraham Lincoln, March 1861 First Inaugural Address, Final Version*, (manuscript/mixed material), Library of Congress, Washington, DC, https://www.loc.gov/item/mal0773800/.

79 Frederick Douglass, "Our Composite Nationality" (speech delivered at Tremont Temple, Boston, December 7, 1869), in *The Frederick Douglass Papers, Series One: Speeches, Debates, and Interviews*, vol. 4, ed. John W. Blassingame (Yale University Press, 1991), 384–387.

80 See Amartya Sen, *Identity and Violence: The Illusion of Destiny* (W. W. Norton, 2006), 2–3.

81 John Rawls, *A Theory of Justice* (Oxford University Press, 1972), 5.

82 And it's what we would all choose if we had to define the "original position" behind a "veil of ignorance," as Rawls describes his thought experiment.

83 Jia Hu et al., "Leader Humility and Team Creativity: The Role of Team Information Sharing, Psychological Safety, and Power Distance," *Journal of Applied Psychology* 103, no. 3 (2018): 313–323.

84 Henry Emerson Fosdick, *The Meaning of Service* (Association Press, 1944), 138.

85 See Isaiah Berlin, *Concepts and Categories: Philosophical Essays* (Oxford University Press, 1980), 96.

86 Alex "Sandy" Pentland, "The New Science of Building Great Teams," *Harvard Business Review*, April 2012, https://hbr.org/2012/04/the-new-science-of-building-great-teams.

87 Edgar Schein, *Organizational Culture and Leadership* (Jossey-Bass, 2004), 15.

88 Vaclav Havel, *The Power of the Powerless* (Vintage Classics, 2018), iv.

89 George Orwell, *Animal Farm* (Secker and Warburg, 1945).

90 See Franz Boas, *Anthropology and Modern Life* (W. W. Norton & Company, 1928), 14–16.

91 For example, look at the intellectual history of racial superiority, including: Arthur de Gobineau, *An Essay on the Inequality of the Human Races*, trans. Adrian Collins (William Heinemann, 1915; originally published 1853–1855); Madison Grant, *The Passing of the Great Race: Or, The Racial Basis of European History* (Charles Scribner's Sons, 1916); Madison Grant, *The Rising Tide of Color against White World-Supremacy* (Charles Scribner's Sons, 1920).

92 Aristotle, *The Politics of Aristotle*, vol. 1, trans. B. Jowett (Clarendon Press, 1885), 3.

93 David McCullough, *John Adams* (Simon & Schuster, 2001), 170.

94 Abigail Adams, letter to John Adams, March 31, 1776, in The Adams Papers: Adams Family Correspondence, vol. 1, ed. L. H. Butterfield (Cambridge, MA: Belknap Press of Harvard University Press, 1963), 369–71.

95 Thomas Jefferson believed in his own biological superiority. See *Notes on the State of Virginia*, 1781.

96 EY, "Could Trust Cost You a Generation of Talent?," accessed August 9, 2019, https://whirlingchief.com/wp-content/uploads/2016/10/EY_Global-Study-on-Trust-at-Workplace-2016.pdf.

97 Robert Putnam, *Bowling Alone: The Collapse and Revival of American Community* (Simon & Schuster, 2000), 21.

98 Ferdinand Tönnies, *Gemeinschaft und Gesellschaft* (Fues's Verlag, 1887). An English translation of the eighth edition (1935) by Charles P. Loomis appeared as *Fundamental Concepts of Sociology* (American Book Co., 1940).

99 James MacGregor Burns, *Leadership* (Perennial, 1978), 11.

100 Carol Dweck, *Mindset: The New Psychology of Success* (Random House, 2006), 121.

101 Franz Kafka, *Letters to Friend, Family, and Editors*, ed. Richard and Clara Winston (Schoken Books, 1977), 16.

102 Nathaniel Branden, *The Six Pillars of Self-Esteem* (Bantam, 1994), 7.

103 See Edward H. Chang et al., "The Mixed Effects of Online Diversity Training," *Proceedings of the National Academy of Sciences* 116, no. 16 (2019): 7778–7783.

104 Paul Ekman and Richard J. Davidson, "Voluntary Smiling Changes Regional Brain Activity," *Psychological Science* 4, no. 5 (1993): 342–345, https://doi.org/10.1111/j.1467-9280.1993.tb00576.x.

105 Carl R. Rogers, *On Becoming a Person: A Therapist's View of Psychotherapy* (Houghton Mifflin, 1961), 33.

106 "Hymn to Freedom," lyrics by Harriette Hamilton, track 11 on Oscar Peterson, *Night Train*, Verve Records, 1963.

107 Jonathan Haidt, *The Righteous Mind: Why Good People Are Divided by Politics and Religion* (Pantheon Books, 2012), 370.

108 Martha C. Nussbaum, *Upheavals of Thought: The Intelligence of Emotions* (Cambridge University Press, 2001), 3.

109 Gerald L. Clore et al., "Affect and Cognition: Three Principles," *Current Opinion in Behavioral Sciences* 19 (2018): 78–82. See also Barbara L. Fredrickson, "The Role of Positive Emotions in Positive Psychology: The Broaden-and-Build Theory of Positive Emotions," *American Psychologist* 56, no. 3 (2001): 218–226.

110 Rachel Carson, *The Sense of Wonder* (Harper & Row, 1965), 45.

111 Ralph Waldo Emerson, *Letters and Social Aims* (Boston: Houghton, Osgood and Company, 1876), 142.

112 ToMiller, Tony. "Partnering for Education Reform." Remarks by U.S. Deputy Secretary Tony Miller at the Church of God in Christ's International AIM Convention in Houston, TX, July 7, 2011. Archived by the United States Department of Education.

113 See James. J. Heckman, "Catch 'em Young," *Wall Street Journal*, January 6, 2006.

114 Martha J. Farah et al., "Childhood Poverty: Specific Associations with Neurocognitive Development," *Brain Research* 1110, no. 1 (2006): 166–174; Bruce S. McEwen and John H. Morrison, "The Brain on Stress: Vulnerability and Plasticity of the Prefrontal Cortex over the Life Course," *Neuron* 79, no. 1 (2013): 16–29; Charles A. Nelson et al., "Cognitive Recovery in Socially Deprived Young Children: The Bucharest Early Intervention Project," *Science* 318, no. 5858 (2007): 1937–1940; Nathan A. Fox et al., "The Effects of Severe Psychosocial Deprivation on Brain Development in Children: A Longitudinal Study," *JAMA Pediatrics* 168, no. 2 (2014): 113–121; Torkel Klingberg, "Training and Plasticity of Working Memory," *Trends in Cognitive Sciences* 14, no. 7 (2010): 317–324; Janice M. Juraska and Cheryl L. Greenough, "Plasticity and the Aging Brain: New Directions in Cognitive Neurodevelopment," *Brain and Cognition* 42, no. 1 (2000): 102–113; Kathryn L. Mills et al., "Structural Brain Development between Childhood and Adulthood: Convergence Across Four Longitudinal Samples," *NeuroImage* 141 (2016): 273–281.

115 Robert Balfanz and Nettie Legters, *Locating the Dropout Crisis* (Center for Research on the Education of Students Placed at Risk, Johns Hopkins University, 2004).

116 This anonymous quote is often erroneously attributed to W. B. Yeats but is no less true.

117 Neil Postman and Charles Weingartner, *Teaching as a Subversive Activity* (Delacorte Press, 1969).

118 This section draws heavily on my personal interviews with Craig from 2014 to 2019 as well as classroom observations conducted in 2019. Disclosure: Craig has taught five of my children in his calculus classes.

119 Why, for example, are females dramatically underrepresented in computer science and STEM majors in college? Undoubtedly, part of the gap is due to an unconscious bias that says they can't excel as well as males in these fields, even though they perform as well as males in K–12 standardized math tests and earn 57 percent of bachelor's degrees today. See Thomas Dee and Seth Gershenson, "Unconscious Bias in the Classroom: Evidence and Opportunities" (Google's Computer Science Education Research, 2017),

https://services.google.com/fh/files/misc/unconscious-bias-in-the-classroom-report.pdf. See also David M. Amodio, "The Neuroscience of Prejudice and Stereotyping," *Nature Reviews Neuroscience* 15, no. 10 (2014): 670–682.

120 Jenna McGregor, "Nobel Prize–Winning Psychologist to CEOs: Don't Be So Quick to Go with Your Gut," *Washington Post*, March 4, 2019.

121 C. Roland Christensen, *Education for Judgment*, (Boston: Harvard Business Review, 1991), 118.

122 Claude M. Steele, *Whistling Vivaldi: How Stereotypes Affect Us and What We Can Do* (W. W. Norton & Co., 2010), 46.

123 From classroom observation conducted on February 14, 2019.

124 See Jenny W. Rudolph et al., "Establishing a Safe Container for Learning in Simulation: The Role of the Pre-simulation Briefing," *Journal of the Society for Simulation in Healthcare* 9, no. 6 (2014): 339–349. Smith's classroom becomes the safe container.

125 See Ernest Hemingway, "A Clean, Well-Lighted Place," in *Winner Take Nothing* (Scribner's, 1933). Craig's practices embody the primary findings released in the Aspen Institute, *From a Nation at Risk to a Nation at Hope: Recommendations from the National Commission on Social, Emotional, & Academic Development* (Aspen Institute, 2019).

126 C. Roland Christensen, "Premises and Practices of Discussion Teaching," in *Education for Judgment: The Artistry of Discussion Leadership*, ed. C. Roland Christensen and David A. Garvin (Harvard Business Review, 1991), 15–34.

127 Babette Bronkhorst, "Behaving Safely under Pressure: The Effects of Job Demands, Resources, and Safety Climate on Employee Physical and Psychosocial Safety Behavior," *Journal of Safety Research* 55 (2015): 63–72.

128 Anya Kamenetz, "Bill Gates on Education: 'We Can Make Massive Strides,'" *Fast Company*, April 15, 2013, https://www.fastcompany.com/3007841/bill-gates-education-we-can-make-massive-strides.

129 Gary Hopkins, "How Can Teachers Develop Students' Motivation—and Success?" (interview with Carol Dweck), *Wire Side Chats, Education World*, accessed January 30, 2026, https://www.educationworld.com/a_issues/chat/chat010.shtml.

130 Richard Florida, *The Rise of the Creative Class* (Basic Books, 2002), 24.

131 Malcolm S. Knowles, "Adult Learning" in *The ASTD Training and Development Handbook: A Guide to Human Resource Development*, 4th ed., ed. Robert L. Craig (McGraw-Hill, 2004), 262.

132 Peter F. Drucker, *Landmarks of Tomorrow: A Report on the New "Post-Modern" World* (Harper & Brothers, 1959), 264.

133 Byung-Jik Kim et al., "The Dark Side of Artificial Intelligence Adoption: Linking Artificial Intelligence Adoption to Employee Depression via Psychological Safety and Ethical Leadership," *Journal of Business Ethics* (2025): 1.

134 Amy C. Edmondson. "Making It Safe: The Effects of Leader Inclusiveness and Professional Status on Psychological Safety and Improvement Efforts in Health Care Teams," *Journal of Organizational Behavior* 27, no. 7 (2006): 941–966.

135 Roderick M. Kramer and Karen S. Cook, eds., *Trust and Distrust in Organizations: Dilemmas and Approaches* (Russell Sage Foundation, 2004).

136 Michelangelo Buonarroti, *The Letters of Michelangelo*, vol. 2, trans. E. H. Ramsden (Stanford University Press, 1963), 207.

137 Carl G. Jung, *Modern Man in Search of a Soul* (Harcourt, Brace and Company, 1933), 226.

138 Susan David, *Emotional Agility: Get Unstuck, Embrace Change, and Thrive in Work and Life* (Avery, 2016), 229.

139 Vincent H. Dominé, "Team Development in the Era of Slack," *INSEAD Knowledge*, May 24, 2019.

140 James G. March, "Exploration and Exploitation in Organizational Learning," *Organization Science* 2, no. 1 (1991): 71–87.

141 A *defensive* innovation is similar to the *sustaining* innovation described by Clayton Christensen, but it's an innovation that you do not initiate. It comes in response to an adaptive challenge in the form of a threat or crisis. See Clayton M. Christensen et al., *The Prosperity Paradox: How Innovation Can Lift Nations Out of Poverty* (HarperBusiness, 2019), 20.

142 See Claude M. Steele and Joshua Aronson, "Stereotype Threat and the Intellectual Test Performance of African Americans," *Journal of Personality and Social Psychology* 69, no. 5 (1995): 797–811.

143 See Steven R. Harper and Charles D. White, "The Impact of Member Emotional Intelligence on Psychological Safety in Work Teams," *Journal of Behavioral & Applied Management* 15, no. 1 (2013): 2–10.

144 Amy C. Edmondson, "Dangerous Silence," in *The Fearless Organization: Creating Psychological Safety in the Workplace for Learning, Innovation, and Growth* (Wiley, 2019).

145 See Christopher J. Roussin et al., "Psychological Safety, Self-Efficacy, and Speaking Up in Interprofessional Health Care Simulation," *Clinical Simulation in Nursing* 17 (2018): 38–46.

146 John Stuart Mill, *On Liberty* (Broadview Press, 1859).

147 Jim Harter, "Dismal Employee Engagement Is a Sign of Global Mismanagement," *Gallup Workplace*, December 20, 2017.

148 Aristotle, *The Nicomachean Ethics*, in *The Complete Works of Aristotle: The Revised Oxford Translation*, vol. 2, ed. Jonathan Barnes, rev. by J. O. Urmson Ross (Oxford University Press, 1984), 1107.

149 Irving L. Janis, *Groupthink: Psychological Studies of Policy Decisions and Fiascoes* (Houghton Mifflin, 1982), 9.

150 Margaret Atwood, *The Handmaid's Tale* (McClelland and Stewart, 1985), 88.

151 Satya Nadella, *Hit Refresh: The Quest to Rediscover Microsoft's Soul and Imagine a Better Future for Everyone* (Harper Business, 2017).

152 See Carl R. Rogers and F. J. Roethlisberger, "Barriers and Gateways to Communication," *Harvard Business Review*, November–December 1991.

153 Marcus Du Sautoy, *The Creativity Code: Art and Innovation in the Age of AI* (Belknap Press, 2019), 11.

154 Celia Swanson, "Are You Enabling a Toxic Culture Without Realizing It?" *Harvard Business Review*, August 22, 2019.

155 Edward O. Wilson, *The Origins of Creativity* (Liveright, 2017).

156 Ben Farr-Wharton and Ace Simpson, "Human-Centric Models of Management Are the Key to Ongoing Success," *Sydney Morning Herald*, May 24, 2019.

157 Stephen A. Schwarzman, "The Mistake That Changed Blackstone Forever: Life Lessons with Stephen A. Schwarzman," YouTube video, 5:26, posted October 13, 2025, by Blackstone, https://youtu.be/hDl2RqHet-o?si=mciKCr9KVSF3okzr.

158 Edgar Schein, *Humble Inquiry* (Berrett-Koehler, 2013), 64.

159 Chris Argyris, "Good Communication That Blocks Learning," *Harvard Business Review*, July–August 1994.

160 Chie Nakane, *Japanese Society* (University of California Press, 1972), 13.

161 Abraham Carmeli et al., "Learning Behaviors in the Workplace: The Role of High-Quality Interpersonal Relationships and Psychological Safety," *Systems Research and Behavioral Science* 26, no. 25 (2008): 81–98.

162 Abraham Maslow, "Safe Enough to Dare," in *Toward a Psychology of Being*, 3rd ed. (Wiley, 1998), 65.

163 Duena Blostrom, "'Nobody Gets Fired for Buying IBM.' But They Should," *Forbes*, November 30, 2018, https://www.forbes.com/sites/duenablomstrom1/2018/11/30/nobody-gets-fired-for-buying-ibm-but-they-should/.

164 Henry Wadsworth Longfellow, "Morituri Salutamus," in *The Poetical Works of Henry Wadsworth Longfellow* (Houghton, Osgood and Company, 1877), 416.

165 Andrew Hargadon and Robert I. Sutton, "Building an Innovation Factory," *Harvard Business Review*, May–June 2000.

166 Gary Wolf, "Steve Jobs: The Next Insanely Great Thing," *Wired*, February 1, 1996.

167 Adam Lashinsky, "The Unexpected Management Genius of Facebook's Mark Zuckerberg," *Fortune*, November 10, 2016, https://fortune.com/longform/facebook-mark-zuckerberg-business/.

168 Alison Beard, "Life's Work: An Interview with Brian Wilson," *Harvard Business Review*, December 2016.

169 Yuval Noah Harari, *21 Lessons for the 21st Century* (Spiegel & Grau, 2018), 223.

170 Paul J. Klimoski and Wei Zhang, "Cross-Level Examination of Team Psychological Safety and Process Innovation," *Journal of Organizational Behavior* 35, no. 8 (2014): 1120–1136.

171 Jeff Dyer et al., *The Innovator's DNA: Mastering the Five Skills of Disruptive Innovators* (Harvard Business School Press, 2011), 46–49.

172 Vivian Hunt et al., *Diversity Matters* (McKinsey & Company, February 2, 2015), 14.

173 Peter F. Drucker, *The Effective Executive* (Harper Business, 1996), 152.

174 Dotan R. Castro et al., "Mere Listening Effect on Creativity and the Mediating Role of Psychological Safety," *Psychology of Aesthetics, Creativity, and the Arts* 12, no. 4 (2018): 489–502.

175 Mihaly Csikszentmihalyi, *Creativity: Flow and the Psychology of Discovery and Invention* (Harper Perennial, 1997), 11.

176 Max Planck, *Scientific Autobiography and Other Papers*, trans. Frank Gaynor (Philosophical Library, 1949), 33–34.

177 Jennifer Luna, "Oscar Munoz: Learn to Listen, Improve Your EQ," *Stanford Business*, January 19, 2019.

178 Chris Argyris, "Teaching Smart People How to Learn," *Harvard Business Review*, May–June 1991.

179 Alison Beard, "Life's Work: An Interview with Yo-Yo Ma," *Harvard Business Review*, June 2016.

180 Manfred F. R. Kets de Vries, "Coaching the Toxic Leader," *Harvard Business Review*, April 2014.

181 Geert Hofstede, *Culture's Consequences: Comparing Values, Behaviors, Institutions, and Organizations Across Nations*, 2nd ed. (Sage Publications, 2001), 107–112.

182 Todd Spangler, "HBO Max Says Intern Sent Mistaken Test Email," *Variety*, June 18, 2021.

183 Mark L. Frazier et al., "Psychological Safety: A Meta-Analytic Review and Extension," *Personnel Psychology* 70, no. 1 (2017): 113–165.

184 Shane Snow, *Dream Teams: Working Together Without Falling Apart* (Portfolio/Penguin, 2018), 47.

185 Irving L. Janis, *Victims of Groupthink* (Houghton Mifflin, 1972), 35–62.

186 Graham T. Allison and Philip Zelikow, *Essence of Decision: Explaining the Cuban Missile Crisis*, 2nd ed. (Longman, 1999), 275–280.

187 Amy C. Edmondson, "Psychological Safety and Learning Behavior in Work Teams," *Administrative Science Quarterly* 44, no. 2 (1999): 350–351.

188 Sidney Dekker, *The Field Guide to Understanding "Human Error"*, 3rd ed. (CRC Press, 2014), 143–160.

189 K. A. Jehn and E. A. Mannix, "The Dynamic Nature of Conflict: A Longitudinal Study of Intragroup Conflict and Group Performance," *Academy of Management Journal* 44, no. 2 (2001): 238–240.

190 Jeffrey K. Liker, *The Toyota Way: 14 Management Principles from the World's Greatest Manufacturer* (McGraw-Hill, 2004), 103–118.

191 Andrew C. Loignon et al., "Shared Leadership, Psychological Safety, and Team Performance," *Journal of Applied Psychology* 107, no. 5 (2022): 819–835.

192 Jonathan Haidt and Greg Lukianoff, *The Coddling of the American Mind* (Penguin Press, 2018), 22–42.

193 Ethan Burris, "The Risks and Rewards of Speaking Up: Managers' Responses to Employee Voice," *Academy of Management Journal* 55, no. 4 (2012): 851–875.

194 Nada Wentzel, "Mental Health, Psychological Safety and Psychosocial Safety—Same but Different?," *APPEA Journal 63*, supplement (2023): S117–S120, https://doi.org/10.1071/AJ22146.

195 Julien Haye, *The Psychology of Risk: Mastering the Art of Risk Management* (London: Risk Culture Builder, 2022), 14.

196 DuPont Safety Resources, *The Bradley Curve*, DuPont, 1995.

197 Maojuan Wang et al., "Value Congruence Regarding Patient Safety Among Nurses and Their Managers and Its Association With Patient Safety Behaviors: The Moderating Role of Psychological Safety," *Journal of Nursing Management* 32, no. 5 (2024): 1121.

198 Robert L. Helmreich and Ashleigh C. Merritt, *Culture at Work in Aviation and Medicine* (Ashgate, 1998), 65–88.

199 Steven J. Spear and H. Kent Bowen, "Decoding the DNA of the Toyota Production System," *Harvard Business Review* 77, no. 5 (1999): 96–106.

200 Hannah Leroy et al., "Psychological Safety, Error Reporting, and Patient Outcomes," *BMJ Quality & Safety* 21, no. 2 (2012): 171–176.

201 Anita Williams Woolley et al., "Collective Intelligence and Group Performance," *Science* 330, no. 6004 (2010): 686–688.

202 Elizabeth W. Morrison and Frances J. Milliken, "Organizational Silence: A Barrier to Change and Development in a Pluralistic World," *Academy of Management Review* 25, no. 4 (2000): 706–725.

203 Irving L. Janis, *Groupthink: Psychological Studies of Policy Decisions and Fiascoes*, 2nd ed. (Houghton Mifflin, 1982), 13.

204 Jennifer J. Kish-Gephart et al., "Silenced by Fear: The Nature, Sources, and Consequences of Fear at Work," *Research in Organizational Behavior* 29 (2009): 163–193.

205 John M. Darley, "Fear and Social Comparison as Determinants of Conformity Behavior," *Journal of Personality and Social Psychology* 4, no. 1 (1966): 73–78.

206 J. R. Dempsey et al., "Program Management in Design and Development," in *Third Annual Aerospace Reliability and Maintainability Conference*, (Society of Automotive Engineers, 1964), 7–8.

207 Danielle D. King et al., "Voice Resilience: Fostering Future Voice after Non-Endorsement of Suggestions," *Journal of Occupational and Organizational Psychology* 92, no. 3 (2019): 535–565.

208 Daisy Grewal, "How Wealth Reduces Compassion: As Riches Grow, Empathy for Others Seems to Decline," *Scientific American*, April 10, 2012.

209 Martin Luther King Jr., "Letter from Birmingham Jail," in *Why We Can't Wait* (Harper & Row, 1964).

210 Adam Grant, *Think Again: The Power of Knowing What You Don't Know* (Viking, 2021), 118–120.

211 Timothy R. Clark, "How a CEO Can Create Psychological Safety in the Room," *Harvard Business Review*, January 23, 2023.

212 Ingrid M. Nembhard and Amy C. Edmondson, "Making It Safe: The Effects of Leader Inclusiveness and Professional Status on Psychological Safety and Improvement Efforts in Health Care Teams," *Journal of Organizational Behavior* 27, no. 7 (2006): 941–66.

213 Fred L. Strodtbeck and Harmon J. O. Hook, "The Social Dimensions of a Twelve-Man Jury Table," *Sociometry* 24, no. 4 (1961): 397–415.

214 Amy J.C. Cuddy et al., "Connect, Then Lead," *Harvard Business Review* 91, no. 7/8 (2013): 54–61.

215 James R. Detert and Ethan R. Burris, "Leadership Behavior and Employee Voice: Is the Door Really Open?" *Academy of Management Journal* 50, no. 4 (2007): 869–84.

216 Alexandra G. Rozovsky, "The Five Keys to a Successful Google Team," *re:Work*, November 2015. See also Mary A. Zellmer-Bruhn and Cristina Gibson, "How Great Teams Make Decisions: A Field Study," *Academy of Management Journal* 49, no. 5 (2006): 953–970.

217 Edgar H. Schein, *Organizational Culture and Leadership*, 4th ed. (Jossey-Bass, 2010), 236–54.

218 Timothy R. Clark, "Building a Culture Where Employees Feel Free to Speak Up," *Harvard Business Review*, August 2023.

219 Charles Dickens, *A Christmas Carol*, in *Christmas Books* (Chapman & Hall, 1843), 72.

220 Émile Durkheim, *The Division of Labor in Society*, trans. W. D. Halls (Free Press, 1984; originally published 1893), 291–310.

221 Ruth Benedict, *An Anthropologist at Work: Writings of Ruth Benedict*, ed. Margaret Mead (Houghton Mifflin, 1959), 451.

222 Alexis de Tocqueville, *Democracy in America*, vol. 2, trans. Henry Reeve, rev. Francis Bowen and Phillips Bradley (Alfred A. Knopf, 1945), 106–107.

223 Paul F. Lazarsfeld and Robert K. Merton, "Friendship as a Social Process: A Substantive and Methodological Analysis," in *Freedom and Control in Modern Society*, ed. Morroe Berger et al. (Van Nostrand, 1954), 18–66.

224 Geoffrey L. Cohen, *Belonging: The Science of Creating Connection and Bridging Divides* (W. W. Norton & Company, 2022), x.

225 Gordon W. Allport, *The Nature of Prejudice* (Addison-Wesley, 1954), 281–282.

226 Robert D. Putnam, *Bowling Alone: The Collapse and Revival of American Community* (Simon & Schuster, 2000), 22–23.

227 Robert W. Livingston, *The Conversation: How Seeking and Speaking the Truth About Racism Can Radically Transform Individuals and Organizations* (Currency, 2021), 228.

228 Timothy R. Clark, "Don't Let Hierarchy Stifle Innovation," *Harvard Business Review*, August 2022.

229 Aristotle, *Nicomachean Ethics*, trans. Terence Irwin (Hackett Publishing, 1999), 1159b.

230 This chapter builds on and expands my original HBR article. See Timothy R. Clark, "How to Challenge Your Organization's Status Quo—Productively," *Harvard Business Review*, May 2023.

231 Frances J. Milliken et al., "An Exploratory Study of Employee Silence: Issues That Employees Don't Communicate Upward and Why," *Journal of Management Studies* 40, no. 6 (2003): 1453–1476.

232 Jane E. Dutton et al., "Moves That Matter: Issue Selling and Organizational Change," *Academy of Management Journal* 44, no. 4 (2001): 716–736.

233 Celia Moore and Kate Coombs, "Five Ways Leaders Can Get People to Speak Up," *MIT Sloan Management Review*, November 20, 2024.

234 Chris Argyris and Donald A. Schön, *Organizational Learning: A Theory of Action Perspective* (Addison-Wesley, 1978), 12.

235 See Timothy R. Clark et al., "How Constructive Dissent Can Unlock Your Team's Innovation," *Harvard Business Review*, June 28, 2023.

236 G. K. Chesterton, *The Thing: Why I Am a Catholic* (Sheed & Ward, 1929).

237 Thomas S. Kuhn, *The Structure of Scientific Revolutions*, 2nd ed. (University of Chicago Press, 1970).

238 Edwin P. Hollander, "Conformity, Status, and Idiosyncrasy Credit," *Psychological Review* 65, no. 2 (1958): 117–127, doi:10.1037/h0042501.

239 Stanford University, "Introduction to Civil Discourse," *Civic, Liberal, and Global Education (COLLEGE 102)*, Stanford Center for Deliberative Democracy, 2022.

240 Mike Allen and Raymond W. Preiss, "Comparing the Persuasiveness of Narrative and Statistical Evidence Using Meta-Analysis," *Communication Research Reports* 14, no. 2 (1997): 125–131.

241 Charles Dickens, *Bleak House* (Bradbury & Evans, 1853), 456; William Blake, "And Did Those Feet in Ancient Time," in *Milton: A Poem* (author, 1808).

242 Elisabeth Noelle-Neumann, "The Spiral of Silence: A Theory of Public Opinion," *Journal of Communication* 24, no. 2 (1974): 43–51.

243 Gerald Dworkin, "Paternalism," in *Stanford Encyclopedia of Philosophy* (Stanford University, 2017).

244 Higher Ed Dive Team, "A Look at Trends in College Consolidation Since 2016," *Higher Ed Dive*, last modified February 7, 2026, https://www.highereddive.com/news/how-many-colleges-and-universities-have-closed-since-2016/539379/.

245 "The Federalist Number 10, [22 November] 1787," Founders Online, National Archives, https://founders.archives.gov/documents/Madison/01-10-02-0178. Original source: Robert A. Rutland et al., eds., *The Papers of James Madison, Vol. 10, 27 May 1787–3 March 1788* (University of Chicago Press, 1977), 263–270.

246 Milton Friedman, "The Social Responsibility of Business to Increase Its Profits," *New York Times Magazine*, September 13, 1970.

247 Alexander Solzhenitsyn, *The Gulag Archipelago* (Harper & Row, 1973), 24.

248 Christine Porath and Christine Pearson, "The Price of Incivility," *Harvard Business Review*, January–February 2013.

249 C. Terry Warner, *Socialization, Self-Deception, and Freedom Through Faith* (Brigham Young University Press, 1973), 2.

250 Carol S. Dweck, *Mindset: The New Psychology of Success* (Random House, 2006), 117.

251 "Hotel California," track 1 on The Eagles, *Hotel California*, Asylum Records, 1976.

252 This section draws heavily on Timothy R. Clark and Alistair Aitchison, "Why Are Some Leaders Afraid of Psychological Safety?" *HR Magazine* (Chartered Institute of Personnel and Development), June 14, 2023.

253 Ralph Linton, *The Study of Man: An Introduction* (Appleton-Century-Crofts, 1936), 115–116.

254 Adam Nossiter, "35 Employees Committed Suicide. Will Their Bosses Go to Jail?," *New York Times*, July 9, 2019, https://www.nytimes.com/2019/07/09/world/europe/france-telecom-trial.html.

255 Robert Waldinger and Marc Schulz, *The Good Life: Lessons from the World's Longest Scientific Study of Happiness* (Simon & Schuster, 2023), 16.

256 Acts 10:28, *Holy Bible, King James Version.*

257 F. A. Hayek, *The Road to Serfdom* (University of Chicago Press, 2007), 70.

258 PSindex® is a twelve-item psychometrically validated scale that we use to measure the level of psychological safety in each of the four stages at the team level. We house the largest normative database for psychological safety in the world.

Index

About the Author

Timothy R. Clark is founder and CEO of LeaderFactor, a global leadership development organization. He has worked with more than three hundred executive teams around the world. Dr. Clark is the author of five books and earned a PhD from Oxford University.

4 Stages Training and PSindex®

If you would like to bring the 4 Stages of Psychological Safety training or the PSindex® assessment to your organization, please scan this QR code:

Berrett-Koehler
PUBLISHERS

Dear Reader,

Welcome to the Berrett-Koehler Community—a global network of changemakers creating positive impact in their lives, organizations, and communities.

Our Mission: Connecting People and Ideas to Create a World That Works for All

We believe transformation is possible. While outdated paradigms of self-interest, exclusion, and hierarchy continue to hold back our communities and organizations, we know that change can happen. That's why we connect people with actionable ideas from leading experts who are already creating the solutions we need.

The BK Way

We're an independent publisher that practices what we publish. Our books, digital resources, and community offerings provide practical pathways for building more just, equitable, and sustainable organizations and lives. Whether you're transforming your workplace, community, or personal practices, our publications meet you where you are with tools that work.

But we don't just talk about positive change—we live it. Through "The BK Way," we put stewardship and purpose before profit. As a benefit corporation, we're legally committed to benefiting all our stakeholders: authors, readers, employees, communities, and the environment.

As our gift to you, claim your free bestselling ebook at bkconnection .com/welcome. You'll also receive fresh leadership insights delivered to your inbox from bkconnection.com/blogs/the-bk-exchange.

You Make the Difference

We're grateful to our readers, authors, and community members, who bring our mission to life every day. Your stories of transformation inspire us and show others what's possible.

Share how BK publications are making a difference in your world at bkconnection.com/impact.

Your friends at Berrett-Koehler

Join the Berrett-Koehler Community

Are you passionate about supporting independent publishing and reading diverse voices and perspectives? Join the BK Community Membership Program and become a part of a vibrant literary community. To support mission-based publishing while saving up to 30 percent on all books and attending exclusive events, visit ideas.bkconnection.com/bkcommunity-join to learn more and become a member.